THE DIVIDED LEFT

P9-CRG-040

Also by Milton Cantor

Max Eastman

Working Class Culture in Nineteenth Century American Life

Black Labor in America
(editor)

Hamilton
(editor)

Men, Women and Issues in American History
(editor, with Howard H. Quint)

Main Problems in American History
(editor, with Howard H. Quint and Dean Albertson)

Sex, Class, and the Woman Worker
(editor, with Bruce Laurie)

Biographical Dictionary of American Labor Leaders
(advisory editor)

THE DIVIDED LEFT
American Radicalism, 1900-1975

Milton Cantor

CONSULTING EDITOR: Eric Foner

American Century Series

 HILL AND WANG / NEW YORK
A division of Farrar, Straus and Giroux

Copyright © 1978 by Milton Cantor
All rights reserved

Published simultaneously in Canada by
McGraw-Hill Ryerson Ltd., Toronto

ISBN (clothbound edition) 0-8090-3907-9
ISBN (paperback edition) 0-8090-0131-4

Printed in the United States of America

Designed by Irving Perkins

Library of Congress Cataloging in Publication Data
Cantor, Milton.
The divided left.
(American century series)
Bibliography: p.
Includes index.
1. Radicalism—United States—History. 2. Right and
left (Political science) 3. Labor and laboring classes—
—United States—History. 4. Socialism in the United
States—History. I. Foner, Eric. II. Title.
HN90.R3C36 1978   322.4'4'0973   78-4974

To Henry Steele Commager—my teacher and my touchstone

Contents

THE DIVIDED LEFT

Introduction

TERMS LIKE "radicalism" and "class consciousness" are difficult to define with any degree of exactness. There is the initial obstacle of explaining something whose ideological content is historically relative and nonspecific; there is the further problem of distinguishing the "true" radical and the precise meaning of working-class consciousness.

If class identity occurs, as Edward P. Thompson has noted, whenever people "as a result of common experiences . . . feel and articulate the identity of their interests as between themselves, and as against other[s]," why did this cohering process not occur in twentieth-century America? What, then, were the special circumstances that produced a failure of radical nerve? Or, stating it differently, why didn't trade unionism lead to class consciousness? For we can make an *ex parte* assertion that, with important exceptions, American labor after 1900—even when working-class militancy waxed—demonstrated a decreasing collective consciousness.

Such a claim, conversely, says something affirmative about American capitalism. To conclude that there was no substantive growth of class consciousness, no repudiation of the occupational-social hierarchies which rested on middle-class values, no labor consciousness

3

dialectically transformed into class consciousness, and, of course, no "festivals of the oppressed"—as Lenin once described the brief moment of revolutionary release—then it may also be claimed that criticism of capitalism and proposals for reform were mainly conceived of in terms of the existing system. And again the nagging question, why is this so? Why didn't criticism of capitalism transcend the capitalist structure and turn toward an alternate economic order? To what extent was the failure to develop a mass demand for total change in the socio-economic structure due to the special historical and geographical circumstances of America? To what extent was it due to the inability of radicals and the movements they shaped to maintain a common ground, especially when the highly volatile issue of gradualism versus revolutionary militancy was at stake? And to what extent may the radical failure be attributed to the acceptance by labor—the putative revolutionary force, after all—of dominant social-economic values?

Some writers have emphasized American exceptionalism. Louis Hartz argued that the absence of a feudal heritage accounts for the failure of socialism in this country; but his hypothesis seems static and ahistorical. It is misleading, it would seem, to infer that socialism was a response to the existence of a feudal aristocracy, that it was galvanized by the existence of aristocratic values and repression. The 1870s and 1880s in America hardly suggest a society devoid of class, given the violent industrial warfare of these decades. In a spin-off from this proposition, Kenneth McNaught, the Canadian historian, concludes that the absence of aristocratic values weakened the tendency to dissent by the intellectual elite and made their cooptation by the "liberal establishment" virtually inevitable, a thesis earlier pressed by Selig Perlman. This absence-of-feudalism argument neatly complements the conclusions of Seymour Martin Lipset. America, he finds, had no feudal "carryovers," "no rigid status groups," and was an "open" society—mobile, dynamic, guided by a middle-class consensus and a common set of individualistic values. Thus he sets forth a familiar explanation for the ineffectiveness of radicals: the high rate of social mobility defused class resentments. That nineteenth-century Europe possibly had a comparably high rate of social mobility is explained away by invoking "ideological egalitarianism." "Beliefs about opportunity in the United States" distinguished Old and New

Worlds. Lipset also emphasizes ethnic, racial, and religious cleavages within the labor movement as factors weakening class solidarity. Early in the century, Werner Sombart's *Why Is There No Socialism in the United States?* anticipated much of this argument. In answering his famous question, he emphasized rising living standards, rather than the pauperization of the proletariat which Marx had predicted. Fluid class lines and an open frontier, he concluded, produced a society which lacked a "settled" working class, offered the "free gift" of the franchise, and attracted newcomers who were seeking to improve their lot.

Other scholars find the root cause of the failure of radicalism in the bitter and divisive factionalism that afflicted socialist parties. There is a surface plausibility in their position. For the history of radical movements is littered with individuals and organizations caught up in the mordant intra-party quarrels over tactics and strategy, immediatism and impossibilism, gradualism and militancy. "Immediatism," as understood by Milwaukee socialist Victor Berger and by labor leader Samuel Gompers, meant adaptation to existing conditions—though many did not relinquish the idea of an inevitable evolution to socialism. "Impossibilists" represented the socialist left. They retained their twin faith in the inherent internationalism and revolutionary nature of the working class. Reforms, they believed, were impossible; and revolutionaries should not encourage labor to seek improvements in the competitive system. Imperialism and war, they concluded, were the logical and inevitable outcome of capitalism.

The immediatists almost inevitably confused means and ends; their tactics evolved into strategy, their ultimates became identified with expedients. The "revisionism" of Eduard Bernstein and Karl Kautsky, German social democrats and socialist theoreticians, was most attractive to them, to the founders of the Social Democratic Party, and to many of America's socialists generally. Reduced to its essentials, Bernstein's formula—the social-democratic methodology—stressed the democratic political process and the reform road to socialism and de-emphasized socialist ideology and objectives. It would ineluctably lead the Socialist Party to act as bargaining agent for labor within the capitalist structure and, in the hands of such "bourgeois collaborators" as Berger, it stressed peaceful change.

To seek *immediate* political and economic goals would produce harsh factionalism within the Socialist Labor Party, as we will see, and would invite excommunication. Such divisive struggle had a paradigmatic quality to it, for it prefigured the ideological warfare that persisted throughout the twentieth century, along with the vituperation, suspicions, and jockeying for power, the harassment and the expulsions. At stake was the legitimacy of the true church. The believer who condemned immediatists and social democrats as "bourgeois reformers," who drummed them out of the SLP or the later Socialist and Communist parties, was proclaiming his doctrinal purity and militancy. Suffice to say that these "renegades" and "revisionists" must also be numbered among America's radicals and cannot be easily read off the stage of history.

Can we, however, attribute the failure of radicalism to this recurring dilemma—the relation between ultimate goals and immediate methods, orthodoxy and opportunism? Would socialism have succeeded if intra-party strife over this issue had been resolved? Perhaps the persuasive but not certain response can be sought in the social and economic realities—though not in quite the same way that Lipset and Hartz, among others, have done. Without seeking any holistic answer, it seems reasonably obvious that American values and realities, and the working-class perception of them, frustrated an effective socialist movement.

Those who stake out a Marxist claim must contend with the bourgeois mentality of much of American labor, the obstacle to radical dreams for a socialist society. As the century advanced, it became clear, the work force became increasingly committed to the dominant values, assumptions, and consciousness of the middle class. The central bourgeois doctrines of self-help, self-improvement, and ballot-box reformism eroded critical elements in nineteenth-century working-class culture. That traditional work-centered culture was replaced by one oriented toward family life and mass entertainment; working-class institutions and values were increasingly absorbed into the mainstream of industrial capitalism; marked class distinctions and militancy were shorn of their threatening and subversive features.

There were some exceptions, to be sure, and labor's insurgent behavior did not suddenly disappear, as developments during and directly after World War I indicate. There were also some relatively powerless segments of the population which retained doubts about aspects of the socioeconomic system—though they, too, accepted it as fundamentally superior to any proposed alternative. More to the point, the overwhelming majority of Americans endorsed the dominant values of capitalism. Indeed, this acceptance became more pronounced after 1900. Intense class conflict, for instance, occurred in the earlier rather than the later stages of capitalism. Such developments were prompted by several factors: conservative ruling elites, the readiness of elected socialists to work within the system, working-class passivity and consent—derived from the strategic vision of union leaders and acceptance of the dominant social-economic values.

Such acceptance was "obtained by consent rather than by force, of one class group over other classes." The description is Antonio Gramsci's, as applied to Italian society at about this time, but Gramsci's assumptions and emphases are also relevant to America. Subtle but pervasive ideological control, not direct political coercion, became the primary means of perpetuating capitalism. Such control was accepted voluntarily. "The 'spontaneous' loyalty that any dominant social group obtains from the masses," he argued, was obtained "by virtue of its social and intellectual prestige and its supposedly superior function in the world of production."

This "social and intellectual prestige" was termed "hegemony," by which Gramsci meant the entire range of institutions, such as unions, schools, churches, the family—the system of values, attitudes, beliefs, morality—which comprised consciousness. These hegemonic values comprised a world view—that "powerful system of fortresses and earthworks" protecting the state. They were easy to popularize in an advanced capitalist society owing to the increasingly intrusive role of the state, the rise of a skilled labor force, the importance of technical expertise, the sophisticated techniques for education and control of public opinion. And they were readily internalized by the working class. For these core values—America's democratic and egalitarian ethos, representative democracy, the fluidity of the class structure— were part of a "general conception of life," a part of those integrated values and attitudes associated with the dominant ruling forces, *and* a part of labor's concerns as well.

It should not be thought that working-class acceptance of hegemonic values and interests was a matter of conscious choice. The dominated are seldom aware of such dominance. And those who dominate rarely do so calculatingly. As Peter Berger has written, "deliberate deception requires a degree of psychological self control that few people are capable of. . . . It is much easier to deceive oneself. It is, therefore, important to keep the concept of ideology distinct from notions of lying, deception, propaganda or legerdemain. Ideologic dominance rather is a mode of consciousness. It is rooted in the needs of a social group—even though these needs may have been transformed by what Marx has called 'false consciousness' or what Malinowski described as myth." America as the land of opportunity, for instance, was one ideological value which fell into such a category; and its consensual acceptance frustrated any realistic appreciation of the inegalitarian and class nature of the society by American labor.

Gramsci, Raymond Williams warns, did not find these consensual values and attitudes unchanging and thereby ahistorical. The dominant culture can change—as we have seen over the past decade—even if there is no change in its central formation. It must "always change in this way if it is to remain dominant, if it is still to be felt as in real ways central in all our many activities and interests." Such change does not mean the abolition of social inequality or the structure giving rise to it; rather, it rationalizes new social and cultural relations *within* the structural social inequality. Hence this "integrated culture" of the elites did not emerge from an ideological vacuum; it advanced in stages, refined and reshaped to the needs and contradictions of capitalism.

Out of these theoretical considerations two related questions emerge: to what degree was the prevailing ideology socialized within the work force and embraced by it, and to what extent has American radicalism reinforced or further legitimized such hegemony? The first question can only be hinted at here, but it does appear to be seamlessly wedded to the second—namely, how, why, and to what degree then has indigenous radicalism reinforced the dominant cultural values? Finally, why has the left failed? Why have Americans so consistently voted against socialist programs when such programs moved outside immediate, issues-oriented reforms? To what extent were elite values truly hegemonic; that is, rarely requiring guns and tear gas to keep the ruled in their place. Such questions are terribly ambitious and beyond the confines of a small volume, and they can be determined only by a direct investigation of working-class attitudes and behavior.

But even for this limited study of modern American radicalism, Gramsci's theory of hegemonic values and institutions is very helpful. Suffice for the moment to note that revolutionary, even radical, third parties have ultimately failed. And for salient reasons: rationalized capital-labor relations; popular support for the dominant social group, which contributed to its stability, particularly in times of crisis; a "false consciousness" which accepted the dominant view that no ruling class existed in America, the great disparities of wealth and power notwithstanding, and which criticized the established social order in the terms supplied by that order; electoral participation, which meant working within those political guidelines that the radical third parties ostensibly despised. To attract the labor vote seemingly demanded emphasis on immediate reforms rather than on an alternative form of society. There existed genuine distress, and reform consequently had great appeal on humanitarian grounds which all radicals shared, but it would provide only ephemeral relief. The capitalist economy, its property and market institutions, remained intact. Indeed, some radicals would argue, state intervention in the form of welfare assistance, social security, unemployment insurance, progressive taxation, workmen's compensation measures, etc., probably helped to limit class conflict and even militated against class consciousness; yet the basic inequities remained, actually becoming more endurable.

Notwithstanding the cooptation of trade-union leaders and the embourgeoisement of the work force, there is no denying labor militancy. Intermittent though it was, it customarily took the form of strikes, union organizing drives, and a push for worker control. By the last I mean the collective effort to control conditions of labor at the workplace—to determine practices in the factory: enforcement of work rules, regulation of dismissals, union recognition, discharge of unpopular foremen, etc. Militancy appeared in industries menaced by Taylorism, the "scientific management" program of Frederick Taylor which would measure each employee's daily labor, the time required for the work, etc., and compute wages on the basis of work done and the time taken to do it. And it also broke out among certain immigrant laborers, whose past included a tradition of labor militancy: Jewish sweatshop workers in New York City's East Side, Italian shoe workers in Lynn, Chicago's Polish shoe operatives, Greek and Polish textile workers in Ipswich in 1913, Slavic newcomers in Pittsburgh's finished steel products industries in 1912, Passaic and Lawrence textile workers in 1919. Most walkouts by immigrants were over bread-and-butter issues, especially cost-of-living increases. Leaders of the Industrial Workers of the World surely converted some of Passaic's and Lawrence's strikers to the IWW's vision of the good society, but, for all its charisma and power, most workers rejected programmatic radicalism and, as David Montgomery tells us, sought better working conditions, shorter hours, and "durable, open, recognized unions."

In any case, labor militancy could not be sustained. It sagged with the depressed economy and rising unemployment of 1909–10, reviving again in mid-1912, especially with the Lawrence strike. There was a virtual "epidemic of strikes" in 1912–13, but they were brief, spontaneous, and usually affected only single shops or factories. Then, toward the end of 1913, prosperity and labor militancy both declined, unemployment climbed, and economic conditions worsened. The war and postwar periods were distinguished by strikes. Again, these walkouts were usually short and spontaneous—with wildcatting locals going out over the eight-hour day or worker-control issues. There is no indication that the radicalization of some striking leaders and the radicalism of outside organizers from the IWW or the Socialist Party (SP) reached deep into working-class ranks or, more significant still, that it had a permanent effect or ideological basis.

These instances of worker militancy between 1901 and 1904 or between 1916 and 1920—and they were not duplicated until the 1930s—do not necessarily indicate any deepening hold of radical-socialist thought or a strongly felt sense of class consciousness. Admittedly the idea of consciousness is complex and broader than formal statements of belief. "Sabotage, syndicalism, passive resistance," as P. J. Conlon, the Machinists' vice-president, claimed, "were a reaction to Taylorism and scientific management," and these responses, like the wildcatting of union locals, indicate that workers were sometimes forced to *act* in contradiction to their stated values and to a whole congeries of middle-class beliefs. Furthermore, there *were* instances of militant socialist unions—the brewery workers, New York's jewelry workers, and the structural iron workers. Significantly, however, as Montgomery has emphasized, these unions were composed of traditional craft workers and dealt with small employers. They stood outside heavy industry, though Taylorism prompted labor militancy wherever it was introduced.

To admit a broader view of labor militancy or even of class consciousness than is generally recognized does not suggest yielding to past or current radical fantasies on this subject. It is important to avoid inflated and generalized claims for working-class consciousness or for the success of socialist thought. We may assume, when all is said, that sabotage and slowdowns do not constitute expressions of an ideological position or reflect adherence to socialist thought. We may still believe that those who governed, who believed in the virtues of capitalism, and who, their reservations notwithstanding, believed it the superior economic and social system, were never in danger of losing control. Strikes, sabotage, and the struggle for worker control do not imply rejection of capitalism. Indeed, the system's dominant values and institutions were on balance more acceptable in the twentieth century than in the nineteenth.

In the years after 1900, and the half century before, the industrial process was doing what Adam Smith (not Marx) predicted (in his early *Lectures* and in *The Wealth of Nations*): it was robbing labor of its "martial spirit" and its native capacity for reflective and critical judgments, and the result was the intellectual degradation of labor rather than heightening class awareness. In the 1870s and 1880s, Americans fought desperately for the right to strike, to form unions, and to press for immediate change. The concessions labor obtained provided important restraints on employer rapacity. But as the new century began, labor's efforts produced only such reforms. The belief of socialists (Daniel De Leon and his followers excepted) that struggle for immediate reforms would lead to humanitarian benefits, as well as a rising awareness of the nature of socialism, would not be fulfilled.

The pre-Civil War years saw the beginnings of a new industrial morality, which emphasized sobriety and self-discipline. Refined after 1865, this new morality was smoothly enfolded into the "job consciousness" of Samuel Gompers and his American Federation of Labor. Gompers knew something—namely, that a substantial majority of America's work force, if it had to choose between strikes and negotiated settlement, between radical violence and the trade agreement (that is, collective bargaining), would choose the more peaceful course. The once socialistic Boot and Shoe Workers' Union of Massachusetts, led by John F. Tobin, a De Leonite in the late 1890s, rejected demands for revolutionary action, much to "the astonishment and anger" of those socialists remaining in the union. Tobin, as John Laslett observes, even urged union members to consider the profit margins of their shoe employers before demanding wage increases and went so far as to break wildcat strikes. Nor were Tobin and his union unique. The Western Federation of Miners adopted time contracts; the International Ladies' Garment Workers' Union, in 1910, negotiated the Protocol of Peace for its industry; brewery workers cooperated with management on pension plans; and the United Mine Workers abided by nationally negotiated trade agreements designed to rationalize labor-capital relations in the mining industry. Considering the decentralized nature of the Federation, it is unlikely that any Gompers ukase would have been heeded—if it had met with strong radical opposition in any of the independent unions which comprised the AFL. Federation leadership could not have thwarted the growth of a mass socialist movement if conditions had been ripe for it.

But Gompers knew instinctively that bread-and-butter unionism struck the proper chord. True, this approach triggered the radical charge of "bourgeois collaboration"; and it was accurate enough. The Federation, even in its earliest years, had a record of equivocation and de facto support of dominant social-economic values and institutions. It was very much representative of what Lenin would term "trade-union consciousness," which is compatible with capitalism. William Pfaff, in *Condemned to Freedom,* described the problem of radicals when they perceived workers as revolutionaries: "Once the worker has won a position of basic economic security and reasonable expectations, he has considerably more reason to be conservative on social issues than the middle-class executive or professional man. . . . For the workingman, everything could be jeopardized by radical change." Socialists are startled by this observation, which claims that improving conditions will buy off worker militancy. And considering the facts of union growth in times of prosperity, we may add a gloss: improved economic conditions bring stasis to any ripening class consciousness or limit union actions to ad hoc economic reforms.

Lenin recognized as much. Hence his distinction between the limited trade-union consciousness, which develops spontaneously, and the "socialist consciousness," which does not. On the one hand, he is asserting, the immediate experiences of the workers are restricted to the problems of their economic struggle; that is, as Eric Hobsbawm writes, to the relations between employers and themselves. But less circumscribed, long-term objectives, socialist objectives if you will, cannot result from such experiences. If capitalism allows for the minimum demands of labor, then trade-union consciousness is likely to drift into acceptance of middle-class ideology; then the working class is likely to act as if the system were permanent, trivializing socialist goals by reducing them to politically irrelevant codas to their "real" activities.

De Leon understood and endorsed Lenin's fundamental distinctions. He also recognized that if socialists acted as if capitalism were permanent, they would contribute to it. Thus he dismissed the struggle over immediate economic issues, finding them irrelevant and "infantile." But he had to struggle against the natural inclinations of some SLP'ers as well as against the more conservative AFL leadership. This leadership calculatingly used the organizing abilities of radicals, so long as they muted their political program and did not seek to build revolutionary or industrial unions that might directly challenge the tradition-bound craft unions of the Federation. It was hardly a painful restraint upon most radicals, since they gave priority to strengthening labor unions, believing that labor's socialist perspective, a fundamental precondition of revolution, would proceed slowly. But radicals failed to realize—in 1900 and thereafter—that a higher degree of political consciousness in the labor movement would alone frustrate the drift into reformism. Only a special effort by a conscious socialist movement, both Lenin and De Leon realized, might prevent that—for the labor movement *and* radical cadres alike.

Socialist-radical attitudes toward equality for blacks and for women were by present-day standards backward indeed. Before the 1930s, for instance, there was scant mention of women among socialists, and the Party's leadership regarded the "women question" as part of the "labor question." SP'ers scarcely differed in their attitude from that held by virtually all Americans: the home must be maintained and women were uniquely suited to rule over it. Socialists, as might be expected, added a modest gloss: capitalism was threatening the home by paying low wages to male breadwinners, forcing females into the work force, and it was also responsible for divorce, prostitution, inadequate housing. Accepting the stereotyped role for women, socialist males scarcely advanced beyond the Cult of True Womanhood. There were some women in leadership positions, to be sure, with Ella Reeve Bloor prominent among them, but they were generally relegated to a secondary place and looked upon with "irritating contempt" by male socialists. After 1910, there were fewer references to the "inferior" sex in socialist journals, but the campaign of women socialists for equal rights did not enlist male support.

The civil rights movement received some early recognition among socialists. Among the NAACP's founders, for example, there were socialists like William E. B. Du Bois, Charles E. Russell, and William English Walling, a major SP theoretician. But there were few rank-and-file black socialists, and only one resolution favoring civil rights was ever passed by a national SP convention before 1912. Indeed, some Party locals and state bodies segregated black and white members into separate bodies. Victor Louis Berger's racist views were well known: blacks constituted "a lower race," he believed. More important, a majority of socialists shared this belief in black "inferiority." Equally significant, the Party was indifferent to anti-Negro violence, and affirmed that socialism was an economic movement exclusively and that the Negro's condition was part of the general "labor problem," thereby rejecting the idea that SP'ers should serve in campaigns seeking social and civil equality for blacks. Socialism would bring equality, the Party affirmed, but it would also bring complete segregation: blacks and whites should not live in the same areas or even work in the same factories. Only with the end of World War I was there any significant rise of interest in the black, in his condition, and in organizing him.

Nor did blacks fare better in the early years of the Communist

Party. None attended the founding convention, for example, and Communists, having split off from the SP, shared the socialist attitudes toward them: the Negro "problem" was linked to that of the unskilled worker. In December 1928, nine years after the first CP convention, there were only 150 to 200 blacks in the Party and scant attention was paid to civil rights. In the 1930s, CP'ers became increasingly attentive to civil rights and proposed the Negro-nation line: "right of self-determination of the Negroes in the Black Belt" of the South—in a way an astonishing proposition, given the Party's understandable hostility to any doctrine that would curb Communism's vaunted internationalism. With soaring black unemployment during the 1930s, the Party swung into organizing work in urban ghettos and among southern sharecroppers. By 1935, it had become a force in black communities. The CP cause was helped by its highly publicized efforts in behalf of the Scottsboro Boys and by its well-advertised, though relatively few, black Party leaders. But blacks never numbered more than 8 percent of the Party's rank and file, and the Negro-nation doctrine attracted few recruits among blacks, owing in part to their expectations within the capitalist structure. This sense of expectancy remained—among them and among women. Consequently, neither group would be drawn to Communist thinking in substantial numbers—even in the 1960s and 1970s. Both the civil rights and women's movements were destined to become powerful political forces, but CP efforts at infiltrating and recruiting within them remained desolately ineffectual.

1 Origins of Twentieth-Century Radicalism: The Socialist Labor Party

THE SOURCES of twentieth-century radicalism are varied and familiar. There were in the nineteenth century the social gospel ministers, who sought to implement the social teachings of Jesus; the Populists, who proposed to eliminate the economic inequities suffered by the dirt farmers of the West and the South; the Nationalist followers of Edward Bellamy, who had their own brand of utopian idealism; the early votaries of Karl Marx, who first emigrated to the United States after the 1848 Revolutions and who would early dominate the SLP as well as the SP after the latter was founded in 1901. Then there were the advocates of cooperative colonies, such as the charismatic Eugene V. Debs, who inadvertently called up millenarian pre-Civil War utopian practices and whose emotional visions as well as quixotic outbursts embodied the contradictions inherent in the Socialist Party itself.

Early-twentieth-century socialism streamed down from the Gospels, the precepts of Jesus, the Enlightenment teachings of Jefferson and Paine. It continued a political movement deeply rooted in farmer and worker experience. It was a mix of social gospel Christians, utopians, Populists, a handful of anarchists-syndicalists, and some Marxist ideologues. Prominent among the last was the Curaçao-born Daniel De Leon. A doctrinaire thinker—he was called a "pope"—and yet imagi-

native and independent, De Leon differed from so many later radicals
in his stubborn refusal to bend to the dictates and dicta of Kautsky,
Lenin, Trotsky, or other giants of European socialism. Volatile, vigorous, militant, he became a vital force among America's radicals. He
had been involved with the Knights of Labor, passed through the
Bellamy movement, became a convert to Marxism and its most prominent scholar in the United States. He entered the SLP in 1890, was ap-
pointed editor of the Party's official paper, *The People,* and for a
quarter century—down to 1914, when he died—shaped a party whose
most distinctive quality was discipline. He sought to make the SLP the
spokesman for the American working class, and his program, though
suffering from some fundamental shortcomings, most completely expressed the current views of the historic left.

Out of the SLP tactics that triggered the intra-party strife emerged
the basic and conflicting programs of organized radicalism: dual
unions versus infiltration, third-party politics versus regular-party activities.

De Leon argued for both an economic and a political assault upon
American capitalism. Rejecting the old SLP tactic of infiltrating the
American Federation of Labor and other "reformist" unions, he contended that the Party should avoid "boring from within." Dual unionism, he predicted, would become the major labor trend after 1900.
This meant large and inclusive unions that would be competitive with
the AFL, would seek immediate reforms for the working class, and
would also educate it toward the larger goals of an alternative economic order. Thus he dismissed "pure and simple" unionism, a
phrase given its classic definition by Adolph Strasser of the cigar
workers. "We have no ultimate ends," he declared in 1883, "we are
going on from day to day. We are fighting only for immediate objects—objects that can be realized in a few years." Such an orientation, De Leon asserted, ignored "existing class distinctions" and "the
close connection there is between wages and politics, it splits up at the
ballot box among the parties of capital, and thus unites in upholding
the system of capitalist production." These diametrically opposed
quotes set down and prefigure the lines of conflict between established
labor bureaucracy and militant radicalism in the twentieth century.

To implement his belief in revolutionary unionism, De Leon helped found the Socialist Trade and Labor Alliance (STLA) in 1895. The resolution establishing it called upon SLP'ers to carry "the revolutionary spirit of the STLA" into all labor organizations, an ambiguous command since it would entail working within the established union structure—while urging the creation of "one class-conscious army." Drawing its initial recruits from the AFL and the Knights, the STLA would openly attack non-socialist Federation locals and double its original 15,000 members.

De Leon's second spearhead against capitalism took political form and pointed to another basic radical strategy after 1900, a third party, a revolutionary political party which would seek a socialist victory at the polls. Economic tactics were meshed with the political: there must be militant class-conscious unions—the archetypal IWW and STLA would unite "the whole working class industrially"—which would support a socialist election victory. The Party's goals would be successfully challenged by a powerfully resistant capitalist economy were these dual tactics not employed.

The observations of IWW organizer Joseph Ettor were fully shared by De Leon. Deploring collaboration with craft unions and capitalism, Ettor declared: "We learned at an awful cost particularly this: That the most unscrupulous labor fakers now betraying the workers were once our 'industrialist,' 'anarchist,' and 'socialist' comrades, who . . . were not only lost, but . . . became the supports of the old and [the] most serious enemies of the new." He went on to attack the "careerist" impulses of AFL officials, a viewpoint which De Leon also shared. De Leon, for his part, found that AFL leaders "are essentially hired men of the capitalists," and "politicians who were sent to keep the toilers in line," and that craft unions betrayed labor by building their economic organization upon capitalist foundations. He rejected short-run and nugatory gains like shorter hours and higher wages, the goals of reformers.

De Leon's ideological purity, disavowal of reform, and high-handed practices produced acrimonious conflict within the Party. As a result, after 1895 the Party suffered from endemic intrigue and fratricide. One anti-De Leonite faction (known as the Kangaroos) gravitated toward Morris Hillquit of the New York City SLP chapter and to Job Harriman of California. Their opposition was both personal and theoreti-

cal, antagonistic to De Leon's iron-fisted rule, his sectarianism and rigidity, as well as to his declaration of war upon pure-and-simple trade unionism and upon the Federation. The issues were clearly drawn, the antagonisms fueled by strong emotions, and, by 1897, the talismanic rhetoric and normative strictures of each side had divided every Party local. Soon there were two leaderships, two headquarters in New York City, two newspapers, and two parties, each claiming legitimacy and each having about half the total 7,000 members.

The centrists concluded that elections were only "for purposes of propaganda," but participation in them became an end in itself: the election of socialists to office became synonymous with the achievement of socialism. Thus these centrists inadvertently equated means with ends, tactics with objectives. And they thereby provide an early example of a recurrent, critical, and seemingly insoluble dilemma confronting organized radicalism; what Svetozar Stojanovic, in a different context, has wisely described as "the finalization of means and the instrumentalization of ends." The means, which included participation in electoral campaigns and union drives, became, in such instances, independent of the initially assigned ends and even replaced them; the means, any number of instances suggest, "acquire their own rhythm and direction," and the gap between them and the ends becomes unbridgeable. The Hillquit faction evolved a socialist practice that turned to the path of opportunism. Its goals became little more than election to office and reforms within the capitalist system.

De Leon, to his credit, stubbornly resisted the lure of "immediate demands." He correctly perceived that Progressive reforms would not awaken working-class consciousness to the level of political struggle. Ironically, however, as Paul Buhle has shrewdly observed, De Leon's insistence upon revolutionary strategy "pointed toward a theory in which all 'outside' forces *including his own SLP* were growing obsolescent if not already unnecessary." In elaborating upon this inherent contradiction, Buhle wrote, "The more one sought in objective class forces the actual liberation of workers, the more the intellectual's role seemed relegated to observer."

De Leon's militancy increasingly isolated him and his followers. "Immediatism," for most SLP'ers, would provide benefits—irresistibly attractive to those seeking adherents and respectability. And, they delusively reasoned, it would also educate the working class in how their class interests differed from everyone else's. The immediatist appeal, with its quick, though ultimately trivial, reformist victories, produced relief if not contentment for American labor—and these relatively easy successes reflect the willingness of a significant entrepreneurial sector to make concessions and union readiness to accept them.

De Leon's arraignment of the AFL's "labor fakers" and of its immediatism was a challenge that would wake the dead. By 1900, Gompers and other Federation officials (like Strasser and P. J. McGuire) had turned away from the interminable theoretical disputes of the socialists, and away from the socialist influences of their earlier years. De Leon's attacks and the formation of the obviously competitive STLA provoked sharp reaction, with Gompers responding in kind. "The work of union wrecking," he acidly observed in *The Federation,* "is being taken up by a wing of the so-called socialist party of New York, headed by a professor without a professorship." American labor, as Gompers perceived it, need not stand outside capitalist society and challenge it. Rather it should seek acceptance and power within the system; and, pursuing this accommodationist viewpoint, he would soon lead the Federation into the National Civic Federation (NCF), a powerful organization of employers, thereby confirming the SLP charge of "class collaborationism."

The flexibility of this major segment of the American business community must be emphasized; its capacity to bend, however grudgingly, to the winds of change. Representing a large bloc of powerful corporate and financial interests, with Mark Hanna and Ralph Easley especially prominent, the NCF concluded that coercion was stupid, that bloody strikes should be avoided, that unions ought to be recognized. Organized labor, Hanna declared, deserves entrepreneurial trust—for when "the concerns and interests of labor are entrusted to able and honest leadership, it is much easier for those who represent the employers to come into close contact with the laborer and, by dealing with fewer persons, to accomplish results quicker and better." Labor mediation and certain social reforms could be conceded, enlightened businessmen like Hanna believed, since they would not endanger capitalism. So the NCF endorsed the trade agreement (collective bargaining) as the vehicle which could direct the growing power of labor into "evolutionary" channels, which could bring orderly processes and industrial peace to a number of industries suffering from mounting labor-capital conflict. John Mitchell of the UMW found this same device to be the essence of trade unionism; so did other labor leaders. For Hanna, "the spread of a spirit of socialism" was as much a "menace" as rising working-class militancy, and, we may speculate, Gompers shared both sentiments. He surely agreed with Hanna that "many of the ills that have crept into labor organization are importations from older countries"; and he was glad to observe that "the American labor unions are becoming more and more conservative and careful in their management, and are not likely to be led away from the straight road by hot-headed members."

So the specter of socialism haunted labor as well as business leaders. But the central thrust of the NCF–AFL alliance sprang from the belief that the industrial program of the former and the objectives of the latter corresponded, that unauthorized strikes threatened both. The NCF espoused social reform after 1905, and by 1909, for instance, it was campaigning actively for workmen's compensation measures. Its views were not simply propaganda for material interests, but expressed a cultural imperative of enlightened entrepreneurs and conservative trade unionists alike.

The De Leonite struggle against reformist tendencies was a harbinger of dilemmas that would confront organized radicalism. One difficulty was never satisfactorily resolved. The SLP's struggle against the easy pursuit of immediate demands effectively cut it off from the realistic demands of America's work force. The result was predictable: the De Leonites became a party of ideological purists, increasingly isolated and sectarian, hopelessly remote from their labor base.

Such tendencies and dilemmas plagued American radicalism. They were further intensified by sharp differences of personality and background among the leadership. Consequently, there were markedly contrasting definitions of Marxist orthodoxy, of proper "socialist" programs, of the good society itself. Continuous and acrid divisions became the fate of all organized radicalism in the twentieth century. More immediately, internecine warfare within the SLP helped set the stage for the Socialist Party.

2 The Socialist Party and the IWW

THE SOCIALIST PARTY of America (SPA or SP) was not born *ex nihilo,* without parents, a child of the "bloomin', buzzin', confusion" of 1901; and it would oversimplify to conclude that the Party was only an amalgam of Debsian and dissident De Leonites. Its delegates had no direct lineage or loyalties to Marx; and when they went to Europe for inspiration, they drew as frequently upon H. G. Wells, George Bernard Shaw, Karl Kautsky, Henri Bergson, and Friedrich Nietzsche as they did upon the gray-bearded founders of Communism. They were anti-capitalist, of course, but more often their ideas derived from Edward Bellamy's *Looking Backward* rather than from *Das Kapital.* To a considerable extent rooted in an earlier tradition of protest and dissent, their members included refugees from the old Populist Party, from Debs's American Railway Union, from the SLP (Rochester faction), from Christian socialism, whose votaries came to socialism through a belief that life on earth could be made into a reasonable facsimile of the Kingdom of God. There were other strains in the Party as well: the boyish romanticism of Jack London, the messianic piety of George Herron, the syndicalist bravura of Big Bill Haywood and his IWW bloc, the do-good settlement worker crowd, the millionaire socialists like J. G. Phelps Stokes, upper-class converts like Robert Rives La

23

Monte and William English Walling, perhaps the Party's most original theoretician, the lineal descendants of German Forty-eighters who belonged to Milwaukee's social-democratic circles, and the culture radicals—bohemian writers and artists—who fought for birth control, women's suffrage, and uninhibited social-sexual behavior. So the SP comprised a mongrel breed. It was an umbrella organization for such diverse figures as Haywood and Berger, who came out of Milwaukee's reform-oriented social democrats; George Lunn, the Schenectady social gospeler who fought municipal corruption and was never a Marxist; and Hillquit, from the De Leonite splinter in New York.

The New Yorkers included many of the SP's intellectuals, and socialism, for them, was not merely a political movement. It was a way of life. They had been nurtured on hot theoretical debate in East Side tenements, accompanied into maturity by Abe Cahan's *Jewish Daily Forward* as well as Marx's *Communist Manifesto,* joined one of the needle-trade unions, and possibly studied at the Rand School, an institution which educated youthful, mostly Jewish, radical youth.

These urban intellectuals shared the same platform with a national, state, and local leadership that was largely working-class. Hence the SP was quite unlike the Progressives, who were middle-class reformers. Not only did it have a solid labor base—with skilled workers, especially class-conscious craftsmen and artisans, liberally sprinkled among them—many of its local officials came out of the ranks of labor, including Eugene V. Debs, its dominant personality. Debs was the hero and symbol of socialism in America. He would have no traffic with the major political parties; opposed capitalism since it was "inherently unjust, inhuman, unintelligent"; emphasized individual rights and private conscience; rejected socialist participation in the AFL; sought what novelist John Dos Passos called "a world brothers might own where everybody would split even." He represented a doctrinal mix, which included a grass-roots populism and a near-mystical sense of self, that was anathema to ideological purists like De Leon. Indeed, he embodied the unity of populist, Marxist, militant trade union, and Judeo-Christian traditions which fused to form the Party itself.

Debs's Social Democratic Party, the predecessor of the SP, adopted a platform at its 1898 convention which outlined the future position of mainstream socialism and trade unionism in the twentieth century. Including fashionable Progressive measures as well as more advanced proposals which were implemented only with the New Deal, this platform was contemptuously dismissed by De Leon as "palliatives." His Party's program at the 1900 convention eliminated some twenty-one of them, including reduction of hours of work, nationalization of mines and transport, public works projects for the unemployed. In rejecting immediatism, the SLP reaffirmed its doctrinal purity—at a time when the rival SDP challenged its claim to a historic mission for the American working class. Such inflexibility prompted many of its rank and file to desert. Powerless to prevent the erosion, De Leon could only deplore it and arraign the Socialist Party as the enemy of American labor, "essentially hired men of the capitalist class."

The SP thus began its "golden age." Its membership more than doubled between 1900 and 1902, and nearly doubled again during the 1904 presidential campaign year. SP immediatists like Max Hayes and Victor Berger were in the ascendant and, until 1914, the influence of left-wing socialists—the impossibilists—was negligible, especially so in the trade-union movement. Eminently practical leaders, Berger and Hayes denied any contradiction between the struggle of labor for immediate needs and the long-run interests of socialism, between being good trade unionists and being radical ideologues. As AFL socialists, they praised the skilled craftsman as "the real American worker," and looking backward, thus reinforced the AFL's archaic class perspectives and failed to grasp changing industrial realities.

Socialist nominees, in these expansive years, captured a number of local political offices, and demonstrated considerable citywide strength in some municipalities. Their supporters included many workers— which is not to claim that many workers were socialists. Indeed Algie M. Simons in 1909 candidly noted that "the actual wage workers . . . are outside" the Party. The SP may have virtually tripled in size in the first decade of its life, but its recruits were frequently tenant farmers of the Southwest, the former Populists, as well as urban radicals and intellectuals—Marxists and utopians—and its officers admitted that the Party had failed to attract the trade-union "family man." Its peak strength nationally coincided with the high point of progressivism, the 1912 national election, when Debs received nearly

900,000 votes. To be sure, it was a small percentage of the national vote (about 6 percent), but it was the highest percentage ever given to a radical candidate.

A coda should be added. There was, it must be cautioned, a sharp disparity between votes and membership; and the large outpouring at elections indicates that the Party was a vehicle of negative protest against existing social-economic conditions, not one carrying people to socialism.

The SP program had the same appeal for labor and for reformers that the Social Democratic Party had once held out. It, too, proposed a long list of "immediate demands" that De Leon scorned: conservation, public ownership of transportation, etc.; and it included some staples of the Populist, Progressive, and Wilsonian platforms, such as workmen's compensation and a graduated income tax. The first SP convention limned the conflict that such programs would generate. The minority left wing, the "impossibilist" or revolutionary bloc led by Simons, the youthful Chicago editor and ex-SLP'er, attacked the "immediatists" who would transform the Socialist Party into a "reform" organization. Hillquit (for both the Springfield and Chicago factions) replied by equating immediate reform goals and ultimate ends. After summing up the immediatist position, Hillquit warned: "If we ever attempt to go before the working class and promise them the cooperative commonwealth in three or four or five years and if they wait six and ten and see no chance of its realization, then we will be much worse off, for they will lose faith in our propaganda." Victor Louis Berger's plea for peaceful change was an inevitable spin-off of the reform position. The Hillquits and Bergers prevailed, by a four-to-one vote, and set the pattern for future conventions and future Party policy.

Successive SP conventions coupled ultimate goals with immediate reforms—as if every reform was one element in a full-fledged socialism. The revolutionary patina, the chiliastic rhetoric, was usually relegated to the platform preamble. So Party platforms were larded with such revolutionary bromides as "emancipating the working class" and "the abolition of wage slavery." The 1901 and 1904 SP platforms insisted that "immediate demands" were merely "remedial measures as means to the one great end of the cooperative commonwealth . . . , a preparation of the workers to seize the whole powers of government.'' Verbal protestations about the purity of the Party and the unthinkability of any compromise with bourgeois reformers abound. But once again, as with the SLP, *causa finalis* was transformed into *causa efficiens,* and vice versa: the ends metamorphosed owing to an obsessive concern with means; the ends became the rhetorical detritus of Party conventions.

America's socialists, then, like their European counterparts, endorsed melioristic legislation. True enough, they relentlessly affirmed the historic mission of socialism, though divided on the course it would take. Right-wing, tactics-oriented socialists like Berger, for example, believed in an inevitable, though peaceful, transition to the good society. However, we must watch what they did rather than what they said. And what socialists sought and implemented when opportunity arose can be considered part of the main current of progressive thought in the dozen years preceding World War I. Some important socialist thinkers candidly admitted as much. Witness, for instance, William Walling's attempt to join Marxist rhetoric to John Dewey's pragmatic reform. Walling urged the Party to encourage and enlist middle-class support; he had the uneasy conviction, shared by other socialists, that the workers alone could not bring off a socialist society in middle-class America.

Successive Party programs and political campaigns brought in members, voters, and election victories in the decade that followed the 1901 convention. That few of the delegates to this first convention, as David Shannon has concluded, ''had more than the haziest intellectual acquaintance with theoretical Marxism'' is true enough—and it is an observation applicable to any SP convention. The ''socialist'' response invariably adapted to the exigent needs of the labor-reformer constituency. The Party, then, genuflected in the direction of socialist purity and internationalism. It remained, however, indigenous, even parochial. Its non-derivative character accounts in part for its easy appeal to middle-class reformers and to selective elements of the work force: old-time Kansas populists, Oklahoma wheat farmers, East Side garment workers, Milwaukee Germans, New York and Chicago intellectuals and culture radicals. Small wonder that economically marginal labor—black sharecroppers, western farmers and miners, ethnic groups from Southern and Eastern Europe—were seldom interested in the Party or soon became disillusioned.

The Party did draw German, Jewish, and some Irish workers, but its efforts to attract immigrants were otherwise largely unsuccessful. More often it was English-speaking workers, or German artisans locked into declining crafts, who tended to become socialist. Plant modernization, decreasing wages, economic instability, and cheap labor—that of the Southern and Eastern European newcomer— radicalized some of the skilled or semiskilled native-born workers. Thus the transition to a mature industrial society, which menaced both the economic security and the achievement perspective of American-born artisans and factory operatives, drove some of them toward socialism. Ironically, then, it was not the unskilled but elements in the aristocracy of labor which were becoming radicalized. Party influence among such trade unionists, and in miner locals as well, as John Laslett has observed, also derived from the populist demand for democracy as much as for a revolutionary alternative to capitalism. In Texas and Oklahoma, states which gave the SP a relatively large vote, socialist strength also reflected an earlier rural radicalism, the ongoing farmer interest in Debs's "cooperative commonwealth" programs. Socialism in these years was a rural movement as much as it was urban; it appealed to Oklahoma's farmers and to Bryanite country generally.

But it was the urban and labor constituency, rather than the agrarian radicals, which confirmed the "correctness" of a non-Marxist and non-theoretical socialism. The theoretical poverty of America's left— and, except for De Leon, not one major theoretician emerged out of socialism in this country—enabled the SP to collaborate with reform-minded Democrats and trade unionists: there were no theoretical strictures to the contrary. The efforts of the Union Labor Parties in 1902 and in 1903 induced Algie Simons, then an "impossibilist," to liken collaboration to "measles and whooping cough in human beings. . . , a disease which seems to effect the Socialist Party in every country at certain stages of its development." The SP's non-theoretical character also enabled it to elect a number of public officials, mostly on the municipal level, in this first decade; and these officials—in Berkeley Butte, Milwaukee, Reading, Lynn, and other cities—were overwhelmingly "gas and water socialists." Milwaukee's Party members were typical, with their demand for municipal ownership of utilities, improved sanitation, adequate school facilities, free textbooks, anti-corruption drives; and socialist Mayor Emil Seidel won in 1910 by campaigning for the elimination of graft in City Hall, expanding welfare services, and the like. A similar socialist program was victorious in the 1910 Berkeley mayoralty race. Such local electoral successes fed the fantasies of Party members and permitted onlookers to conclude that "we are all more or less socialists today," which reflected the definitional problems afflicting the SP itself.

Admittedly, some socialist locals balked at immediatism. The 1902 Chicago convention declared, in its majority report, that "municipal ownership . . . and other reforms . . . will bring no lasting relief to the working class, until these industries pass into the control of the working class." But SP'ers in office prided themselves on being realistic—attuned to the electorate's needs. So they readily worked within the guidelines of progressivism, especially those below the national level. Small wonder that the potential constituency of tenant farmers, and marginal and unskilled workers, were dissatisfied with Party tactics. Or that progressive intellectuals such as Charles Eliot of Harvard could enthusiastically endorse municipal "socialism" as practiced in Milwaukee, Schenectady, and Berkeley. Eliot personified the Brahman elite and his reactions are highly suggestive. The "socialism" he approved of did little more than coopt dissidents—workers and intellectuals alike—and inadvertently helped rationalize the system. The benefits of this "socialism" were negligible. But its contributions to social order and stability hastened acceptance of the business civilization and confirmed the beneficence of its values.

The issues which troubled voters received scant attention from the major parties—at least until socialists won office. Then local politicians woke up and made some programmatic adjustments or entered into fusion against this menacing third force. While machine bosses became more attentive to the needs of their constituents, some socialists lost touch with reality. For example, J. G. Phelps Stokes, the millionaire socialist, interpreted the 1910 election as a victory for radical thought. It was not. The Cleveland *Plain Dealer* offered a more accurate appraisal:

> Towns which have chosen Socialist mayors have done so by way of vigorous protest against the conditions of government permitted to flourish under some Democratic or Republican regimes. . . .
>
> Communities which tire of being continually misrepresented by either or both the other parties sometimes turn in despair to a well-organized Socialist Party as a means of effecting their temporary relief. When the people of a town rise and use this weapon, however, it seldom means that they have endorsed Socialism.

The political experience of cities like Cleveland and Philadelphia confirms this estimate. When a socialist reformer was elected, that was the end of the matter for the voters; they then returned to their original party loyalties.

SP'ers paid a high price for what Eduard Bernstein called their "partnership" with liberals. They became markedly conservative on such matters as Negro rights and immigration—indeed no different from the AFL on such issues—and even tolerated rampant anti-Orientalism as well as the exclusion of black applicants from the lily-white locals of southern socialists.

Thus the SP, unlike the SLP, adjusted to political and social realities. Such adjustment meant reforms, which socialists predicted would deepen the contradictions of capitalism, make them the political beneficiaries, and hasten the revolution. This was the blueprint which they followed. They would be voted into office, mostly municipal, by the industrial labor force, which, in fighting for its own immediate interests, would develop a revolutionary consciousness. They were in effect very much an American political party, a regional and ethnic amalgam that responded to what pragmatists called the "felt necessities" of the work force of the age.

Debs's charismatic role and influence should not be discounted in explaining Party successes. He *was* a romantic and a visionary, he shunned machine politicians, and he caught the imagination of his time. But ultimately it was pragmatic operators like Hillquit and Party mechanics like Berger who formulated Party programs and policies and who had their way with the rank and file. And under their influence the SP, recalling Trotsky's contemptuous yet appropriate description, indeed became a party of dentists—notwithstanding Debs and the farmer-miner sectors. Such a party would never launch major recruiting drives among those who worked the soil or among the unorganized industrial work force. To the contrary, it was, from the outset, ambivalent about agrarian labor, and the 1901 Unity Convention, for instance, voted not to take a specific stand on the "farm problem" or on the Party-farmer relationship.

By 1910, according to Buhle, the Party confronted "certain fundamental choices" on how best to expand its base. The options were obvious: continued participation in the political process or organizing the industrial work force. James Weinstein contends that emphasis on the electoral process was the SP's most effective tactic and that the IWW stress on alternate methods, while giving it a "romantic appeal . . . did not approach the Socialist Party in its impact on contemporary life." He is right, it would seem, and the Party's choice between options was really not debatable since socialist policies were shaped by practical-minded functionaries. But their opportunism guaranteed SP conformity to social-democratic methods. Ultimately it fractured the organization, would perforce lead to neglect of the "ultimate aim" of revolution and socialism. Finally, such thinking also underlay the practices of liberals, of those who worked for piecemeal change through legislation and the ballot box.

In 1912, the socialist tide was rising, though it was barely distinguishable from the Progressive upsurge of that election year. If one includes the liberal Wilsonian Democrats and the Roosevelt Republicans, it may be said that four out of every five voters chose candidates to some degree critical of abuses within the existing system. The SP showed marked electoral strength nationally: Oklahoma's militant socialist farmers, then near to organized rebellion, gave 16.6 percent of the state's vote to the SP; Nevada, Montana, Arizona, and Idaho also had a considerable socialist electorate; and the combined vote in Ohio, Pennsylvania, Illinois, and California surpassed that of New York. No fewer than 1,200 municipal officials—including fifty-six socialist mayors and many more aldermen and city councilmen—were elected, and there were now socialist police chiefs as well as state legislators.

But those who voted for them did not believe they were choosing between fundamental and incompatible alternatives.

Socialists thereby lost the initiative to Wilsonian liberalism. Democratic liberals joined with corporate liberals and AFL conservatives to press home such immediate social reforms as the Federal Trade Commission and workmen's compensation. In so doing, they dramatized the superfluity of American socialism and contributed to its decline. Ira Kipnis concluded that the SP gradually destroyed itself by racism, opportunism, and the lack of inner-Party democracy. Not so, declares James Weinstein. There was "no serious decline after 1912," he has found; "the Party grew in strength and popularity during the war."

Notwithstanding Weinstein's claims, SP membership began to slide after 1912, and the Party was heading into trouble. By 1915, Michael Bassett has determined, the Party "was a floating remnant, a protest group trying to maintain its identity while able to contribute less and less to serious discussion about the future of American society." The great debate over America's entry into World War I briefly revivified Party fortunes—since the SP served as a vehicle of antiwar protest. But the prewar Party was in crisis, even before European hostilities forced an agonizing decision upon it. There were declines in finances, membership, and voter support. The 1912 vote for Debs had been over 900,000; the 1916 presidential vote for Allan Benson was 590,000.

The seeds of SP decay may partly be attributed to the 1912 victories of socialist reform candidates. This reform game was rigged at the start, since the majoritarian reformers could hold out prizes and power as well as the reward of respectability. Besides, unlike socialists, they were not ambivalent about reforms; they could give unqualified support to such civic reforms as the commission and city manager proposals or the good government leagues. Moreover, such reforms reduced the influence of both labor and the SP in local government.

In 1916, moreover, Debs was not on the hustings. The SP fielded Allan Benson, who ran a weak campaign. Then, too, the fusion device—used by Democrats and Republicans collaborating on the local level—brought victories over SP candidates, even though, as Weinstein demonstrates, socialist votes for a given nominee might be substantially greater than in 1912. There was also a mounting number of socialist trade-union defections to the Democrats, a trend becoming significant by 1916. The tendency had always been there, if only because union benefits depended partly upon union willingness to bargain collectively; that is, to accept the capitalist economic framework as a starting point.

Once Wilson took office and began to initiate reform measures—such as the La Follette Seaman's Act, the Workmen's Compensation Law, legislative prohibitions on the products of child labor in interstate commerce, among others—most of the socialist-oriented trade unions moved into the Democratic camp. Thus the International Association of Machinists, with a long record of support for populism and for socialism, greatly benefited from the Democrat-sponsored Adamson Act (which established an eight-hour day for all interstate railway workers) and shifted from public endorsement of Debs in 1912 to Wilson in 1916. The United Mine Workers had a big socialist minority in some mining districts; however, many miners turned to Wilson in 1916. Similarly the Brewery Workers, openly socialist before the war, having long been dominated by German-born radicals, as Laslett found, acknowledged that Wilson had an enviable record of labor accomplishment and grudgingly endorsed his re-election.

These defections are significant. They suggest that Wilsonian reforms were an important factor in the erosion of trade-union support—that sine qua non of socialism. Nor, in accounting for Party membership and election losses, should we forget the successes of the unions themselves—as they fought with and within a stubborn but ultimately resilient capitalist system. Their very successes were made manifest in economic benefits and governmental reform measures. Surely, we may speculate, they contributed to a diminished radical militancy.

The ease of the political crossover, for even radical labor, suggests not so much the absence of classes, as Louis Hartz would have us believe—classes there were and are in American society!—but an absence of class awareness and its concomitant, class conflict. Instances of labor militancy abound—born of the workers' ability to close down an industrial department, or a factory, or a region's factories or mines. These occurrences evoked an exhilarating sense of power but produced little fundamental change. Furthermore, labor's recognition of its collective power was intermittent at best, directed toward immediate goals and rarely fed at the springs of socialist theory. SP literature, like that of progressives and muckrakers, was drenched in the argot of class and class consciousness, though its readers, more often than not, were urban middle-class reformers or intellectuals rather than the average worker. Neither they nor urban factory operatives, nor members of the AFL's craft unions, were greatly agitated by official and unofficial violence in the Northwest's labor camps or among Colorado's miners and California's migrant workers. With some exceptions (e.g., the ILGWU), a sufficiently consensual agreement existed: the viable political and economic institutions would be respected.

Thus virtually all traditionally militant unions came around to support the Democratic Party in 1916. The AFL did not require conversion; it had been recruited earlier. Not that the course of Gompers' Federation commitment to orderly business-labor practices and to Wilson went without challenge. For instance, the socialist trade unionist Max Hayes received a third of the delegate support when opposing Gompers at the AFL's 1912 national convention, which reflected the radical upswing in 1912 as well as the residual socialist support within the Federation.

There is no wish to deny the existence of radical workers, most apparent, perhaps, among the native-born—the skilled and semiskilled who had high expectations. But that conventional wisdom which sees the immigrant as docile needs some revision. There were, of course, the highly publicized walkouts at Passaic, Paterson, and Lawrence in 1912. But there were other newcomers who carried radical traditions and doctrines in their baggage and who joined trade unions in urban areas—such as Jewish socialists and Italian syndicalists in New York City's jewelry trade, who went on strike in 1916, and in the union of structural iron workers, who walked off their jobs at the end of the war. There were the Greek and Polish cotton-mill strikes in Ipswich in 1913; the Lithuanians, Poles, and Hungarians who walked out of Pittsburgh's National Tube Company in 1912; the 1915 strike at Remington Arms in Bridgeport; and, of course, the spontaneous 1909 walkout at the Pressed Car Steel Company in McKees Rocks, Pennsylvania, which, in its first phase, united Eastern European labor and the slightly better-paid native-born co-workers. These strikes and others are significant: they occurred in industries being rationalized by scientific management and the introduction of mass-assembly technology, prompting strikes over wages as well as worker control, and they demonstrate that semiskilled and unskilled immigrant factory labor could be radicalized.

The SP seemed blind to the resurgent labor militancy which characterized the prewar period, and continued to concentrate on the ballot box. The IWW was an immediate beneficiary, which discomforted Party members and which intensified factionalism. The problem of tactics continued to torture radical exegetes. Divisions were also sharpened by personality clashes, by nuances of rhetoric, by verbal thrusts and ripostes about deviation from orthodoxy, by clashing visions of the road to power and of the coming social order—with each side claiming that it preserved, in Debs's resonant phrase, "the revolutionary character of our party."

Algie Simons, a National Executive Committee member, opened an old wound in 1909—by invoking the impossibilist charge that the AFL "comes much nearer representing the working class than the Socialist Party." These impossibilists were then in the minority and, before 1917, had only a negligible voice. Relegated to the rhetoric of position papers which scorned short-run goals, they refused—much like De Leon—to countenance anything less than the overthrow of capitalism. That they did not bolt suggests that similarities of style between them and the right-wing immediatists were possibly more important than substantive doctrinal differences. For all their infighting, the antagonists remained in the same house. The earlier quarrels were of this sort—of highly polemical form, rather than of substance.

Still there *was* a left wing, however elusive the term may be, however much it was a mood and a style rather than a program. And though the impact might be delayed, it was on a collision course with the "bourgeois reformers" within the Party. There appeared to be no possible resolution of the issues dividing them.

The Industrial Workers of the World exhumed the old issue of immediatism, presumably interred with the De Leonite expulsion. The IWW also triggered controversy—over "orthodoxy" versus "opportunism," "direct action" versus "political action," the wisdom of the general strike, industrial sabotage as a tactic, the violence of syndicalism. Its beginnings were in Chicago, in January 1905, when a group of about thirty labor and socialist leaders, meeting on the initiative of the Western Federation of Miners, agreed to hold a founding convention six months later. The "Manifesto" of January 1905 prefigured things to come. It attacked craft unionism and emphasized the need for industrial unions, thereby earning the early and lasting hostility of the AFL:

> Craft jealousy leads to the attempt to create trade monopolies. . . . Craft divisions foster political ignorance among the workers, thus dividing their class at the ballot box as well as in the shop, mine and factory . . . [whereas] one great industrial union embracing all industries . . . should be founded on the class struggle . . ., should be established as the economic organization of the working class, without affiliation with any political party.

The IWW, then, would organize the whole factory or, better yet, the whole industry into One Big Union.

In June 1905, William D. Haywood set the tone for this "Continental Congress of the working class," which represented about 70,000 workers. He assailed the AFL for prohibiting Negro applicants, for its policy of immigrant restriction, for not being "a working-class movement." The delegates incorporated his sentiments into a "Declaration of Principles" which became part of the preamble to the IWW constitution. When De Leon's STLA merged with the IWW, socialists were further troubled. But Debs defended the new organization. He urged workers to join it and "help it fulfill its mission, and thus hasten the emancipation of the working class and the brighter, happier day for all humanity."

The IWW's values and tactics were set forth at this first convention. Committed to socialism in the broadest meaning of that term, the delegates hoped to attain it through industrial, not craft, unions, using the weapons of the strike, the slowdown, and the general strike. Industrial unions would embrace skilled and unskilled alike, as well as sectors of the work force overlooked or excluded by many AFL unions—such as women, blacks, and immigrants. IWW strongholds were in the logging camps and harvest fields of the West, among the unskilled and the disfranchised. IWW'ers thus were unique in American labor history; they would organize the unorganized and the unskilled—rather than those in the factories who were already unionized. They sought to attract those most alienated from the American dream; hence the IWW charged low initiation fees and even lower dues. They arraigned business unionism and claimed that trade-union welfare systems were "coffin benefits." Their organization would be open and anti-bureaucratic, inclusive and not exclusive, like the Federation, and would unionize those whom the AFL ignored.

A debilitating conflict almost immediately erupted in IWW ranks. Indeed, divisiveness, rather than strikes, seemed to preoccupy the leadership in its early years. At least three factions surfaced: those who envisioned the IWW as the economic arm of the political socialist movement and would go the ballot route; those who, like SLP'ers, would subordinate politics to the economic goals of labor; and those who were anarcho-syndicalist, wholly rejecting political means in favor of revolutionary industrial unionism. The first sector dropped out almost immediately; the second in 1908, when IWW convention delegates, a majority of whom were western loggers and migratory workers, proposed to win economic concessions by direct action—which was roughly defined as strikes, boycotts, and sabotage.

Notwithstanding a façade of ideology, this conflict assumed the shape of a power struggle between two rival blocs. Each agreed that the IWW was dedicated to the destruction of capitalism through direct action. The issue was who would command the troops. Eventually, at the 1908 IWW convention, De Leon was expelled and Haywood emerged victorious. Unlike De Leon, he always considered political action within the mental framework of the unionist at war with the state apparatus. Not that the issue was ever starkly reductive. *Solidarity,* the organ of the eastern Wobblies, rejected "anti-political sectarianism" and later editorialized: "The IWW at its birth was committed to a program of 'political action' while at the same time forbidden to endorse or affiliate with any 'political party.' "

The IWW saw itself as the leading force in "the historic mission of the working class to do away with capitalism." But it was vague and contradictory about how the system would be changed, about tactics. Sometimes Wobblies would use the vocabulary of violence and endorse all nonpolitical means, including revolution. Occasionally they went beyond rhetoric; they drove tacks into fruit trees, hammered spikes into logs, set fire to hop fields. Often, however, the violence attributed to them was committed by their enemies—vigilantes, police officials, state police and militia, employers who were embattled owing to IWW-inspired strikes. Indeed, as Melvyn Dubofsky has observed, even the IWW language was frequently nonviolent. Haywood, during the 1912 Lawrence strike, stated: "I, for one, have turned my back on violence. It wins nothing. When we strike now, we strike with our hands in our pockets."

Nor was their rhetoric the only ambivalent and contradictory thing about the IWW. For one, Wobblies never clearly defined the general strike, perhaps the ultimate weapon in their arsenal. Nor did they ever precisely outline the structure of the new society, sometimes calling it the "cooperative commonwealth" or "industrial communism." Finally, while the revolutionary language was often uncompromising, the Wobblies were more flexible than their slogans might suggest. For while they retained a vision of ultimate revolution, they also contributed to or led labor stoppages to gain immediate demands.

The 1909 strike at McKees Rocks, Pennsylvania, was of this nature. The company involved had pioneered techniques of worker efficiency and work rationalization so central to Taylorism. The strike was in response to the speedup, wage decreases, and vastly increased specialization. The IWW leadership conducted itself along customary narrow business-union lines rather than indulging in revolutionary sloganeering. The issues, as the Wobblies saw them, were wages and hours. Elsewhere, the IWW reacted in similar fashion. They sought union contracts for the unskilled and worked to improve the conditions of labor. In so doing, they reasoned, they would help develop a sense of class power.

But this commitment to unionism *and* revolution was undertaken at a peril. It produced the classic confusion over means and ends. "Class war" was elevated by IWW doctrinal purists to an anti-political tactical level, where it became an exhilarating end in itself. And ultimately the emphasis on tactics failed the most crucial test. Short-range objectives—significantly, those also sought by established and non-revolutionary trade unions—were never transformed into a higher consciousness of class and the revolutionary proletariat of Marx's vision. For instance, IWW membership tailed off sharply after the 1912

Lawrence strike had finally been won; and, by late 1913, the Wobblies' local was once again limited to a few hundred members. So the IWW'ers did indeed fight for concrete improvements—and were beaten and jailed and killed for their efforts—but Wobbly activism was not followed by any marked raising of class consciousness. Much as in Lawrence, the 1913 Paterson strike of silk workers was characterized by militancy, and its Wobbly leadership was decidedly nonpolitical in outlook. The strike, however, did not conclude with a permanently radicalized constituency or labor organization. As in Lawrence, there was a rapid decline in IWW members—which suggests that the union here, too, served as a useful and convenient weapon to secure limited goals.

When defining itself as a revolutionary force, opposed to capitalism, the IWW was not viable; when emphasizing the limited objectives of bread-and-butter unionism, it prospered but was unable to develop any durable appreciation of socialism within the work force. The IWW thus suffered from a familiar and inherent defect: as a union it had to work for immediate ends and these could not be revolutionary unless charged with a revolutionary theory and consciousness. But if it did not seek immediate improvements for its workers or if it emphasized such theory, a union could not become successful, as Wobblies learned to their regret.

This is not to discount the nature of the IWW's organizing drives among the unorganized and unskilled—which did have a revolutionary content, the bread-and-butter concerns notwithstanding. These drives represented the most blunt challenge to capitalism, and employers understandably feared Wobbly organizers. But immediatism, we've suggested, corrupts the revolutionary purpose of destroying class society. While denying its syndicalism, the IWW insisted it was an industrial union; and, after 1913 especially, it emphasized direct action.

Immediatism was also the SP's objective, and the two organizations maintained a fragile coalition until 1913. In theory, they both drew from the same ideological springs: both opposed capitalism and both sought the good society, but neither went beyond a reductivist Marxism or explained how the promised end would be achieved. Such fuzziness contributed to their joint reliance on short-term goals. So they shared the irony of the radical experience in America. Committed to immediate demands and to eventual revolution, they accelerated the growth of both strong trade unions and regulatory legislation. Their successes, however, contributed to working-class acceptance of a consumer-oriented middle-class culture. Ironically, then, they strengthened the class system and the dominant values of the society.

Obviously, all this was inadvertent. The IWW struck in the belief that their occasional and local successes would bring about revolutionary consciousness and unionism. And by 1917 they had a record of notable labor victories to their credit: the McKees Rocks strike of 1909, the successful "free speech" fights which frightened local conservatives from San Diego to Sacramento, and the creation of the powerful Agricultural Workers Organization. By 1917, then, the Wobblies seemed like a permanent fixture on the labor scene. But, even more than the socialists, they had to face the realities of World War I and the concomitant domestic repression, and they barely survived.

From the outset, the SP and the IWW had maintained only an uneasy spirit of cooperation. Both searched for the good society, but socialists would find it primarily by means of the ballot box while, in theory at least, the Wobblies stressed direct action and violence when justified. Until 1912, SP'ers continued to find the IWW the focal point for a *ralliement à gauche*. Publisher Charles Kerr, the Chicago socialist, put it succinctly in 1910: "The main function of the Socialist Party has been and still is its work of propaganda and education. . . . Something more than voting is needed to overthrow capitalism, and revolutionary unionism is the something more."

In 1912, however, the two organizations came to a parting of the ways. Haywood by then had become emblematic of union-Party alignment (which Debs incidentally also favored) and of the "direct action" or revolutionary forces within the SP. His tremendous popularity among workers made him a power in socialist circles. Indeed, he was the only nationally known socialist leader on the left, and he was the only left-winger on the eight-man National Executive Committee of the Party, receiving the second-largest number of votes in an election that constituted a defeat for the leftists. Haywood admittedly despised the law, justified direct action, and favored the general strike, and though, as noted, he did not repudiate the political process, he was nonetheless vulnerable to the charge of being anti-politics and of advocating violence.

Haywood had stood in the wings while the increasingly conservative Simons and the radical theorist William Walling quarreled bitterly, among other things, over Simons' tenacious attempts at a rapprochement between the SP and the AFL. Perhaps he should not have stood aloof—for the sniping between left and right wings would eventually determine his own fate in the Party. Although Simons was censured by Party locals, a determined right-of-center coalition developed. It included Simons and Berger as well as Hillquit, John Spargo, and Robert Hunter—and it was on a collision course with "the Haywood element," which conceived of the IWW as synonymous with the labor movement.

Straws in the wind appeared in 1912. The socialist local in Yuma, Arizona, moved Haywood's recall from the National Executive Committee—with the New York Central Committee, in a Hillquit-engineered move, providing the necessary second. The Lawrence strike victory, however, so enhanced Haywood's reputation that the New Yorkers embarrassedly withdrew their vote a few days later. Then the turbulent 1912 convention voted an amendment to the SP constitution which made opposition to "political action" or advocacy of "sabotage, or other methods of violence as a weapon of the working class" grounds for expulsion. Intent on curbing those who would admit the possibility of violent revolution, it failed to intimidate Haywood. "I believe in sabotage, that misunderstood word . . . ," he affirmed. "There is no revolutionary action which can be too strong if we will only throw the capitalist class back." The Party's New York State Committee then accused him of inciting workers "to use direct action and sabotage," urging immediate steps to bring about his recall. The referendum vote on the recall passed easily. This vote, and the subsequent defection of his followers, robbed the Party of its most militant and uncompromising elements. More than ever, the SP was now a body of reformers, openly committed to the ballot and believing the loss of an important minority would be compensated for at future elections. But 1912 would not be the harbinger of a glorious new era for socialism in America.

3 Culture Radicalism, 1900-1917

ORGANIZED RADICALISM had become part of the liberal and reform mainstream. But leaders of America's "high culture," including the so-called culture radicals, continued to feel isolated. Significantly, their isolation, indeed their occasional alienation, did not have doctrinal roots—for all the rhetorical façade that justified their rejection of middle-class values. These culture radicals were neither organized nor a clearly defined category. They included socialists and anarchists, bohemians and devotees of Mencken, young Jewish intellectuals and their Wasp counterparts—critics like Van Wyck Brooks, who ironically sought to stimulate an American cultural renaissance. More often than not, they regarded themselves as socialists, though they did not think in terms of a political insurrection.

Most culture radicals shared the same magazines, the same idols, the same fashionable parlor game of *epater le bourgeois*. They agreed on many antipathies, as Daniel Aaron wisely observed, and had some spiritual ancestors in common. They honored a Protestant-evangelical radicalism which stemmed from the Hebrew prophets, the undiluted precepts of Jesus, the haunting cadences of Jefferson and Emerson, the dithyrambs of Whitman, the passions of civil resistants like Thoreau, and the preachings of the social gospelers. They also drew upon a culture that was international—a mix of art, literature, free love, social experimentation. They did so to create life styles that would upset and challenge the middle class; their counterculture was dedicated to overthrowing Victorian morality that no longer represented life in America. They combined a romantic defense of individualism with a critique of capitalism, but they were relatively uninfluenced by the ideas of Europe's gray-bearded revolutionary prophets of a half century earlier.

Not that all culture radicals denied rhetorical homage to European ideologues, including the explicitly Marxist. But in truth they thought of themselves as more pragmatic and scientific-minded than Old World socialists. They were not "party" people, unlike their offspring in the 1930s. Some, of course, joined the Socialist Party, but their tenure usually was brief, and they retained a sense of independence and individualism which the Hillquits repudiated. While not explicitly and consciously rejecting those "smelly little orthodoxies," as George Orwell acidly called them, they instinctively recognized the accuracy of John Reed's observation that "the class struggle plays hell with your poetry." And they thought of themselves as poets first—as creative people—rather than people of politics. Consequently, they saw a poem or a painting in aesthetic terms, and their criticism of capitalist society was the result of a very personal moral commitment, the theoretical sources of which were not sufficiently important to involve them in doctrinal considerations. Their art was never subordinated to politics or to political criteria.

For the culture radicals, then, ideology was employed more flexibly than it would be in Europe. Their radicalism, in this halcyon first decade of the new century, must be defined in terms of emotional commitments and not theoretical constructs. Like many "radicals," they can hardly be distinguished from liberals and progressive reformers in these years, and, like the SP, they were increasingly fashionable. Socialism *seemed* to be gaining a foothold under Debs's leadership and to be growing into a mass movement; and the reform wave then washing over political parties stimulated new ways of thinking about societal problems. Those most influenced were the children of middle-class and upper-class America, especially the educated Wasp middle class. Harvard, for instance, was touched by a spirit of intellectual insurgency, as young men like Brooks, Lippmann, and Reed have reminisced.

The Intercollegiate Socialist Society (ISS) began in September 1905, with Upton Sinclair as its founder, and Jack London, Hillquit, and Walling among its most prominent members. It proclaimed that college youth could no longer afford to ignore socialism, or be ignorant of its programs. Under ISS auspices, London made a colorful tour of the nation's campuses. He criticized the "passionless pursuit of passionless intelligence" and urged undergraduates to respond to the great social challenges facing them. And they did respond. Between 1910 and 1913 ISS campus chapters mushroomed almost everywhere except in the South. "Many of America's foremost progressive economists, writers, and technicians . . . ," one of its leaders recalled, "received their first impetus to social thinking in the college chapters of the ISS." Indeed, the membership list was such that the ISS enhanced the respectability of the Party itself.

Though most youthful radicals remained outside organizational forums, their lives were forever affected by the critical ambience around them. It was a "renaissance," John Reed later wrote of his Harvard years, and it made him realize "there was something going on in the dull outside world more thrilling than college activities." Not all undergraduates were like him or Van Wyck Brooks—Anglo-Saxon, Protestant, middle-class, native-born; some were German Jews, but they were all part of American high culture. Members of another radical constellation, Russian Jewish immigrants or their children, received a handsome education at the City College of New York, or were autodidacts out of New York or Chicago slums. They were drawn to verbal battle that intensified and honed their thought, which derived primarily from Marxist texts—though they simultaneously read Horatio Alger's juvenile guides to success. Inspired by Benjamin Franklin as well as Engels and Voltaire, they became active left-wing socialists.

Whatever the group (and these two roughly defined circles did not dominate: there were the Pounds and the Eliots, radical in another and apolitical way), whether native-born or immigrant, Anglo-Saxon or Jew from the *shtetl,* middle-class or poor, product of Ivy League or tuition-free schooling, whether committed to political radicalism in organized form or not, they mingled in Greenwich Village and received their postgraduate education there. So in this friendly enclave of low rents, quiet, twisting streets, cheap grocery stores and restaurants, they created the Village's reputation as an oasis for artists and rebels. Each radical circle started with some degree of alienation from society, was touched by some of the detritus of parochialism, and each greatly appealed to the other. And amid the Village's bookshops, art studios, saloons, and salons, long-haired poets and short-skirted women, Columbia University's Protestant undergraduates like Randolph Bourne, German Jews from Yale like Paul Rosenfeld, and East Side Jews from City College like Morris R. Cohen, artists like John Sloan and literary critics like Brooks, sat down together to a rich intellectual feast. They talked passionately about the prospects of American art and letters, about the variegated world of European thought and culture, becoming less insular and more sophisticated in the course of it.

One radical circle, made up of Europeans, thought primarily in political terms, though the distinction between them and the native-born intellectuals should not be unduly stressed. Neither felt they were Jews or Protestants; nor did they feel an acute sense of nationality. Rather, as Joseph Freeman recalled his days with *The Masses* (commenting on his own sense of Jewishness), he and his Jewish radical friends felt they were "Westerners initiated into and part of a culture which merged the values of Jerusalem, Egypt, Greece and ancient Rome with the Catholic culture of the Middle Ages, the humanistic culture of the Renaissance, the egalitarian ideals of the French Revolution, and the scientific concepts of the nineteenth century." Of the last, Marxism was primary, and it made "socialism" seem to them "the apex" of Western and humanistic civilization. From these sources was their political radicalism fashioned. And even the less literally political circle sought at the least to improve the quality of national life. They were, as a whole, more interested in reform—of education, culture, sexual and social relations—than in strictly political issues. They held to a loose system of attitudes, a consciousness of their social group, not to a class or a party. The culture radical sought to construct a world view, one differing from the dominant middle-class culture; and if he did not exactly menace the social system, as many claimed, he nonetheless arraigned and outraged those clinging to the prevailing values.

Culture radicalism was manifold and shifting—and perhaps these are its most salient qualities. Judging by its history, it seemed at times to consist of a succession of spasmodic local movements of protest and passion, which did little more than chill liberals and alarm conservatives. Culture radicalism, so diffuse and so elusive in definition, was shaped by a tradition of dissent and by new voices—strange doctrines about man and society, such as Bergsonism, pragmatism, anarchism, Marxism. It drew upon the egalitarian, primitive, plain-speaking strains of a populist and insular radicalism. It also drew upon, among others, Thorstein Veblen, Friedrich Nietzsche, Henrik Ibsen, and Sigmund Freud, with the last convincing many of the necessity of sexual self-expression. Freud would throw many culture radicals back upon introversion and the unconscious, and a decade would pass before they rediscovered a symbiotic relationship between the individual and society. Until the late twenties, they were concerned primarily with purging the psychic and social restraints imposed upon the individual; they would conclude only in the 1930s that such restraints were products of life in a repressive society. And taking the next inevitable step, they would combine political and social change with artistic and spiritual liberation; anything less than such a combination left many of them cold.

Returning to these earlier years, it is obvious that literary and artistic insurgency was at least linked to social insurgency as well as to a bohemian life. The result was a radicalized consciousness that was broad if not deep. At the turn of the century, bohemia was not yet surrogate for revolt against middle-class values or for social radicalism, being merely expressive of occasionally unconventional attitudes. But by 1910 bohemians had come to feel estranged from the small communities in which most were reared, from the nation's values, and, of course, from their parents. Thus bohemianism mixed with the unstable properties of American radicalism.

Political and culture radicals customarily traveled in different orbits, each displaying a principled antagonism toward the other. There were infrequent exceptions: John Reed, a romantic and revolutionary symbol for his age, was one, for he was both a Party member and a culture radical; however, we may guess that Party functionaries were as dismayed as his friend Max Eastman by Reed's paean to romantic individualism and his visceral, anti-theoretical commitment to radical experimentation. Art Young, also of *The Masses,* recalled the archetypal radicalism of the day: "We were sailing out, so to speak, with no charts but our untried beliefs and a kind of confidence that any way might be better than the old way." Such sentiments were cold comfort to Party officials.

Ad hoc alliances between political and cultural radicals were not entirely absent. When the controversy swirled around such issues as birth control, easy divorce, the rights of labor, or even artistic and literary freedom, it was possible to find collaborative efforts. John Reed's exertions in behalf of the Paterson silk workers and the massive fundraising pageant staged at Madison Square Garden provide a model of sorts: the collaboration of artists, writers, and dramatists in the cause of labor and of the IWW.

But alliances of political and culture radicals were rarely harmonious. It is an old problem. Artists contributing to *The Masses,* for instance, can testify to the recurrent tensions and difficulties. From December 1912, when Eastman, then a young philosophy instructor out of Columbia University, took over its reins, *The Masses* was devoted to socialism, anarchism, and paganism, the humorous and the irreverent. Its columns were filled with talk of syndicalism, Marxism, free love, birth control, cubism, Freudianism, the new woman, the new poetry, the IWW. Its artists—such as John Sloan, George Bellows, and Stuart Davis—were governed by a desire for personal freedom, not "scientific procedure toward a goal." This distinction, the difficulty in reconciling art and doctrinal sympathies, is hardly unique or unfamiliar; rather it confronts radicals in every age. Writers and critics may have had an easier time of it. They seem to have overcome more readily the traditional division between art and politics, indeed even between their art and their personal lives.

For example, such prominent radical writers as Eastman, Floyd Dell, and Emma Goldman, the notorious anarchist and activist, considered themselves both political and sexual radicals. They bridged the gap easily. Eastman was a putative Marxist theoretician and a socialist, and so he occasionally lamented the bohemian life style of so many radicals. He condemned, like the Party orthodox, "the puny, artificial, sex-conscious simmering in perpetual puberty of the grayhaired Bacchantes of Greenwich Village." But bohemianism was as central to him in the prewar period as radical political and social thought. What Eastman sought, as he stated, was "a carefully thought-out program of class struggle." And what he really deplored—and what he shared as well!—was the ability of most radicals, John Reed and others, to live one way, as bohemians, and to think and work another way. But he was also discomforted by this very schizoid quality in the magazine which he edited—and by the popular Village ditty which surely struck home:

> They draw nude women for *The Masses*
> Thick, fat, ungainly lasses—
> How does that help the working classes?

Small wonder that organized radicals were unhappy with the journal and its followers. *The Masses* also urged its readers to "enjoy the revolution" and it had a sense of humor, a quality lacking at Party headquarters. W. J. Ghent, a well-known socialist writer, charged that the magazine was financed by "rich men and women of that nebulous middle world which lies somewhere between the Socialist movement and the world of bourgeois complacency." It converted no workers to socialism, he asserted, and it lacked doctrinal coherence for its readers. "It has found no trouble in mixing Socialism, Anarchism, Communism, Sinn Feinism, Cubism, sexism, direct action and sabotage into a more or less harmonious mess. It is peculiarly the product of the restless metropolitan coteries who devote themselves to the cult of Something Else; who are ever seeking the bubble Novelty even at the door of Bedlam."

Those who guided *The Masses* were vulnerable to such charges. Eastman, for one, took pride in his impure radicalism. Very much like Reed, and also lionized by culture radicals, he could write "pure" poetry with his right hand *and* revolutionary tracts with his left; he could pay homage to scientific socialism *and* romanticize the anarchist; he believed in the "common worker" *and* in Nietzsche's superman; he endorsed disciplined Party work *and* the spontaneous life style of the bohemian; he attacked religion and embraced a pagan attitude toward nature; he thought of the artist as an artist, not as a social critic, and he idealized the Poet. Contradictions and ambivalences, then, were rife in the ranks of culture radicals. Some of them were aware of the dangers of compartmentalizing their ideas—placing political commitments in one box and views on the function of culture in another—but, aware or not, they could not resolve the dilemma.

Though the culture radical was unable to manage a synthesis of art and life, he still had a disproportionate voice in the shaping of the nation's culture. His staying power was remarkable, all the more striking when the assertion of an alternative life style inevitably throws most Americans into panic and rage. Not only did he persist, his values became increasingly generalized after midcentury, so that what has been described as a "youth movement" in the 1960s is in some ways scarcely more than a widespread recurrence of a pre-World War I phenomenon.

4 Organized Radicalism and World War I

EMPLOYING VERY different tactics, the IWW and SP enjoyed some successes down to the outbreak of European hostilities. Neither was numerically strong: the IWW at its peak had about 100,000 members, and the SP vote, which was larger than its membership, amounted to only a small fraction of the national total in 1916. Both had to face critical challenges which came with the war in the form of mounting official and extralegal violence against their adherents. Overseas conflict brought down the furies upon Wobbly leaders and rank and file alike, and their organization was smashed on the rock of government repression. If it did not mortally wound SP organization, it effectively eliminated locals in rural areas.

But the war at first seemed a boon for America's socialists. Before the war, after all, there had been a dramatic decline in the socialist vote. The disappointing showing of Allan Benson in 1916 owed in part to his weak candidacy and to Wilson's "peace" slogan—the man "who kept us out of war"—which many socialists found attractive. Reed, for instance, supported the President in 1916, while Eastman, demonstrating tortured logic, criticized the Party for nominating Benson and then voted for him while endorsing Wilson. The Chief Executive, he declared, "has not succumbed to the epidemic of militarism." The vigilantly radical *International Socialist Review,* in censuring

Berger's Milwaukee *Leader* for attacking Wilson, took the same position: "To howl suspicions of militarism against a president who kept the working class of America out of war during a hair trigger period is a species of treachery to the working class that does no good."

That a number of socialists found Wilson's campaign slogans appealing was oblique testimony to the Party's hardening antiwar position. But the SP's views were obvious two years earlier. From the outset it understood the conflict to be one of imperialist rivalries and it publicly marked off the socialist position from that of the two major political parties. Notwithstanding the general decline in Socialist Party voters, James Weinstein has pointed out, the number of socialist lawmakers in state legislatures increased from twenty in 1912 to thirty in 1918. Certainly the Party, with its antipreparedness and antiwar line, made a partial comeback after 1917. In 1917, it took an unequivocal position against American intervention and became a vehicle of protest. In the April 1917 local elections, it did exceptionally well in the cities and rural areas of Minnesota, Kansas, Iowa, Illinois, and Wisconsin, owing to its opposition to American entry into the war, and it markedly increased its vote in November 1918. Ironically, this growing popular support was at the expense of the long-sought legitimacy. That is, the very position which attracted protest votes unleashed an intensive assault against the Party—and such attacks served to restrict Party efforts and weaken Party organization.

These local successes heartened Party leadership. So did the war itself. Even the SP left wing did not take the grim view of the conflict that one might expect. Indeed its position, though wholly unpublicized and unacknowledged, was often comparable to that embraced by the acolytes of liberalism and social justice. Louis Fraina echoed the fondest hopes of John Dewey and the war liberals. Possibly the most important left socialist of the time, Fraina denounced the war and even "the duty of national defense"; nonetheless, he thought the war would bring an irreversible trend of collectivism in its wake. "War is a socialist opportunity," the New York *Call* candidly proclaimed. "There is no cause for despair," Debs counseled in 1915. "The world is awakening and we are approaching the sunrise." "Let the war go on," Eastman urged, "for the sake of the German people and of all nations." And Benson also affirmed, "Let the war go on."

The Party's official position was in marked contrast. In August 1914, the National Congressional Campaign Committee, which had been established to direct Party work, adopted the slogan "Starve the War and Feed America"; by October, the SP's National Executive Committee specifically approved an antiwar campaign—to be "carried on systematically through the *American Socialist* and the Socialist press"; and one national committeeman moved that "the Socialist Party of the United States prepare to call a general strike as a protest should the United States start to mobilize her troops for war." Benson ran on an antipreparedness campaign plank in 1916 and the Party platform of that year declared that "the competitive nature of capitalism is the cause of modern war." Conflict under capitalism, Hillquit affirmed, was unavoidable. But Louis Boudin, another Party official, found "no inevitability about war, such as is supposed to flow from the very existence of the competitive system."

Extending these theoretical convolutions, a clause in the 1916 Party platform proclaimed that disarmament was "essential to an assured and permanent peace." Walling was among those who demurred. "Our opposition to war," he agreed, "must be based on our opposition to capitalism." But he went on to the conclusion, regarded as disastrous by some pacifist-inclined socialists, that "war can be abolished neither by armament nor disarmament." The SLP, incidentally, endorsed this position, but it struck at the Party's lack of any "coherent and effective program of action." And its voice, the *Radical Review,* made another accurate and telling observation when affirming that socialists like Berger frequently advanced "uneconomic" causes of the war, such as "national and race hatred."

The SP promoted war protest meetings, demonstrations of "mass opposition" to the conflict, an export embargo, anticonscription drives. By so doing, it cut loose from European socialists—after urging them to stand firm and to "exert every influence on their governments to accept American mediation." But socialists abroad conformed to nationalist impulses, frequently joined war cabinets, and ignored the pleas of America's antiwar leadership—much to the embarrassment of SP members. Isaac Hourwich, a leading socialist editor, observed: "The plain and unvarnished truth is that the Socialist Parties do not differ in their attitude toward the war from the capitalist

parties of their respective countries." Socialist internationalism, he lamented, "has proved but an empty sound." Joseph Freeman agreed. So did most left-wing Party leaders who, like Fraina and Boudin, were stunned by European socialist defections.

Various Party locals urged condemnation of Europe's parliamentary socialists "who have seen fit to support the militaristic policies that are arraying the workers of Europe under the various nationalistic banners in defiance of our international programs." The Party, affirmed one local, should expel any socialist holding public office who "officially approves of or votes for any appropriation of public moneys in support of the army or navy of the United States."

Ultimately this became the Party line, and by it the SP staked out exclusive ground. Socialists now could put some distance between their Party and the Wilsonian war liberals, and could repudiate liberal policies within the theoretical framework of Marxist analysis. For the first time perhaps, they advanced policies qualitatively different from those of liberal reformers; moreover, they were consonant with orthodoxy: the proletariat should only engage in class war against the bourgeoisie; all other conflict resulted from imperialist rivalry.

Paradoxically, in taking this orthodox line, Party leaders weakened their organization, especially in the West. Yet they instinctively knew that it was an issue to which a considerable number of voters would respond. And the Party did relatively well in these years, we have seen, regaining strength and members lost immediately after the European conflict began. So the SP, almost intuitively—much like its intuitive choice of domestic reform issues and of meliorism—turned to tactics that paid off politically. As early as mid-December 1914, the Party's National Executive Committee endorsed a "national campaign for national and international disarmament and international peace," an innocuous program which liberals and even old-line pacifists could endorse and which produced growing support. And it is ironic that the one socialist party which remained true to the vaunted principles of internationalism—which reaffirmed that the worker had no country and that socialism knew no national boundaries—was the one most nearly destroyed by its principled stand. There is the added irony that the record of America's socialists until 1917 was one of being reformers par excellence, unlike socialists overseas. But when the showdown came in 1914, it was the Europeans who turned opportunistic with a vengeance.

Socialists, then, were of two minds on every aspect of the war—on its potential impact upon the United States, on the proper response to European socialists, on the 1914 Proposed Manifesto and Programs of the Socialist Party of America on Disarmament and World Peace—which was greeted with especially vehement disagreement over the no-indemnities and disarmament clauses. There was a clear antiwar majority, but the overseas conflict hardly produced consensus. The antebellum factional squabbling continued and intensified at times. Before 1914, however, this internecine struggle did not tear the Party apart. The SP's very elasticity, its theoretical vagueness, was, absurd though it may seem, a source of strength—for it enabled conflicting groups to remain under the socialist umbrella. But the growing firmness of the official line after 1914 made it more difficult to cushion the friction. Socialists could no longer embrace a doctrinal variation on the accepted dogma and be ignored or tacitly accepted as members in good standing. Increasingly, the left came into its own.

The Party had long been divided into a left and right wing, with a reformist center that was philosophically closer to the right. Haywood's expulsion had triggered an exodus which reduced the "reds" to less than a quarter of the total membership. Those who remained retained a community of interest and were a recognizable faction. The war did not immediately generate any visible friction because the reformist elements, including right-wingers like Berger, supported official Party policy—though some would have preferred a milder antiwar position.

David Shannon is obviously right in concluding that the Party, preoccupied with domestic issues and confident of success by gradual means, "was poorly prepared for the outbreak of war." Though some socialists welcomed it in 1914 and 1915, many vacillated between despair and the hope that America, in Dell's words, would assume "the role of peace bringer." Despair was the more understandable. Human decency, scientific enlightenment, fidelity to socialist principles—all were challenged or diminished by the war. "There are evidently flaws in our human nature which makes our idealism a tragic joke," Dell concluded; while Hillquit, also conveying the sense of shock, admitted that "in common with hosts of others I was dismayed by the sudden collapse of human reason." Both Dell and Eastman, in what was a mindlessly un-socialist conclusion, attributed the conflict to "blind tribal instinctualism" and "a native impulse of our constitution." Such views derived from Nietzsche and Darwin, then in fashion in intellectual circles; they had little to do with Marx, who was uncompromising in his perception of capitalist wars as flowing from economic causes.

Floyd Dell's hopes for America as "peace bringer" and mediator were shared by many liberals, pacifists, and socialists. This proximity to pacifists troubled Party leadership. Pacifists threatened to cut into socialist strength and erode its popular base. Moreover, their organized peace societies did not share Marxist canons. Even moderates like Hillquit feared that cooperation with peace groups would impair the Party's integrity and constituency. They worried over the parallel between the Party's official position and that of the new peace societies, such as the Women's Peace Party (WPP) or the American Union Against Militarism (AUAM). As *Class Struggle* protested editorially: "We are not pacifists . . . we are ready to fight for our ideals." Yet the Party's emphasis on mediation, which continued through 1916, made it virtually indistinguishable from these peace societies. There was the Hillquit-Debs delegation to Wilson in December 1915, urging upon the President a conference of neutrals, which would mediate between the belligerents; so did a second Party deputation, led by Hillquit and James Maurer, the Reading, Pennsylvania, socialist, in 1916; and Meyer London, the only socialist congressman, proposed arbitration. Benson in 1916 proposed a national referendum on the issue of war, which assumed that a popular mandate for belligerency would have been acceptable to the Party, as it was to a number of peace societies, including the AUAM. The Party's very first proclamation on the war, as Shannon rightly concludes, "might have been written by any peace group."

Randolph Bourne complained in 1916 that the spreading socialism on America's campuses was "full of the unfocussed and unthinking." The journals of adult socialism reflected the same. *Blast,* the *New Review, Class Struggle,* the *Radical Review,* the *International Review,* and *The Masses* variously interpreted the conflict as a traders' war, a militarists' war, a munitions makers' war, a war between feudalism and capitalism, between democracy and autocracy, and so forth. Hillquit and the 1916 SP platform declared that "the competitive nature of capitalism is the cause of modern war," that it is "one of the natural results of the capitalist system."

Vagueness added to the ambivalences. Pre-1917 SP peace proposals were non-specific and non-programmatic. Expressing the hopes of many socialists, the New York *Call* candidly stated: "What we are looking for, the one thing we are thinking about, is how far this war will advance the cause of Socialism and Social Revolution." For those who urged prolongation of the conflict, such a goal was sufficient; for the socialist bloc which would speedily end the conflict—the so-called "immediatists"—the remote possibility of war-cum-revolution was a distraction. It diverted Party leaders from the chore of working out a specific peace program.

The left wing, in any case, offered little in the way of details. "It is our task to prepare for peace, not to bring peace," Fraina ingenuously explained, after he had denounced the 1915 Party program as "apologetic, incompetent, and pro-German." This program, however, would be virtually identical to that later announced by the Bolsheviks, calling as it did for no indemnities, national self-determination, no military or arms exportations; and one senses that Fraina's splenetic opposition derived more from the fact that Hillquit and reformer elements were influential in framing the platform than from any substantive objection. In any event, Party policy became menacingly specific by 1916—but hardly toward the end of initiating or organizing a peace movement. Workers were urged to refuse "to mine the coal, to transport soldiers, to furnish food or other supplies for military purposes, and thus keep out of the hands of the ruling class the control of armed forces." Such proposals implied a general strike, which Meyer London had already proposed. But there was little talk of it among socialists, or of how to implement it, and an earlier motion to this effect—in the event "the United States starts to mobilize her troops for war"—died in Party convention "for lack of seconds." The left wing did, to be sure, talk of "mass action," but it would not or could not go beyond resistance to recruiting drives "by means of mass meetings, direct demonstrations, and educational propaganda,'' and strikes against industrial conscription.

One reason for this failure, we may surmise, was the existing theoretical confusion and policy divisions. Another was the wavering loyalties of many socialists. The immediatists and others as well were in general agreement, even if only privately shared, on an Allied victory. Hillquit, Haywood, Fraina, Eastman, *et al.* all held this view. The real dilemma was how to be against Germany and to condemn all the belligerents at the same time. The 1916 election and Wilson's candidacy only exacerbated matters—witness the tortured logic of the Eastmans and Reeds in voting for the incumbent.

Spargo and Simons reveal further ambiguities. They spoke out against preparedness but were for the Allies. In opposition to the Allies was a pro-German, pro-embargo bloc and Russian-Jewish Federation elements, a powerful socialist constituency joined out of hatred of the Czar. Still another schism occurred. Pro-Ally socialists like Charles Edward Russell upheld preparedness, which was consistent, but the Simons-Spargo-Benson group did not. Nor did this dispute coincide with long-standing ideological divisions. The Party's left wing supported preparedness; but so did right-wing leaders like Berger, Russell, and Ghent. Hillquit equivocated on most issues. He affirmed only the isolationist argument that the United States was immune from attack by foreign powers. Eastman, meanwhile, had come around to an antiwar and antidraft attitude by 1917, after supporting Wilson's re-election.

One trend in SP ranks became increasingly apparent: the moderate centrists grew weaker and the left wing began to dominate Party policy sessions. The membership adopted a program in 1916 which included self-determination for all peoples, opposition to all military appropriations, and mandatory expulsion of any elected socialist "who shall in any way vote to appropriate moneys for military or naval purposes, or for war."

Developments in 1917 led to an enduring, irrevocable schism and eventually to the formation of new radical organizations. These developments would create anguish for a Party dominated by gradualists and reformers—who were reluctant to break with their traditional allies, now known as "war liberals," owing to their support of Wilsonian measures.

While a crisis of faith occurred among socialists, the nation moved toward involvement overseas soon after the November 1916 election. On January 9, 1917, the Kaiser decided to resume unrestricted submarine warfare—to begin on February 1. Wilson then announced a break in diplomatic relations with Germany. Some weeks later came the Russian Revolution, and Kerensky's provisional government was immediately recognized, on March 22, thereby clearing a major obstacle to America's entry on the Allied side.

Alarmed by events, troubled and embittered by divisions in Party ranks, the National Executive Committee determined to avoid the fate of European socialists. It called an emergency convention for April 7, in order to take on the inevitable declaration of war. Nearly two hundred "tense and nervous" delegates assembled at St. Louis's Planters Hotel, but by this time Wilson had appeared before a special session of Congress (on April 2), urged recognition of a state of war, and received legislative assent. Party delegates thus faced the challenge that their European counterparts had earlier failed to meet. What should America's socialists do? Could they support the war effort? Should they declare continued opposition to conscription and to war, and withhold all support of wartime programs?

Hillquit urged this latter course, predicting that the war would end in European revolution. Algernon Lee, his close associate, assailed Wilson: "The working men of the country were deceived by the cry 'He kept us out of war.' " Adolph Germer angrily declared: "Wilson has not kept us out of war and I have no reason to stand by him." Kate Richards O'Hare expressed the dominant mood of a convention at which moderates on the war were significantly absent. "I am a Socialist, a labor unionist and a believer in the Prince of Peace *first,* and an American second." She continued: "If need be, I will give my life and the life of my mate to serve my class, *but never with my consent will they be given to add to the profits and protect the stolen wealth of the bankers, food speculators and ammunition makers.*"

That a majority of the delegates shared Kate O'Hare's sentiments became obvious when they chose her to chair the Committee on War and Militarism. This key fifteen-member body conducted the main business of the convention. Its majority resolution, written by Hillquit, Lee, and Charles Ruthenberg, the militant Cleveland socialist, emerged out of four days and nights of bitter wrangling. It reflected, in its class-conscious tone, the growing strength of the left wing, even while symbolizing the continued unity of the shaky left-center alliance. This resolution was signed by eleven committee members—with Marxist theoretician Louis Boudin writing a slightly different antiwar version and the right-wing Vermont socialist John Spargo submitting a prowar minority resolution urging cooperation with Wilson's administration.

The convention's majority report violently condemned the war, encouraged "all mass movements in opposition to conscription," declared America's entry "a crime against the people of the United States." The more extreme passages rejected defensive as well as offensive wars, urged a general strike, and implied the worker-has-no-country doctrine of the left wing.

This report—known as the St. Louis Proclamation—received 140 votes to 31 for Boudin's and only 5 for Spargo's. Submitted to the membership, it was overwhelmingly approved: 21,000 votes for it and about 350 against. Almost every socialist periodical supported it and denounced the war. The position of left-wing journals like *Class Struggle* and *The Masses* was predictable, and they opposed conscription and the war with a single-minded tenacity. But even right-wing journals, such as *St. Louis Labor,* hailed the antiwar stand of the delegates; and right-wingers like Berger, and centrists like Maurer and Hillquit, joined in. Indeed, there was no predictable correlation between left or right and prowar or antiwar positions. If some right-wingers were opposed to the conflict, some left-wingers, such as Walling, Rose Pastor Stokes, and Frank Bohn, supported intervention. Nonetheless, a near-unanimous position generally prevailed. The harmony was such that *Class Struggle,* the most important theoretical organ of communism, praised Berger's conservative leadership and regretted that Wisconsin did not send him to the Congress in November 1918.

The détente, however, was deceptive and ephemeral. Indeed, even before the majority report emerged from committee, it was obvious that sharp divisions remained. There was simply no way to reconcile left-wingers like Ruthenberg and rightists such as Spargo. The former flatly declared: "The workers are never justified in taking part in any war waged by any state in the control of capitalism," while Spargo stated: "The arming of a people to defend itself is not necessarily militarism, as we use the word. I favor universal progressive disarmament but it is not the duty of a democratic state surrounded by armed autocracies, to disarm itself." That a number of Party members agreed with Spargo and joined him in leaving the SP further emphasizes the confusion and volatility in socialist ranks. That the antiwar majority report would split Party membership was inevitable.

The very names of those who defected indicate a further blurring of ideological lines. Walling, Bohn, *et al.* belonged to the left wing; so, too, did Simons, who had bitterly arraigned European socialists in 1914. Benson, Spargo, Stokes, and others belonged to the reformist right wing, though there were right-wingers, such as Berger, Hillquit, and Maurer, who held pronounced antiwar views. The declaration of war, then, and the appeal—of Eastman, Dell, Fraina, among others—that Germany be "smashed as the indispensable condition for universal peace," sharpened that "contradiction within socialist ranks which," Freeman recalled, "we could neither understand nor resolve."

This antiwar majority report sharpened long-standing divisions. It accelerated the quiet exodus of prowar socialist trade unionists and the highly publicized desertion of the prowar party leaders. It also speeded the end, so Daniel Bell tells us, of the precarious balance of socialist forces and strengthened the "impossibilist" left-wingers. Hillquit and the moderates, sensing the growing trend toward militancy, paid the price of continued loyalty: they moved toward an antiwar position which consequently further weakened the voice of social-democratic action. In a sense—and it is bitterly ironic—the parliamentarian tactics eventually brought down its advocates. For America's socialists, unlike their European comrades, did not have large legislative delegations, electing only two congressmen (one in 1910 and one in 1914 and 1916). This very lack of substantive electoral gains smashed their hopes for a mass socialist consciousness; thus they were able to remain truer to socialist principles in war than socialists of the Old World.

Socialist leadership had good reason for nervousness about SP proximity to the organized peace movement. Many socialists were prepared to join a broad antiwar coalition which included the new peace societies and unattached peace workers. They may have officially disavowed advocates of an unqualified pacifism but they occasionally all worked together.

The AUAM, one of the newer peace societies, included Lillian Wald as chairperson, John Haynes Holmes, and Rabbi Stephen Wise, pacifists all—with socialists like Eastman liberally sprinkling the leadership. The Union provided one vehicle of organized opposition to conscription and to the war itself. Once the United States intervened overseas, socialists and peace workers alike became increasingly isolated and by mid-April 1917 they began to consider some cordial organizational entente. They found their model in the workers' councils of socialist Russia; and the indigenous form, they hoped, would actively resist both Wilson's and Gompers' prowar policies.

The declaration of war and the Conscription Act provided the catalyst for both pacifists and socialists; the March revolution in Russia and the Bolshevik peace proposals inspired their program. Peace workers "turned from a negative policy of protest against war to constructive proposals for an early peace." Socialist moderates, including the entire leadership, joined in stressing a peace campaign, rather than "mass opposition" to war and conscription, which had been at the heart of the St. Louis Proclamation. Hillquit's mayoralty campaign of November 1917 was one of studied moderation, affirmed an observer, and the candidate told New Yorkers that "we want a speedy but general and negotiated peace." In the course of seven months, Hillquit had moved far from the St. Louis platform—to the point of a negotiated cease-fire. Socialists, he contended, did not advocate violation of laws, which seemed implicit in the majority report. By November 1917, then, the SP seemed more remote than ever from its proclaimed role as the revolutionary vanguard of the working class. Not only was it participating in the electoral process, it was also talking conciliation rather than militancy or violent opposition.

Clearly, then, most socialists and pacifists were ready for a joint effort. A series of spring meetings took place in 1917 at which representatives of the WPP, the AUAM, the Emergency Peace Federation (EPF), and the Socialist Party participated—to develop a peace policy which could be agreed upon. Out of their deliberations came the May 30–31 meeting and the First American Conference for Democracy and the Terms of Peace. Its tone was set by James Maurer, who attacked the AFL for its predictably pro-administration position, and by Eastman, among others, who condemned both Wilson and Gompers. Opposing conscription and militarism, various delegates urged that sturdy pacifist vision of "international cooperation to maintain peace." It was this two-day conference which spawned the People's Council of America, a united front of socialists and pacifists which also included single-taxers, immigrant radicals out of the garment industry, union activists drawn from the Cigar Workers and United Mine Workers, officials of such Jewish groups as the Workmen's Circle, whose commitment to peace derived from anti-Czarist and anti-capitalist impulses as well as from enthusiasm for the Bolshevik Revolution.

Socialists played a prominent role in Council affairs. Moderates like Hillquit and Berger were among Council leaders, and Debs, Maurer, Algernon Lee, *et al.* joined its ranks. They gave it contour and coloration. It was the Party's objections to the war, together with its anti-capitalist rhetoric, that shaped the public image of the Council and that isolated it from the national consensus.

The socialist-pacifist alliance was a fragile one and the Council was early beset by difficulties, both internal and external. But events on the outside could also work in its favor. The Bolshevik accession to power gave a lift and immediacy to Council efforts. Council literature emphasized the model of the "new Russia," and one broadside exhorted: "Fellow workers of the United States . . . why don't you do the same thing here that your brother-workers are doing in Russia?" We need not linger here on the details of this campaign to capture the loyalty of American labor, nor describe the fund-raising difficulties or the deepening schism between right- and left-wing socialists within the Council, especially on the issue of recognition of Bolshevik Russia.

Thus the Revolution at first brought fresh hope to the People's Council—and to the Socialist Party as well. But it would add a Red Scare to the existing anti-German sentiment and increase the determination of those who would crush socialism. The SP became a casualty of the war, unlike their European comrades, who supported their wartime governments. Party leaders adhered to the ideals of the Second

International, rejected the practices of overseas socialists, and became the target of law-enforcement agencies and criminal prosecutions.

The IWW, with its unequivocal opposition to the conflict, was even more of a victim. Officially, the Wobblies tried to ignore the war and remain neutral. The conflict, Haywood declared, was "of small importance compared to the great class war." That Wobbly leaders tried to mute talk of sabotage—never much more than talk anyway—and of opposition to the war was to be expected, given the nation's prowar sentiment. Their tactics did not help. The IWW became the object of federal and state espionage laws, of state criminal anarchy and anti-insurrection statutes, of government-encouraged hysteria, of nationwide raids on private homes and Wobbly meeting halls. Their headquarters were attacked, records seized, leaders jailed, members fined and deported. Their treasury and energies were depleted in the course of defending the arrested leaders; indeed, the Wobblies were now completely on the defensive, and effectually destroyed under a rain of legal and extralegal blows.

Revolution in Russia struck like a thunderclap in the radical camp in February 1917. Then, a day after America's November 1917 elections, came the Bolshevik accession to power and it immediately and powerfully affected United States foreign policy. Urged by his allies to support the White Russian forces opposed to the Red Army, Wilson at first opposed intervention and counseled patience, but he found Anglo-French pressure irresistible and, subsequent to a series of improvisations too detailed to recount here, the President ordered a token force of 5,000 American troops to Murmansk and Archangel.

Lenin's rise to power had another effect on Wilson. It cleared the obstacles blocking enunciation of the Fourteen Points and endorsement of the socialist proposals of no annexation, no indemnities. As a result, it persuaded many of Wilson's battle-weary radical antagonists to shift their position. The socialist *Appeal to Reason,* for instance, now became an administration supporter. Most SP members, granted, remained antiwar and anxiously watched presidential policy vis-à-vis Lenin's regime; but many remained stubbornly anti-German and waffled on the capitalism-breeds-war formula. The Kaiser had to be defeated, they reasoned; otherwise socialism in Russia was endangered. Joseph Freeman, for example, found Germany's destruction "essential

to the defense of the workers' republic.'' Hence, along with other radical students, he joined Columbia University's ROTC in early 1918. In
April 1918, Algernon Lee and five other socialist aldermen in New
York City voted to support the third Liberty Loan. Thomas Van Lear,
the Minneapolis socialist machinist, announced his support of the war
in June 1918; three socialist aldermen in Chicago voted for a loyalty
resolution; working-class heroine ''Mother'' Jones, for the first time,
urged labor to buy Liberty Bonds. Clearly, then, the old socialist order
was in the process of change.

The Revolution would have a more lasting effect upon organized
radicalism than it did upon Wilsonian policies. Eventually it would
widen the fissures in SP ranks. At first, however, these centrifugal tendencies were not apparent. Seemingly everyone left of the political
center rushed to Russia's defense. The image of a raw and vibrant
land, free from the economic and spiritual slavery that beset capitalism, was exhilarating. Progressive reformers and culture radicals, even
the ''war liberals,'' hailed events in Russia as a quantum leap forward.
Disillusioned by the excesses of war, repression at home, the rabid
postwar nationalism, and a peace that sought ''to disintegrate the German nation,'' the war liberals were demoralized. They wanted to be
converted—and their conversion was instantaneous. Liberals like
Reinhold Niebuhr, progressives like Frederick Howe, old bull ele-
phants like Theodore Dreiser, the editors of *The New Republic*—all
burned incense at the shrine of Bolshevism. The Revolution served as
a useful foil, as a way to validate their critique of the United States.
For some it helped maintain a near-chiliastic faith in the possibilities
of a restructured society. The journalist Will Durant affirmed, in sentiments that Debs, Eastman, Emma Goldman—socialists and anarchists alike—shared: ''The new social order is coming, and that is all
there is to it.'' For other reporters, such as Lincoln Steffens and
Eugene Lyons, who rushed to a besieged Russia, the reaction was
much the same. Writing from 1917 Petrograd, Steffens found that the
Revolution held out lessons ''for the more orderly but equally profound struggle that we are having at home.'' To culture radicals,
events at Moscow served as self-fulfilling prophecy. They readily
agreed with Eastman's assessment: ''What made us rub our eyes at
Russia is the way all of our own theories are proving true.'' The Revo-

lution, then, clashed with the strain of hopelessness produced by war and the Versailles peace settlement. Now both liberals and radicals had the paradigm of a young socialist republic to compare with the materialism and corruption at home.

A cult of Russia flourished. The worshippers compared the passion and spirituality of the Slavic soul with the domesticated and prosaic vision of Americans. They had insisted upon the experimental and the improvisatory. They had laid siege to contemporary American culture, assaulting the provincialism which they wished to escape. They had read *America's Coming of Age* like a breviary, sponsored little magazines like *The Masses*—with its heady mix of art and humor, the experiential and the impertinent; its ardent support of, *inter alia,* syndicalism, socialism, free love, birth control, suffrage reform. That Moscow endorsed these reforms—seemingly so eminently and intelligently humane—contributed to Russia's enormous appeal for feminists, progressives, social workers, liberals generally. Their response has been chronicled at length elsewhere; and, needless to say, Trotsky was right, they would never be more than "fellow travelers."

But the effect of the Revolution upon the American worker was of more serious concern for organized radicals; and, as John Laslett tells us, it reinforced socialist thinking in some sectors of the labor movement. Most AFL trade-union officials praised the March 1917 insurrection in Russia but recoiled after the Bolsheviks seized power in October. Not so the socialist-infiltrated Amalgamated Clothing Workers. And not so the ILGWU with its urban Jewish and Italian radicals. It assessed the October 1917 events as "the first time in the history of the world [that] the workers showed a determination not to allow themselves to be defrauded of the fruits of their victory by their master classes."

Negro socialists like Claude McKay expressed similar views. A long editorial in one journal ended with the ringing exclamation "Long live the Soviet Union." "If to fight for one's rights," a second Negro socialist journal stated, "is to be Bolshevist, then we are Bolshevist." Even the SLP was not immune to the contagion of pro-Russian attitudes. National secretary Arnold Peterson joined the membership in supporting the Revolution, though he initially had reservations. The IWW did not share the misgivings of its General Executive Board and eventually the Board called upon members "to assist the Soviet Government of Russia in fighting the world battle against capitalism." Emma Goldman's *Mother Earth,* an anarchist journal, was filled with praise for the Bolsheviks, and her autobiography also confessed to an immediate loyalty to the Revolution. The equally anarchistic voice of Alexander Berkman, which found expression in his journal, *Blast,* celebrated the Revolution as "the greatest event of modern times," an assured success which would "soon illuminate the whole of Europe and possibly of America . . . , bringing with it the downfall of war and tyranny everywhere, [and] ushering in the birth of a really free and beautiful new world." In short, virtually all radical groups and journals could unite on this issue at the outset; whether they did so with warm and appreciative rhetoric or with the language of special pleading depended on peripheral loyalties and attitudes.

Events following the Revolution continued to produce an unprecedented unanimity. Witness, for instance, reactions to three critical issues: support of the White armies, the landing of American troops on Russian soil, and United States recognition of the Soviet government. William Hard's condemnation of the State Department for its support of Admiral Kolchak, the White Russian leader, was published in *The New Republic,* but might have appeared in *The Liberator,* then *The Masses'* successor. M. J. Olgin, a prominent Jewish-Russian radical, received space in the pages of *The New Republic* for a highly favorable account of Soviet industrial development. The two most critical foreign policy issues—intervention and recognition—evoked similar responses. Allied landings in August 1918 were a final shock for liberals, driving many to an emotional and frequently physical Russian pilgrimage. And so Floyd Dell jumped bail and fled there; Reed went on journalistic assignment; Steffens and Albert Rhys Williams joined them; and black radicals like Claude McKay and W. E. B. Du Bois found in Moscow a new day for mankind.

Having voted for Wilson in 1916, Eastman now condemned the President's "self-righteous emotions" and asserted that the Murmansk-Vladivostok landings revealed "the piratical purpose at the heart of the war for democracy." The "hands off Russia" theme of his nationwide speaking tour in 1919 would be adopted by virtually all socialists and Communists. The SP's National Executive Committee protested "against the use of troops in Russia and demands the immediate withdrawal of Allied and American armies from that country."

The issue of recognition produced the same near unanimity among liberals and radicals. The former provided considerable leadership but their views merely underscored those advanced by the entire left wing. For example, the Friends of the Russian Revolution, having changed its name to the Friends of New Russia, was an early sponsor of recognition at a December 1917 mass meeting. A Soviet Recognition League was organized. Its purpose, Alexander Trachtenburg stated, was "to conduct meetings, to furnish the press with true reports about the doings of the Soviet Government of Russia, and to urge official recognition of the Soviet Government." Supporting its aims, Reed declared, "The Soviet Government of Russia is here to stay; it is based on the almost universal will of the Russian masses."

This spontaneous solidarity was not long-lived, however. For the left-wing socialists, until now shaded by the dominant parliamentarian center, were immensely strengthened by the Bolshevik Revolution and the rise of the Third (Communist) International. The new International dramatized the quarrel over the timetable for the revolution and turned the initiative over to the impossibilists. Another rupture was in the making, and along clear-cut ideological lines.

At a founding session of the SP's left caucus, held in Brooklyn in the winter of 1916–17, Leon Trotsky, Nikolai Bukharin, Alexandra Kollontai, Ludwig Lore, Louis Fraina, and Louis Boudin (the last three being the editors of *Class Struggle*, the replacement for the *New Review*) were among about twenty socialists in attendance. The left wing's approach became immediately apparent when both Fraina and Trotsky attacked the SP for not resisting conscription more militantly and for not turning to sabotage. A formal left-wing caucus, meeting in New York in February 1919, adopted Fraina's manifesto, which became known as the Left-Wing Manifesto. It denounced socialists everywhere for not turning "an imperialist war into a civil war—into a proletarian revolution." Their failure was attributed to "dominant moderate Socialism" which accepted the "bourgeois state as the basis of its action" and which sought to attract "tradesmen, shopkeepers and members of the professions" rather than the true working class.

Fraina concluded with a denunciation of America's socialists for failure to exploit the "formidable industrial unrest," and with praise for Russian Communists for adherence to "true revolutionary socialism." Americans, Fraina counseled, should overthrow their government and replace it with workers' councils, modeled after those in Russia—the Soviets.

This conflict over means was heightened by the SP's ethnic problems. In 1912, the Party had seven Foreign-Language Federations. Autonomous ethnic bodies of 500 or more members of similar national origins, these federations were relatively independent of the national office owing to language and cultural barriers. They constituted about a sixth of the membership in 1912 and, seven years later, swelled to over a third, with especially large increases in the Russian groups. They were, moreover, increasingly militant and a powerful voting bloc at SP conventions; and they were obviously moving toward the no-compromise position of the Bolsheviks. By late May 1919, the Party's National Executive Committee suspended seven of the federations. Many of those who would leave the Party after the clash of late summer and who would form the Communist parties not only were foreign-born but were also recent immigrants from Eastern Europe. They were all more aware of conditions in their homelands than were native-born Party members and they naturally identified with the Bolshevik Revolution and the new International.

This International also sharpened the old quarrel between immediatism and legislative reform impulses. One major article of socialist faith was that revolution would occur only under conditions of advanced capitalism and, notwithstanding the Russian experience, this proposition remained an iron law. Revolution, it was affirmed, would come to those countries that could be characterized by large-scale capitalism and capitalist accumulation. The Third International, it followed, pressed for immediate insurrection in the West. Conflict over this issue sharply polarized SP membership.

This renewed factionalism over impossibilism was different from that of the past. The earlier conflict had not led to schism. For that something more was needed—the triumph of the Bolshevik Revolution, the glamour of the new Soviet Republic, and the edicts of the International. True enough, there was a massive wave of strikes in 1919, led by the steel and coal walkouts—the "formidable industrial unrest" noted in the Left-Wing Manifesto. There were the actual conditions of life in postwar America, the facts of a brutally repressive anti-radicalism, the failure of Europe's socialists to remain faithful to their fiduciary obligations. But it was Russia's requirement—of insurrection in highly industrialized capitalist countries—that was most influential in sharpening the internecine warfare and triggering the split.

In sum, the example of successful revolution abroad was so powerful, and, it must be emphasized, the task of developing socialist doctrine relevant to advanced capitalism in the United States so incomplete, that the Bolshevik model and policy dictates were decisive. Perhaps the left's leading theoretician, Fraina believed that events in Russia signaled "the end of exclusive concentration on parliamentary tactics." The time had now come for the workers of all lands to "annihilate the rapacious regime of capitalism." Fraina would refocus SP emphasis upon mass action—by which he meant bringing "mass proletarian pressure on the capitalist state" and shifting efforts from the legislatures to the shops and the streets. The *New York Communist,* which he and Reed edited, reflected the euphoria released by the Revolution and anticipated an upsurge of revolutionary consciousness among America's workers. Reed himself had earlier disdained the Party, the IWW being his revolutionary ideal. But Bolshevism's ascendancy changed all that; he turned from the Wobblies, with their anti-political stance, and drew closer to the socialists, especially to the left wing. SP'ers, he and Fraina insisted, must now "withdraw from active cooperation in reform movements and . . . devote their energies to organizing the proletariat so as to make its strength felt directly."

Party moderates—those centrists who had "cooperated with bourgeois and essentially reactionary organizations," as the New York leftists charged—found the International's appeal for immediate insurrection was as impossible as it had been when proposed in the prewar years. The war, if anything, seemed to have increased corporate power and tightened corporate control over the economy. So these centrists stood on the old rock of liberal reform. Confronted by wartime repression and postwar anti-radical measures, they appealed to traditional libertarian canons and rights. The idea of soviets, or workers' councils, in the United States seemed more remote than ever. "Revolution in Russia," Berger wrote to Hillquit, "had been one thing." Russia had been "beaten," both economically and militarily; moreover, the Bolsheviks "absolutely controlled the trade unions." But "none of these conditions prevail in America." To the contrary, he observed, the war, and labor's cooperation with the administration, had "strengthened capitalism, reaction and *treason* within the working *class*. We can learn from the Bolsheviks," Berger concluded, but "we cannot transfer Russia to America." Eastman, now a left-wing spokesman, rejected such contentions. He insisted that America's workers were interested in the Soviet experiment. Berger "fails to realize," Eastman continued, "that the idea of 'Workers' Councils' is far more closely and directly related to the immediate lives and interests of the working class than an economic philosophy can ever be."

The Revolution in this way refueled old feuds. And, if possible, these were further intensified by social turbulence at home and abroad—the Seattle general strike, the Boston police strike, and the wave of walkouts in the United States; the revolutionary disorders in Hungary and Germany. But it was Bolshevism which became the most divisive of issues. Personalities and past issues were involved, as they were in the right-left splits of prewar days. But the salient contention was over the applicability of the Revolution to the United States. The appearance of the Third International generated a factionalism so violent that it was qualitatively different from that of the past. The International meant a new and dangerous challenge to the centrists. All socialists, one directive stated, "must be absolutely subject to the full-powered central committee"; and they must "sever all connections with the petit bourgeois and prepare for revolutionary action, for merciless civil war."

The left wing, greatly encouraged by such activist policies, vigorously defended the decision not to admit America's moderate socialists into the International. "It is not our 'support' but our *solidarity* with them," Eastman declared, "that the Communist republics have a right to demand." The militants were further strengthened when the U.S.S.R. (in January 1919) dispatched an official emissary who frequently "conferred" with New York's left-wing leadership. They now had the initiative and captured twelve out of fifteen seats on the National Executive Committee (NEC) when a national referendum was conducted in the spring of 1919. But the old leadership, charging fraud, set aside the election returns, investigated them, and then proceeded to the systematic elimination of the left wing. In May, the old NEC suspended the seven Foreign-Language Federations, the core of left-wing power, and about half the membership. It also purged entire state organizations and many city locals as well. Its work was devastating. In January 1919, the Party had recorded its second-highest membership in history, almost 110,000; after the purges fewer than 40,000 remained. Repurified, with two thirds of the membership expelled, the NEC then felt confident enough to call for a convention.

Meanwhile the left (mainly the federations and the Michigan state socialists) attempted to consolidate, organized branches in some cities, and issued a "call for a national convention for the purpose of organizing a Communist Party in America" (to assemble in Chicago on September 1, 1919). It also adopted a "manifesto," which amounted to a formal declaration of war. For it now affirmed that "there can be no compromise with laborism [that is, a labor party] or the dominant moderate Socialism."

Thus the inevitable fragmentation again took place. An impatient minority, mostly the Slavic-language federations, denounced compromise with the moderates and determined to found a Communist Party. But most of the native-born delegates to New York's National Left-Wing Conference, held in mid-June 1919, successfully opposed this move. These "American" delegates had no wish to cut themselves off from their potential base, that militant labor sector which had belonged to the IWW and which sought to remain within the regular SP organization.

In Chicago, meanwhile, the regular Party convention opened on August 30. New York's left-wingers John Reed and Benjamin Gitlow, who had opposed the call for a separate Communist Party convention on September 1, now tried to be seated; but their credentials were challenged, a fracas resulted, and they were expelled. Thus the old moderate-conservative minority retained leadership and control. A bloc of left-wing delegates—about a fifth of those present—then joined New York's left downstairs from the regular meeting, in the building's billiard room. Failing to achieve a rapprochement with the

Foreign-Language Federation impossibilists, the New York-led bloc issued a report which called for workers' councils like those in Soviet industry, praised the IWW as the model for industrial unionism, and proclaimed itself the Communist Labor Party (CLP). Two days after the SP delegates had convened, the secessionists from the Slavic federations, as well as the Michigan state socialists and the Fraina-Ruthenberg group, met in yet another convention and organized the Communist Party of America (CP). One party had split into three.

Thus did the Revolution and the Third International reinvigorate the left opposition, catalyze a virtually new bloc, and endow it with self-confidence and legitimacy. Hillquit had observed as much: each left wing which appeared in 1918–19 "was entirely different in origin and character" from the pre-1917 left. The International, by its successive ukases, also set the stage for an unhistoric and mechanistic application of the Bolshevik experience to the United States. In so doing it prepared the ground for further conflict. Hillquit's warning actually prefigured the major criticism to be directed at the Communist Party: "to support Russia in all its struggles," he warned, "does not mean, Comrades, that we abdicate our own reason, forget the circumstances surrounding us, and blindly accept every formula, every dogma coming from Russia as holy, as a Papal decree."

5 The Twenties

TRAVELERS' REPORTS constantly refreshed the hopes of those, Communists and non-Communists alike, who looked to Russia for inspiration. Isadora Duncan, the famous dancer and symbol for her age, wrote an enthusiastic letter about her visit in 1921: "I am convinced that here in Russia is the greatest miracle that has happened to humanity for two thousand years." John Dewey, Stuart Chase, George Soule, Rexford G. Tugwell, and countless other American writers hailed Soviet planning as a model for the industrial society at home. The Soviet Union, Soule declared, "offers the first experiment the world has ever seen in economic planning on a national scale for peace-time purposes," an experiment, liberal reformers like him agreed, that was yielding remarkable returns. Further to the left, *The Liberator,* in 1924, described how a dairy and poultry farm cooperative, then being organized in Chicago, planned to move to the Soviet Union.

The early rapture waned somewhat—with unpleasant reports of Soviet bureaucracy and the prosaic economic aims of the new society. "By 1922," Joseph Freeman recalled, "a reaction against the intense hopes generated by the Russian Revolution had set in among American liberals. The New Economic Policy inaugurated by Lenin seemed to them a betrayal of Communism." Floyd Dell also noted a shift of

73

attitude among America's culture radicals: "After a brief enthusiasm, the intelligentsia has for the most part become indifferent to the new order in Russia—an indifference which masks a secret temperamental antipathy." But the disenchantment was hardly a trend in these years. Travelers' accounts continued to pour in, counterbalancing disappointment with the less than innovative economic goals of Bolshevism. Journals like the *New Masses* and the *Modern Quarterly* relentlessly pumped out articles on Soviet life. Scott Nearing and Anna Louise Strong, as well as liberal "fellow travelers" such as Louis Fischer, *The Nation*'s Moscow correspondent, and Walter Duranty of *The New York Times*, were a few of the better-known journalists who filed fervent descriptions of the new society. Russian poetry and prose, translated by Mayakovski and Ilya Ehrenburg, reached American shores: so did many Soviet films, such as *Chapayev* and *Potemkin*, which fused revolutionary themes and exciting new film techniques.

Organized radicals managed to collaborate, on an ad hoc basis at least, on the issue of U.S.–U.S.S.R. relations. But their unity was fragile and occasional rifts appeared—portents of an uglier and bitter fratricide. The left-wing socialists—most of whom were now Communists—moved worshipfully toward the Moscow shrine and the Third International. But as early as 1920, socialist centrists began to hedge. The SP's National Executive Committee declared that the conditions for affiliation laid down by the International were "absolutely incompatible with the position of our Party." Hillquit refused to "accept all the new doctrines"—to "accept for this country, for any other country, for all countries, the special institutions and forms into which their struggles have been moulded by special historical conditions." The left-wing promptly accused him of "thrusting his knife in the back of Soviet Russia" and charged that his Party "has bartered its Socialist soul for votes and offices." Eastman, writing in *The Liberator*, took "a certain aesthetic pleasure" in seeing Hillquit indignant because Zinoviev "has 'excommunicated' him from the Third International as a 'traitor' and an agent of the bourgeoisie"—after Hillquit's "minority machine" had itself excommunicated some 60,000 socialists. There is a continuity about these charges and countercharges; they prefigured the bitter clashes and schisms to come.

Although the 1920 majority report of the Party's Committee on International Relations, reflecting continuous SP ambivalence, criticized the new International along the lines suggested by Hillquit, few socialists expressed doubts about the U.S.S.R. at this time. There were exceptions, of course. Benjamin Schlesinger, socialist vice-president of the ILGWU, opposed an AFL proposal urging American recognition of the Russian government. And in the same year, 1922, the *Jewish Daily Forward* began its devolution into a strong proponent of anti-Communism and anti-Bolshevism.

In general, however, the various radical elements managed to maintain a positive attitude toward Russia—at least until the late 1920s when the CP, beginning its Third Period, resorted to policies which had an alienating and negative impact. The 1921 position paper of the Workers Council stated the case: the November 1917 Revolution gave "back to us our lost ideals"; it provided a "powerful romantic appeal" which pulled socialists away "from a world of hopeless, cheerless realities in a flood of enthusiasm"; and it also inspired the Communist Party, in 1919, to act "as if the Russian Revolution had been bodily transplanted upon American soil."

The SP disputed this last claim, and thus continued the long-standing and basic quarrel between centrists and left-wingers. But it also sundered socialists and Communists after 1919. So the basic issue in this period was not, as some have thought, the status of the new Communist state; rather it was over the imminence of socialism at home. America's Communists accepted the dicta of the Third International, predicted immediate revolution for the West, and would work for it; socialists did not. Such differences would soon produce acrid controversy and simplistic formulas which endured for a half century. With Eastman's early reductionist description, the lines of conflict become obvious. He concluded that the clash was simply between "revolutionary Marxians" and "diluters of Marxian theory"—which suggests an antagonism existing since the 1890s. He made things deceptively uncomplicated.

Former socialist A. C. Townley founded the Non-Partisan League in North Dakota in 1915. It soon spread through the Midwest and even into Colorado, Idaho, and Washington—before collapsing in 1925. The League did not at first enter third-party candidates, but supported those Republicans or Democrats friendliest to its program. By 1920, however, League candidates had been elected to federal, state, and local office. The NPL, together with smaller labor and farmer-labor parties, accounts for the considerable political agitation in postwar America—largely neglected by students of the 1920s.

These farmer-labor movements seemed to justify radical expectations of change. In Chicago, in 1922, the conference for Progressive Political Action (CPPA)—commonly known as the Progressive Party—was organized. It would run a third presidential candidate but would not organize as a third party. The railway unions were its prime movers, but moderate socialists, some AFL'ers, and farmer-labor delegates as well as insurgent midwestern Republicans could be counted among the delegates. When, a year later, Chicago's farmer-laborites deserted to the CPPA, socialists refused to join them because they doubted whether such an alliance would lead "to the establishment of a really powerful political party."

Success by social-democratic standards, therefore, seemed to be the gauge of officially sanctioned socialist approval. Yet two years earlier, Hillquit had inconsistently condemned the farmer-laborite national campaign because it "succumbed completely . . . to the besetting vice of 'practical' American politics, the sacrifice of principle for the desire of momentary political success." Sensitive at that time to "the selling of the soul for votes," and aware of Debs's injunction against such cooperation, Hillquit rejected coalition.

But delegates from the Workers Party (the legal and aboveground CP)—demonstrating a powerful social-democratic mentality—could not resist the invitation of the newly formed Federated Farmer-Labor Party. They had good reason to succumb: their representatives had earlier been snubbed by the CPPA; they were political pariahs until this entente beckoned; and they sought political power within the normative democratic framework—which was highly significant and a harbinger of things to come. Ruthenberg, the WP chieftain, was actively seeking trade-union support, consonant with Comintern directives. He advocated Communist defense of "all genuine labor unions" and publicly endorsed short-term farmer-labor demands. So they joined the Farmer-Labor Party and came to its convention of July 1923 because they anticipated a leadership role in a new mass third party, not because they wished to overturn capitalism. Ruthenberg did include the pro forma requirement of working for the dictatorship of the proletariat, but the debilitating social-democratic seeds were early sown; the Party would increasingly concentrate on means, largely neglecting revolutionary ends.

Each of these political alliances—the SP'ers with the CPPA and the Communists with the Farmer-Laborites—was brittle. The latter compact could withstand no strain whatsoever, and surely not the kind that Senator Robert La Follette placed on it. La Follette had been endorsed by the CPPA convention of 1925, with Hillquit—no longer troubled about "the selling of the soul for votes"—among those seconding the nomination. Despite Debs's order to "keep the red flag flying," Hillquit led the SP into the third party's "non-socialist" campaign. SP'ers proposed to dismantle the present "iniquitous system" entirely and "establish a federation of Soviet republics," but that was rhetoric: they joined a reform party and failed to keep the red flag flying.

La Follette was the logical candidate of the Farmer-Labor Party, and even Communists had rationalized their endorsement. But La Follette declared that the June 17 Farmer-Labor convention in St. Paul could "not command the support of the farmers, the workers, or other progressives" because of the "fatal error" of admitting Communists into the coalition. The latter, he asserted, were acting under "orders from the Communist International in Moscow." This brisk condemnation, and La Follette's distaste for third-party politics generally, resulted in a disappointing and devitalized convention. In a larger sense, it contributed to the failure of the farmer-labor movement, since it also suggested the inability of radicals to agree upon a common course.

The willingness of radical parties to work within the political system and to pursue reformist goals applied to the CPPA and Farmer-Laborites alike. Both really did no more than roll out the old Populist and Progressive buggies to meet the 1920s. The CPPA platform, for example, supported public ownership of the nation's railways and waterpower, direct election of the President, the initiative and referendum, a popular referendum in the event of war (unless there was an invasion), the nostalgic pledge to take arms against monopoly and "special privilege." To such a platform, midwestern progressives had never been cold—and radicals had never on principle opposed it.

These same social-democratic and non-revolutionary inclinations imbued the efforts of socialist youth. Most disaffected students, James Wechsler has recalled, were engaged in one of two major radical trends: either they shared in that revolt in manners and morals common to middle-class youth as well as to culture radicals, or they sought to reshape American society. The latter concern absorbed members of the Young People's Socialist League (YPSL, the anti-war youth arm of the SP after 1913), though the League itself did not recover from the Red Scare until the mid-twenties. It also appealed to the socialist-inclined ISS, which changed its name to the League for Industrial Democracy (LID) in 1921. The growing ISS concern "for a new social order based on production for use and not for profits" became apparent at its conventions of 1919 and 1920. With the theme "The American Labor Revolt: Its Meaning," the 1919 meeting featured speakers like William Z. Foster, then secretary of the Committee for Organizing Iron and Steel Workers. The conferences were still intercollegiate in the sense that they were the principal meeting places for ISS members and that the Society used them to educate delegates in the "new social order." But the ISS had few active college chapters by 1920. Various campus clubs dropped the name "Socialist Club" in favor of titles such as "Social Science Club" and "Social Problems Club." Thus by 1920–21 the ISS no longer had an effective college base and had to rely upon sympathetic liberal organizations, so that the decision to rename it was inevitable.

Repression was a way of life on campuses after the war. Restrictions on speakers, on outside affiliations for student political groups, on the faculty's right to speak, especially if the speech was left of center, was another reason for college clubs to adopt innocuous names like "Politics Club." Such restrictions produced a liberal reaction, and issues of free speech and academic freedom became increasingly important. Colleges, however, were not forums for revolutionary ideas and ideals, the views of frightened college administrators and professors notwithstanding. Teachers complained that students judged English literature on political rather than aesthetic grounds, but the undergraduate mood was largely liberal and anti-rational rather than doctrinaire socialist.

One final observation about the student movement seems appropriate to the Socialist Party itself. For all of the ferment among students in the 1920s, there was little continuity or organization, the latter being virtually destroyed by wartime repression, which continued into the next decade. The Socialist Party was also shaken by government attacks—by denial of seats to its elected representatives, deportation of its alien members, harassment of its leadership and its newspapers. In part, its weakening was due to the strength of vigilantism and, conversely, to the erosion of conventional democratic policies and politics. Ironically, Party effectiveness depended upon the effectiveness of existing libertarian mechanisms.

The SP was obviously diminished by wartime and postwar losses in membership owing to the defection of the prowar sector and to the spin-offs of radical militants. The rise of competing organizations, the CP and the CLP, also deprived the Socialist Party of its most youthful and vigorous members. True enough, the Party did not diminish in size, since its opposition to the war, as Weinstein has demonstrated, increased its numbers and prestige. Indeed, Party membership in 1919 was almost at its 1912 peak. In 1920, while still in prison owing to his conviction under the Espionage Act, Debs managed to roll up over 900,000 votes for the presidency, the largest ever given to a socialist. But the Party was different now. Its membership had shifted sharply eastward, and, in addition to this geographic swing, its rank and file had a mounting foreign-born constituency as a result of the Bolshevik Revolution. Those Party sectors that most prospered as a consequence of the Revolution followed Moscow's directives that socialists seize power immediately. Thus the very revolution that enhanced the prestige of the SP contributed to its division and undoing.

The now "pure" Socialist Party, no longer distracted by the militants, was attracted to British Fabianism as more appropriate to the American experience than Bolshevism. It slowly moved away from close identification with the Russian Revolution. By the 1925 convention, then, socialist delegates were openly hostile to the Bolsheviks, and most members agreed. A steady stream of defectors left for the Communist Party, producing a further attrition in support and strength. Socialists would briefly endorse the La Follette campaign of 1924, withdraw their endorsement in 1925 when the CPPA failed to create a permanent third party, and soon reach their nadir. They would never again come close to capturing a popular or working-class sector. They could count on isolated pockets of Party strength, but the Party had little mass appeal in the era of Calvin Coolidge. By then it had become an isolated sect.

Like the Socialist Party, the CP and CLP had their provenance in the old radical tradition, appealed to the same constituency, and advanced virtually identical programs. Both fought the battle of immediate demands versus ultimate goals; both officially shunned immediatism and piecemeal reforms; both departed from SP practices. New York leftist and CLP'er John Reed contemptuously rejected the policy "of electing Aldermen and Assemblymen to office, where they turn into time-serving politicians," and of "explaining that Socialism does not mean Free Love." The bolting militants had asserted that their parties would not seek peaceful reforms, or permit—unlike Europe's socialists—degeneration into the "loyal opposition"; they would be agents of revolutionary change.

The Communist Party program categorically affirmed that its elected representatives "shall not introduce or support reform measures." Similarly, the CLP directed its political candidates to emphasize that "the chances of winning even advanced reforms of the present capitalist system at the polls is extremely remote; and even if it were possible, these reforms would not weaken the capitalist system." There is only one demand, it continued, "the establishment of the Dictatorship of the Proletariat." Anything less, such as immediatism, would lead to reformist contentment with trivial gains. "Craft unionism is out of date," CLP charter member William Dunne declared; "it is too late for industrial unionism; mass action is the only thing."

Thus the Communists, in Bell's words, had revived Max Weber's ethic of "ultimate ends." Unlike the socialists, they rejected in theory the mandate of responsibility for the daily problems confronting men; they had instead, in these early years, a quasi-religious, almost mystical faith in a new social order. Party efforts among workers could develop the "revolutionary implications" of strikes and could evolve into street demonstrations which would catalyze a broadly based "revolutionary mass action." Then, as Louis Fraina believed, there would be an armed uprising and the dictatorship of the proletariat.

Such a vision was founded on a Whitmanesque assumption that all men were brothers, by a misperception of the realities of national economic and political life, by a selfless devotion and total loyalty to the Communist cause, by a pathological hatred of those who strayed from it. Such unshakable faith found its source in the Bolshevik Revolution.

For those possessed of such faith, for these founding members, there could be no cooperation with liberals and reformers, no ad hoc alliances as in the past. The CP specifically attainted the Socialist Party, the Farmer-Labor Party, the Non-Partisan League, the People's Council, etc., as groups under the ban; and the CLP operated on the same assumptions. In effect, their policy harked back to De Leon and his rejection of immediatism; the isolation of the historic left from the vast majority of the American people continued.

But, as Theodore Draper concludes, the Communist parties did not abandon political action. Indeed, they assumed the necessity of it. In theory, however, they took a jaundiced view of "parliamentary democracy" and gave priority to "revolutionary propaganda." Party political work was not customarily thought to be an avenue to social-economic power—which in theory could only be gained through insurrectionary action, from a general strike to revolution itself: capitalism would not be overturned by elections but by the destruction of the power apparatus. So electoral participation was considered useless as a means of bringing long-run qualitative change. Nonetheless, the Communists ran candidates for political office. They entered the presidential race in 1924 and thereafter turned toward parliamentarianism and unionism, a direction hardly designed to usher in the new social order. In brief, as Gabriel Kolko shrewdly concludes, just as socialism was bureaucratized in the prewar period, so Bolshevism in the United States was being social-democratized after 1924.

The Communist position was consistent with the historic role of organized radicalism in the trade-union movement. The first Communists also affirmed dual unionism: the Reed-Gitlow CLP endorsed the crippled IWW and condemned the AFL. The Fraina-Ruthenberg-led CP did the same, and it proposed a "general industrial union" embracing independent unions, unorganized workers, radical AFL locals as well as the IWW. Its position was theoretically consistent with past radical doctrine which assumed that the immediate demands of trade unions would corrupt revolutionary goals. But Communist activities in trade unions, unlike the proclaimed theory, were unclear and inconsistent. CP'ers were active in union shops, recognized that dual unionism isolated them from the labor movement, and could point to their experiences in the 1926 Passaic textile strike or to the futile, Communist-led National Miners Union, which William Z. Foster had organized. Foster had actually reversed himself. He was committed to working within the existing union movement and opposed to dual unionism. The Profitern (Red International of Labor Unions), however, dictated the official line and Party leadership did not deviate.

Russian Bolshevism created the most difficulties for Communists, especially the need for unconditional loyalty to the Communist Third International (Comintern). The CLP stressed the necessity of an "American" movement, one not controlled by the foreign-language sections—which prompted the CP's conclusion that the CLP and SP retained a symbiotic relation: "It is appropriate that the Communist Labor Party, which has not yet severed the umbilical cord binding it to the Socialist Party, should express this treacherous ideology of 'Americanism.' " The CP reaction was predictable. After all, foreign-language sections made it the larger party: the Russian-born members alone represented 25 percent of the total, and, combined with Eastern Europeans, about 75 percent; only 7 percent of the rank-and-file were English-speaking, and 3 percent of those came from Ruthenberg's Michigan bloc. The CLP, on the other hand, drew its support from former western strongholds of socialism—states such as Oregon, Washington, and Kansas—and had a far greater native-American leadership.

The infant Communist movement, then, remained beset by squabbles and locked into that social isolation which rendered it tiny and helpless. Government repression, especially the Lusk and Palmer raids, further isolated it, forcing both Communist parties underground—which left them even less influential. Defections reduced the total Communist membership to about 25,000, with some disconsolately estimating it at 10,000, a four-fifths decline.

The turn underground with all that it meant—membership cards eliminated, local Party charters destroyed, ultra-secret meetings—had been ordered by the Comintern, which sent its first instructions in January 1920. Both parties were directed to close ranks with the

IWW, in order to smash the AFL, to engage in agitprop (agitation and propaganda), to work within the military, and to amalgamate. Thus the Comintern assumed the right to intervene, which it did on a world-wide scale, and thereby established a lasting precedent—the forged link between Moscow and New York City. That its conviction of the class struggle "entering the phase of civil war" in advanced capitalist countries, including the United States, misjudged the American scene is less significant than the assumption that "the Socialist Fatherland" is the vanguard of world revolution and that fealty must be paid to it. The CP's executive secretary, Ruthenberg, agreed with this directive, but the foreign-language federations, especially the Russian leaders such as Isaac Hourwich, balked at any amalgamation with the CLP—which would threaten their powers. Finally an exasperated Ruthenberg, with Jay Lovestone among others, denounced the Eastern European-dominated Communist Party as a "Federation of Federations," bolted the National Executive Committee, and was joined by about 3,500 members, a majority of the English-speaking rank and file. In effect, a third Communist party now existed, born of cultural and linguistic divisions as much as political. Like the one guided by the arrogant Russian federations, it retained the old name—so as to legitimize its claim as the official party and as the carrier of Communist orthodoxy; and each now wooed the suddenly attractive CLP, with the latter coming to terms with the new Ruthenberg organization.

From this point, the trend was toward seeming unity of the new allies. They called a secret Unity Conference for May 1920, and the United Communist Party emerged, with Ruthenberg being its most influential figure. Most of their energies continued to be devoted to internal warfare rather than to warring against capitalism, the "class enemy," a debilitating course which would be repeated *ad nauseam* over the next decades.

Lenin's brief text *Left-Wing Communism: An Infantile Disorder* contributed to the factionalism. Read religiously by Communists everywhere, it was nothing less than a declaration of war on all Party ultras, with emphasis upon two "errors": refusal to participate in "bourgeois parliaments" and refusal to work in "reactionary trade unions." Coming from the paradigmatic revolutionary, its directives were stunning: Communists were ordered to establish a tightly knit and strictly disciplined party, but one that was a legitimate political organization. They were to engage in electoral work and to infiltrate—"boring from within"—and not attempt to destroy existing trade unions such as the AFL. Lenin was ordering compromise with the enemy whenever appropriate. The world revolution was not imminent, he indirectly admitted, and it would be a disaster for Communists to assume as much. Immediately falling into line, the UCP declared for mass action and alliances with non-Communists.

The Comintern at its Second Congress in July 1920, implemented Lenin's message and enacted his "Twenty-one Conditions." Further, it pressed the cause of unity on the UCP and the Russian federation comrades, and forced the warring antagonists into negotiation at still another unity convention, a clandestine congress which convened at Woodstock, New York, in May 1921. Intervening again in late 1921, the Comintern drew up "The Next Tasks of the Communist Party in America," one of which was to become a legal party. Since it came from Moscow, the ukase had to be obeyed, but it triggered another schism, of those who, romanticizing the underground life, refused to "go legal"—some 2,000 according to Lovestone, then a Party official. Ironically, given the directive from Moscow, the dissidents were mainly in the Party's foreign-language sections—which, when purged, formed the short-lived United Toilers.

Much as Lenin and the Comintern directed, the CP then officially repudiated both the anti-political and dual-union tactics, which had the effect of disowning the IWW effort to "artificially" create "new industrial unions" and "the policy of the revolutionary elements leaving the existing unions." It chided those members who endorsed political activities as a means of improving labor conditions, but confused rank-and-filers by pledging participation in city, state, and national election campaigns, thereby entering the parliamentary house and vitiating the revolutionary creed.

Lenin's primer and Comintern pressure were the prime movers in founding the legal Workers Party, the aboveground surrogate for the underground CP. It sought a mass base, supported the United Front—in accord with the Third International's ukase of February 22, 1922—and worked in the labor and political arenas. Its program omitted any mention of soviets, revolutionary action, the dictatorship of the proletariat, and, Weinstein has concluded, the WP "meant a full cycle return to the Socialist Party position of 1919 . . . [and] it included a set of limited demands."

But formation of the WP ignited further explosive divisions in January 1920—in yet another demonstration of the inability of organized radicals to maintain a common ground, of a weak organization suffering further debility, of the continuity of ideological clashes. The Party's left opposition, mostly Trotskyites, rejected the idea of a public party, preached a revolutionary politics, and, in effect, defied Moscow and the 1922 directive to bury CP–CLP differences. This defiance was boldly assertive: "The so-called Workers Party is a menace to the proletariat of America. It is a party of dangerous compromisers, opportunists and centrists, masking themselves as Communists." This new conflict, then, was something of the usual paradigm: the ideologically "pure" versus the pragmatists who would collaborate for immediate objectives.

CP tactics and thinking continued genuflecting toward Moscow. Invoking "Bolshevization," a term which indirectly ordered: "Remain loyal to the Kremlin," Russian leadership insisted upon and secured absolute obedience. This policy intensified the drive to cast out dissidents and formally ended any independent activities. The Ruthenberg-Lovestone leadership, at all times obeisant toward Moscow, accepted its marching orders unhesitatingly and happily greeted the Comintern prediction, which had no basis in reality in 1924, that "the upward economic movement in America has undoubtedly reached its end—the crisis has come." "Bolshevization" meant a skewed perspective in regard to domestic needs. Thus Communists, rather than adapt practices to changing national circumstances, looked to the Kremlin for guidance and continued down the road that they would travel for decades to come.

By patterning Communism at home in the image of Bolshevism abroad, the Party was wracked by clashes involving personality cults, ego rivalry, and character assassination. Witness, for example, the struggle for control of the *Daily Worker* in August 1925, when the Foster faction took over the newspaper's offices, helped by revolvers, and held out against Ruthenberg supporters for thirty-six hours—until Comintern intervention settled the dispute; that is, until the next year, when new clashes produced new mediation by Moscow.

Bitter debate, then, was usually settled by cablegram from or a quick trip to Russia. Commenting on the practice, Trotskyite Max Schachtman asked, "Can anyone in his right mind imagine leaders of socialism like Lenin, Trotsky, Plekhanov . . . , Debs, De Leon, Haywood . . . racing back and forth between their countries and the seat of the Second International, appealing to its Executive to make the decisions on what policy their parties should be commanded to adopt?" But in the 1920s Moscow spoke—and was heeded. Revolution was the dream, Russia embodied it, and so, as Stephen Spender recalled, it "meant above all never criticizing the Soviet Union." Virtually the entire American left looked toward the East, which surely was a factor in its inability to arouse wide popular support during the Depression decade. That the SP was less dependent on the U.S.S.R. than most was not because of any principled decision of its own—indeed, initially it regretted the situation.

In any case, CP membership was increasingly limited to the faithful who unquestioningly accepted the basic theoretical assumptions upon which policy was founded; namely, capitalism was in crisis and socialist humanism was equated with the U.S.S.R. Party leaders inevitably compared the growth of Russian socialism with the worsening economic situation at home. Capitalism obscured this parallel, Foster complained, since it was "deeply anxious that the masses do not get this message" about Soviet society.

These trends were not confined to the CP. Its left and right opposition were no more than agitational centers in the 1920s, exchanging bitter reproaches and charges when not flinging them against Communists. The lines of hostility were much like those of the past, though the issue of Russia's relevance for the American scene added another dimension. Older socialists like Hillquit and liberals such as Lincoln Steffens continued to support the Bolshevik Revolution, but for a growing number of culture radicals, such as Eastman and Reed among others, the god was beginning to topple. Labor leaders like Haywood, Fraina of the socialist left, anarchist Emma Goldman, who watched in horror the killing of Kronstadt's mutinous sailors, were now lamenting the mounting power of Stalin and asking questions about the liberation of Russia's working class. The romantic revolutionaries had made Bolshevism and the amelioration of man's condition synonymous. They had been inspired by the freshness and lyricism of the Soviet experiment. But where they had once thought it prefigured a new humanism, more and more they began to comment upon the mushrooming bureaucratic apparatus, Trotsky's self-emasculating loss of leadership, the corrupting power of the *apparatchiki*.

The Russian cultural scene provided further confirmation and had added poignance for unattached radicals as well as liberals. They had all been captured by the creative outburst of Russian literature in the 1920s, by the fresh artistic talent and experimentation in the Soviet Union. The growing Party controls on this new art, the reduction of men of letters to propagandists for the state, the collusion of artist and bureaucrat, the ostracism of the creative innovator—his economic boycott and eventual dispatch to a labor camp—guaranteed a ripening disenchantment among culture radicals as well as liberals.

Events at home were no more promising. Randolph Bourne was right! Liberalism seemed to be irrevocably shattered by the war. The carnage in Europe and the secret betrayals at Versailles made a mockery of the humanistic belief in social reconstruction, of the liberal conviction that education and intelligence could bring a steady march of civilization. Progressivism, after La Follette's last fling of 1924, was now a memory, existing as a congeries of reform values rather than as a serious national political movement. The great 1919 strike wave had subsided; so, too, had the struggles for the eight-hour day and for worker control over the conditions of work. By the early 1920s, owing to conflict over such issues, three million workers had been unionized. But trade-union membership dropped over the decade as a whole as the American Plan swung into high gear, with its national network of open-shop associations and company unions. The triumph of Americanization left industrial unionism—witness the United Mine Workers—in disarray and most mass-production operatives without a collective voice. Finally, AFL leaders had become hardened bureaucrats, committed to the continuation of capitalism and to the perpetuation of their power.

Meanwhile, another inspiration of the past was disappearing. The IWW continued its slide downward, helped along by the Justice and Labor departments, by a slack construction industry, by Communist successes in siphoning off Wobbly members, by the IWW's failure to sink roots in the trade unions, and, finally, as Eastman described it, by the intangible "lethargy of age," an exclusivist vision that was remote from the instinctively gregarious earlier radicalism.

Lastly, there were the major liberal journals, such as *The Nation* and *The New Republic,* which trumpeted the durability of capitalism. They campaigned against Prohibition, favored higher farm prices, urged stronger regulatory commissions, and would recognize Russia. But they showed no more daring. Culture radicals, with the gradual dimming of the ignis fatuus of Bolshevism, shared their programs and protests. Both would crusade for reforms and demonstrate against the "civic murder" of Sacco and Vanzetti. For the rest, culture radicals would scribble out their frustrations in the little magazines, such as the *Modern Quarterly,* Victor Calverton's remarkably ecumenical journal. They felt powerless to shift national opinion about the nature of capitalism and some secretly longed for an economic disaster that would produce a reshaping of society. They believed, with the CP's leading cultural spokesman, Mike Gold, that "this depression, this cowardice, this callousness and spiritual death will not last forever among the youth of America. This mean decade of ours will pass on." But apocalyptic visions were for the closet and what openly prevailed was a mood of futility. Calverton summarized it aptly:

> With the dominant parties there are no significant issues at stake, and with the minor parties what issues there are have either been weakened by compromise or obscured by an unfortunate, although courageous, denial and defiance of reality. Nowhere is there light or hope. The radical movements of Europe have little meaning or application on American soil. American radicals are isolated from the American scene.

Of course, being who they were, culture radicals could not be entirely bullish about their country. They did not have any answers, not any more, but they could still heap scorn on the Babbitts and the bourgeois majority, arraign the stupidity of their countrymen, repudiate the middle-class faith of their fathers, and, much like antebellum culture radicals, attempt to throw off dominant social assumptions. They may have considered themselves socialists—a word with little theoretical or technical substance—but they now avoided discussions on the political roads to socialism. Rather they experimented with art and dress and life styles, rallied around such writers as Van Wyck Brooks, and sought to be midwives to a cultural renaissance.

Socialists, too, were on the defensive, and even more resigned to the dim prospects for social change. They had reverted to past, less militant ways, especially after their application to the Third International was rejected. More than ever, the Party was an ethnic organization, and as much as before it emphasized parliamentary practices and infiltration of established trade unions. By 1925, the SP was clearly isolated from earlier sources of power—that coalition of farmers, unionists, and intellectuals which had made it a genuine political party.

Frustrated by the Third International, by internal feuding, by successful CP raids on its membership, by Non-Partisan League inroads upon agrarian SP'ers, the Party became a liberal reform organization once again. Only now it was an empty husk, its glory years behind it. The Communists had taken over the role of raising radical consciousness, and they displayed the militance, energy, and willingness to sacrifice that had once been the hallmark of socialism. By the middle and late 1920s, SP'ers had slowly swung away from their defense of the Russian Revolution and adopted anti-Soviet attitudes that were comparable in tone and substance to those then appearing among culture radicals.

The SP was unlike the Communist Party in still another way. Its leaders lacked the youth and vigor of such officials as Foster and Earl Browder. Debs died in 1926, but his last five years lacked his characteristic forcefulness owing to the rigors of prison life. Berger was an able leader until he died in 1929, but, devoted primarily to his Milwaukee political machine and congressional constituency, he had never become an important national figure. Hillquit was so hardpressed financially that his law practice increasingly occupied his energies. Only under the vigorous guidance of Norman Thomas did the Socialist Party's fortunes bottom out and begin a slow climb back.

A Presbyterian minister in earlier years and a follower of Walter

Rauschenbusch, Thomas was an early convert to the social gospel, to Christian pacifism during the war, and gradually to socialism. Thus he came to the Party through the ministry and not, like Debs, out of the working class. As a college graduate, he appealed to intellectuals, again unlike Debs, whose strongest constituency was in the labor movement. In 1928, he was his party's presidential nominee, conducted a robust national campaign, and received a respectful hearing even in non-socialist circles.

The Socialist Party's 1928 program was clear-cut: public works programs to put the four million unemployed to work—and "at hours and wages fixed by bona-fide labor unions"; federal unemployment insurance and old-age pension plans—to be financed by corporate taxes; and, in foreign affairs, an internationalist and pacifist outlook consonant with Thomas' beliefs. The last included international disarmament, League membership, Philippines independence, and the "speedy recognition of Russia" despite its "despotic and brutal" dictatorship. Federally financed public works, government-operated unemployment insurance, prohibition of child labor—these had been staples of liberal and reform politics for a half century. Socialists, to be sure, did not neglect a plank proposing "collective ownership of natural resources and basic industries," but Party leaders muted such socialist aspects of the 1928 platform. Their proposals, then, remained largely in the old progressive tradition, responding to grievances and urging measures familiar to the supporters of Bryan, Roosevelt, Wilson, and La Follette. Thus putative opponents of capitalism once again failed to appreciate the continuity of means and ends and, unduly emphasizing means, allowed them to "acquire their own rhythm and direction." They thereby made means independent of assigned ends, and even permitted means to replace these ends. Such consequences were virtually inevitable, given the apparent fluidity of class structure, the relative weakness of the class struggle, systematic governmental repression, and the Party's failure to capture the imagination of America's work force. Not surprisingly, then, a visitor from Mars might wonder whether there was any difference between socialists and other reform groups, even between Norman Thomas and Alfred E. Smith, socialist and Democratic Party candidates for the presidency.

Thomas' Christian idealism had drawn him to the Fellowship of

Reconciliation (FOR) and the religious left before he turned socialist. With peace worker Devere Allen, he edited FOR's *World Tomorrow,* the leading journal of Christian pacifists and political radicals. His smooth transition to socialism was made easier by fundamental changes in the nature of pacifism. Earlier peace workers, for instance, had unhesitatingly endorsed America's Christian and commercial expansion. The new pacifists were no longer satisfied with official explanations for American intervention overseas. They turned less credulous and more skeptical; they were, in a word, radicalized.

These new pacifists had a growing relevance in the interwar years. The war, sweeping over the old peace movement, exposed it as morally bankrupt or hopelessly outdated. It generated a host of new groups and new faces, including A. J. Muste and Jessie Hughan, who founded the War Resisters League (WRL) in 1923. It joined with others in promoting issues that had long agitated peace workers, such as mediation of international disputes and "limitation of armaments." What was unprecedented, however, was their collective willingness to go beyond the customary pleas, to take open and sharply critical anti-administration positions on the great foreign policy questions of the day.

FOR was typical in this regard. Established in 1915, it became the major group of radical pacifists. John Haynes Holmes, Harry Emerson Fosdick, and John Sayre were its early leaders, but the Fellowship after the mid-1930s came under Muste's bold and brilliant influence. FOR members asked the hard, and for them interrelated, questions— about class war and the exploitation of labor. Like Walter Rauschenbusch, himself an early FOR member, the Fellowship embraced social Christianity and arraigned capitalism, insisting that human society be transformed so that it resembles Christ's Kingdom. It entered into contemporary labor conflict and came to believe that war was rooted in economic injustice, concluding that antiwar attitudes, in order to be meaningful, must be related to efforts to restructure society. Thus Muste admittedly "came to embrace the view that only revolutionary action by the working class and other elements under the leadership of a vanguard party would bring in a new social order."

Roger Baldwin, who had impeccably pacifist credentials, flatly declared: "To accept absolute pacifism is nowadays to retire into an ivory tower—with a good chance of finding this tower overturned ere long in the hurricane of social change by violence which is sweeping the world.'' Baldwin is here alluding to the mounting Italian-German aggression of the late 1920s, and his view reflects the sense of urgency which then beset pacifists. Frequently, these peace workers were also responsive to the economic hard times at home. Their number included Christian socialists like Niebuhr and the outspoken Harry Ward of Union Theological Seminary, and the growing depression swelled their ranks. They drank at the springs of a socially oriented religion, characterized labor disturbances as ''class struggle,'' and often identified Christ with the working class. The FOR majority, for instance, favored Norman Thomas' socialist candidacy and shared a political and social radicalism with socialists as well as with left-leaning liberals.

Well informed about the dangers of Fascism, these new peace workers willingly joined radical-led Popular Front groups in the 1930s, but a mounting number recoiled from internationalism. Like most Americans, this pacifist bloc moved toward isolationism and vowed ''never again.'' Reflecting a national mood, and a time when textbooks played down battlefield heroes and the war-toy market slumped, it grew in size and number.

In February 1928, at the plenary sessions of the Third International, the notorious Third Period was imposed on the international Communist movement. It followed an initial stage, 1919–21, culminating in the abortive Communist insurrections in Germany and Hungary, and a second in which the U.S.S.R. acknowledged the stability of capitalism and sought peaceful diplomatic exchanges with the West. This Third Period, then, assumed that capitalism was destabilizing and, as Stalin proclaimed, ''the era of capitalism's downfall had come.'' Consequently, the Comintern's Executive Committee announced a ''left'' turn, an ultra-revolutionary phase quite unlike those of the pre-1928 years. It was now time to take the offensive, to turn ''class against class,'' to discredit the solutions proposed by pacifists, non-Communists, and social democrats. Pacifists, liberals, and social democrats were not distinct from Fascists, all reflecting the same repressive bourgeois state apparatus. Ultra-militance, sectarian politics, revolutionary rhetoric: this was the style.

Thus Upton Sinclair, who guided End Poverty in California (EPIC), that non-ideological and lower-middle-class movement which would seek to elect him governor of California, was a "social fascist." Roosevelt would also be so charged in the early 1930s. But it was the Socialist Party which bore the brunt of the Communist assault. It was designated the "hangman of the Revolution," and Thomas, once dismissed as a middle-class reformer, was now a "hypocritical apologist for the bloody rapacities of Wall Street."

Third Period policies would transform the CP into an exclusivist, isolated revolutionary body of the faithful—almost an impersonal agency in behalf of the oppressed, united umbilically for the sake of that service. It would conform to Plekhanov's *salus revolutiae suprema lex,* and, if the revolution, that is, the U.S.S.R., demanded it, everything—democracy, liberty, individual rights—must be sacrificed to it. It would be the ideal Trotsky had adumbrated. "We can only be right with and by the Party," he wrote, "for history has provided no other way of being in the right."

The Comintern's prognosis about the long-awaited death agony of capitalism led inevitably to distortions of American realities. So, as Coser and Howe report, when the New Orleans streetcar workers went on strike in 1929, followed by skirmishes with the police, the *Daily Worker* reported that "again the workers of the South have, with elemental force, delivered heavy blows against the capitalist exploiters and defied the armed forces of the state." And when some members of the Young Communist League "graduated" into the CP, they were proclaimed heroes who "will lead the Red Army to the United States." Thus Moscow's directives led Party leaders to see events at home through revolution-stained lenses. But no Red Army and no revolutionary proletariat appeared. These directives, as a consequence, also produced disappointment, discontent, and desertions.

Jay Lovestone had been Ruthenberg's right-hand man, succeeding him in 1927, when Ruthenberg died. But he had made some serious tactical and theoretical errors during the two years which followed. There was, for example, Lovestone's proposal of "exceptionalism": the unique features of American economic and political life, with the United States then enjoying Coolidge prosperity, distinguished it from other capitalist countries. Hence the Comintern's dicta about the decay of capitalism and the imminence of world revolution, as well as the mechanical application of Marxism-Leninism, appeared irrelevant to specific American conditions.

Lovestone made another mistake. He had praised Nikolai Bukharin, an opponent of Third Period policy, as "an authority of the Communist International," and the endorsement had been duly noted by Stalin, who had a long memory and was an injustice collector par excellence. Lovestone's belated denunciation of Bukharin early in 1929 was only one more instance of self-abasement. It helped him not at all. The techniques—slander, for instance—which the Lovestoneites had perfected, and which had been used to steamroller the Trotskyites, contributing to their expulsion, were now employed against Lovestone himself. Shrewdly summing up the factionalism between the Lovestone and Foster blocs, Stalin depicted the American Communists as

> competing with each other and chasing each other like horses in a race . . . feverishly speculating on existing and non-existing differences within the Communist Party of the Soviet Union. . . . The Foster group demonstrate their closeness to the Communist Party of the S.U. by declaring themselves "Stalinites." Lovestone perceives that his own faction might lose something. Therefore, in order not to be outdone, the Lovestone group suddenly . . . carries through a decision calling for the removal of comrade Bukharin from the Comintern. . . . Let the Fosterites try to beat that!

Before Lovestone's fall from grace, Trotsky's adherents in the CP had rallied around their persecuted leader, especially after he had been driven from Russia. Reflecting thereby the struggle for power within the Kremlin, an anti-Trotsky majority of Communists, including Lovestone and Foster loyalists, joined in a heresy hunt against Trotskyism and, on October 27, 1928, drove the left opposition—led by James Cannon and Max Schachtman—into exile; the Lovestone right would soon follow them.

These divisive struggles were like shadows on the cave wall, unrelated to American realities and working-class concerns, and apparently mattered little to those on the outside. But they had a consuming hold on those involved. The post-Lovestone CP suffered few further en bloc defections over the next decade, but the increasingly monolithic Party paid a heavy price for its discipline—in the form of individual expulsions and a massive turnover of membership. Cardholders declined from 16,000 in 1925 to fewer than 10,000 by 1928, when only the "pure" remained to confront the "social fascists." Thus the old chestnut about the largest party being that of ex-Communists has a factual basis. The purged and the deserted joined others in disgrace, worked quietly for their changeless goals, or devolved into bitter anti-Communists, or supplied the government with a stream of informants in the 1950s, or even assisted the CIA spy culture of these years with a stable of converts.

The Trotskyites, on the other hand, continued to be depleted by splintering. Upon being ousted from the CP, they published *The Militant* and, in May 1929, formed the Communist League of America, Left Opposition, which "faction" sought to remain within the Party orbit and thereby "correct" its views. But one Trotskyite bloc, led by Albert Weisbord, believed the revolutionary cause could best be served outside the CP, and it founded the Communist League of Struggle in 1931. Weisbord's departure was a harbinger of things to come, for the tiny Trotskyite sect continued to subdivide.

Trotskyite impact upon an important literary-academic coterie, which included Eastman, Dos Passos, Lionel Trilling, Louis Hacker, and others, became marked in these years. For example, when *Partisan Review* was conceived in 1934, its founding figures—Sidney Hook, Philip Rahv, William Phillips—being unreservedly antagonistic to "Stalinism," gravitated to its most vociferous enemies. But Trotskyism did not hold them for very long. Some would join the staff of the *Modern Quarterly,* begun in 1937 by a group of disaffected radical intellectuals, but differences immediately developed among them and the journal barely lived out the year. Thus schism characterized non-attached radicals as well as those in organized parties.

Even while recognizing the concrete realities of Depression America, therefore, all radicals were crippled by discord and doctrinal rigidity. To some degree they all inconsistently sought the unattainable—substantive change within the capitalist structure. The 1929 Crash and Depression were encouraging signs; so, too, was the rising unemployment and serpentine bread lines. Marx had said it all in *Capital:* "The more developed a society . . . the more glaringly does the social question emerge": and he noted that "pauperism is making the most gratifying progress'' in the United States. Radicals were heartened by the economic signs and by the literature of prophecy. They gave at least rhetorical attention to conditions at home, and they actively sought to improve labor conditions. But they gave their heart to the internal struggles, to that factionalism which spilled over into inter-party affairs, and which reflected the utterly poisonous ambience of these isolated little oases of radicalism. Thus each group lashed out at the leadership and alleged theoretical "deviations" of its rivals, with each the self-appointed custodian of "correct" revolutionary ideology. There is, it follows, a curiously schizoid quality to American radicalism in the late 1920s, and an element of unreality about their words and formulas.

6 Depression Days

THESE BITTER radical divisions of the late 1920s and early 1930s took place against a backdrop of economic decline, of hunger, joblessness, shantyvilles. The panic days of October and November 1929 were followed by deteriorating conditions. The industrial plant slowly shut down, inventories piled up, factories went on half shift, incomes plummeted, the number of jobless mounted daily, municipal and state relief agencies began to run out of funds, the cities were filled with hungry men and women, and a dull sense of unease replaced the buoyancy of the twenties. But surprisingly few Americans, however grim their plight, gave up on the capitalist system. They stubbornly refused to believe that it had failed. Rather, as Alfred Bingham, a prominent liberal social observer concluded, they took the blows "patiently and quietly."

It is a familiar story. Depression spiraling out, shattering faith in the efficacy of Herbert Hoover's voluntary measures, reviving the hope of socialism as a humanizing force, an agency of social resurrection. But this confidence was limited to radicals, liberals, and culture workers. Their response is equally familiar. Many liberals turned away from laissez-faire imperatives to advocate government intervention in the economy; many writers and artists, having retreated to private concerns and emphases on style in the 1920s, renewed their social commitments; radicals and liberal intellectuals found the Depression decade a time for social idealism, for critical appraisal of the social-political order, for rejection of the claim that capitalism led a charmed life. They were, as Edmund Wilson recalled, "exhilarated at the sudden expected collapse of that stupid gigantic fraud. It gave us a new sense of freedom. It rekindled hope for change." It seemed obvious, as *The New Republic* declared, that "the old recipes of 'rugged individualism' and uncontrolled competition are insufficient." And, it continued, "our mechanized civilization has advanced to a point where it cries out for planning and control in the interests of all."

The League for Independent Political Action (LIPA) was one outcome of such thinking. It included many of the major American reformers—Oswald Garrison Villard, Harry Laidler, Dewey, Muste, Niebuhr, Stuart Chase, Paul Douglas, W. E. B. Du Bois. Its opening statement, in 1928, denounced both major parties, broke with the past, espoused an advanced program of economic planning and expanded social welfare. Its members were largely interested in establishing a new radical party which would oppose capitalist competition, implement a democratic socialism, restore the true community—and which, unlike agrarian archaists, would use the new technology and social engineering toward these ends. Their party, moreover, would benefit all wage earners and show Americans the way out of the economic wilderness. Many of these reformers gathered around *Common Sense,* the journal which Bingham and Selden Rodman founded in 1932. *Common Sense* set forth the LIPA program—which included large doses of technology, collectivism, planned abundance. LIPA would also cooperate with the Socialist Party, but neither socialists nor trade unionists gave more than halfhearted support, much to the disappointment of these youthful liberal intellectuals.

Representing a broad stratum, this left-liberal vanguard soon began to split up. Dewey, for instance, worked within the old progressive guidelines and liberalism—which he always understood to be a relativist and experimental social philosophy. The issue was that of the special interests versus "the people," as he saw it, and he tried to walk the narrow line between significant reform and a radically new social order. Herbert Croly and Walter Lippmann also viewed reform as essentially the task of social engineering and proposed that government power be used to minimize social conflict. Indeed, nearly all these collectivist liberals feared populist democracy and spontaneous political agitation that worked outside orderly institutional life. Some, however, were resigned to the death of liberalism. Confronted by the deepening economic crisis, Lincoln Steffens spoke for them in perceiving that "we liberals, the world over, have had our day."

Rising unemployment and declining relief funds seemed to liberals to require more drastic economic surgery, a root-and-branch social transformation. Some, like Bingham, drew on the rich heritage of American dissent: "There is material enough in American history for a [revolutionary] tradition without importing Cossacks and Kulaks from Russia." Others looked to the Russian experience or even to the CP, whose Comintern-dictated ultra-leftism now seemed more justified: the revolution perhaps could soon begin.

Most of this liberal vanguard, however, did not join the Communist Party. Rather they considered themselves part of an undifferentiated left and were more prepared to consider alternatives to capitalism than were earlier progressives. They were also more ready to consider some variety of Marxism, since it seemed to be an oasis of philosophical certainty in a world shaken by economic crises. Indeed, those who described themselves as "Communists" in this decade were more likely to be committed to Marxist analysis and not to the CPUSA. Recalling his radical involvement, Irving Howe described how Marxism "gave us a language of response and gesture, the security of a set orientation. . . . It felt good 'to know' . . . even in our inexpert hands Marxism could be a powerful analytic tool and we could nurture the feeling that, whether other people realized it or not, we enjoyed a privileged relationship to history."

The culture radicals who urged cultural freedom as a sine qua non emerged out of the privatized life of the twenties, worked in publishing and politics, and often lived in New York. Despite political and ideological variables among them, many supported Communist candidates in the 1932 elections. But they increasingly criticized the U.S.S.R., gravitated toward the Trotskyite bloc of Victor Francis Calverton and James Burnham, and found a forum for their theoretical formulations in the *Modern Quarterly* or contributed to the influential

Partisan Review (founded in 1934). For them—for writers like Freeman, Calverton, Dwight Macdonald, and Edmund Wilson—the Depression vindicated their youthful convictions. But, unlike radicals of the 1920s, they no longer spoke to an empty house. Nor did they reflect the national mood of public resignation. Rather they shared with even pro-Communist culture radicals the view that the United States stood poised on the threshold of social change, that capitalism was nearing its end, that their vision of the cooperative society seemed vividly imminent. And so everywhere there was rekindled radical activity, refreshed confidence, revived insurgency.

More than ever, Russia shook them all with the force of a religious conversion. Many willingly suspended judgment about ugly events in the U.S.S.R. or defended them—and with an emotional intensity which precluded objective assessment. Liberals pleaded Russia's cause on non-ideological grounds: the Soviet Union allowed, indeed encouraged, experimental social models and institutions. In the light of conditions in the United States, the means employed in Russia seemed justified. For the U.S.S.R. stood as a reproach to Depression America, with its Hoovervilles, hobo jungles, soup kitchens, demoralized farmers, joyless youth. "The idle youth," Eastman later recalled, were "in search of a standard to rally round, a crusade, a consecration"; Russia offered it. For all the Bolsheviks' follies, their achievements were emphasized, their sense of purpose inspiring. Liberal journals were eager to affirm Russia's cultural and social superiority, an alternative way of life and reality, a unique set of social conditions. They sent out their correspondents—Waldo Frank, Louis Fischer, Joshua Kunitz, Frederick Schuman—who journeyed in the spirit of pilgrims to a legendary shrine.

The trinity of socialism-pragmatism-Russia converted an impressive group of liberals, academicians, and culture radicals into Russophiles. Though many remained unattached and reactions varied, some of them turned toward Communism. The results were inevitable. For it led to an obsessive loyalty to the U.S.S.R. which would narrow and impoverish radical theory at home and which defined fealty to socialism in terms of fealty to Russia—more precisely, to the Stalinist model. Those liberals and radicals unable to accept slavish Party discipline and Seventh Congress dictates were often borne by similar enthusiasms into the Socialist Party.

Unlike the CP, which entered the 1930s with a tattered remnant of 7,000 card carriers, a bad reputation for splintering, and an unfavorable public image, the Socialist Party would be partly revived by Depression conditions. The economic downturn confirmed its diagnosis of capitalism and brought socialists some small satisfaction. Within days of the October 1929 crash, hopeful signs appeared as SP candidates were relatively successful in local elections. By early 1930, the SP had a larger rank and file than at any time since 1923 and no longer seemed comatose, though it lacked the optimism of the antebellum years.

For all his charisma, Norman Thomas could not hold things together, with warring personalities and world crises dividing socialists and crippling their Party. The SP's very composition assured internal problems. Its mix of pacifists, older Jewish trade unionists, youthful militants of LID, was highly volatile. Its disputes of the 1920s continued to erupt fitfully. Beginning in 1931, the youthful left wing challenged Hillquit's leadership. These "romantic leftists," as Niebuhr called them, were more militant than the Old Guard (Hillquit, James Maurer, James Oneal, Algernon Lee), who, by virtue of age, occupied senior leadership positions in the Party. Their "fundamental differences of view," as Hillquit acknowledged, took the form of open sympathy toward the U.S.S.R., criticism of parliamentary tactics, demands for more active union policy. Youthful militants like Paul Blanshard proposed that the Party endorse "the efforts being made in Russia to create the foundations of a Socialist society." Thomas, largely distrusting his own generation, leaned in their direction. He sought, however, to modify this sweeping endorsement, while Old Guardists like Oneal, the *New Leader* editor, opposed it and went down to defeat.

The ablest of the Old Guard, Hillquit came under siege in the early 1930s. His work as counsel for two oil companies left him vulnerable. So did his New York City location—with many midwestern socialists seeking a grass-roots party, one not dominated by Easterners or those imitating European socialists. Hillquit's death in 1933 ignited a power struggle between the two warring factions, namely, the left versus Old Guardists like Lee, Oneal, and Louis Waldman, New York's unpopular Party leader.

The left wing pressed a Declaration of Principles upon the delegates to the momentous 1934 Party national convention. It pledged support of the U.S.S.R., proposed to meet "any international war . . . by mass resistance," and would take a non-parliamentary route to power, thereby raising the prospect of revolution. The last gave substance to the specter haunting Old Guardists, though not even the most militant bloc, such as the Revolutionary Policy Committee, subscribed to armed insurrection.

Thus the Old Guard campaigned on a number of fronts, both within and outside of the Party. Communists were the external foe since they, too, rejected the tactic of a peaceful parliamentary road to socialism. They were everywhere, especially in the garment trades, and to be fought everywhere—a commitment, an obsession even, which profoundly distorted Old Guard perceptions of the world. This passionate need to defeat CP'ers dominated the right wing. And this need, so Thomas feared, took precedence over any effort to offer alternative radical programs. Thomas had earlier expressed concern over Old Guard social pathology. "It is thoroughly unhealthy," he wrote Hillquit in 1926, "that the one issue on which a great many of our comrades tend to arouse themselves, the one thing that brings into their eyes the old light of battle, is their hatred of communism." Thomas carried the day, Waldman's impassioned plea against the 1934 Declaration—as "anarchistic, illegal, and communist"—being rebuffed. Nor did Waldman's hysterical charge in the following year that Thomas was "the conscious or unconscious tool of the Communist Party" convince the Party's rank and file.

Passage of the 1934 Declaration was the turning point. The cleavage evolved into a struggle so bitter, so uncompromising, that further cooperation was impossible. And matters were further exacerbated by the entry, in growing number, of youthful radicals out of universities and theological seminaries. These radicals equated the Kingdom of God with socialism, believed it attainable on earth and in their lifetime. Some were Christian pacifists; others were revolutionaries; and virtually all were in search of a militant cause. Hence they were hardly the safe social democrats desired by the Old Guard—whom they called "slowcialists"—and they founded the *Socialist Call,* in opposition to the right-wingers' *New Leader.* By May 1938, New York's Old Guard, the key rightist group, bolted the Party—with Waldman acting as the Pied Piper. Following him were New York's leading socialist unionists, major socialist institutions such as the Rand School, and the Pennsylvania state majority, specifically the influential Reading Old Guard. Then Bridgeport's socialists, led by Jasper McLevy, "disaffi-liated"; and so did factions in the Indiana and Oregon state organiza-tions as well as some in the important Jewish federations, including Abe Cahan's authoritative *Jewish Daily Forward.* Many of the dis-sidents joined the Social Democratic Federation (SDF), which was simply a social-political extension of their New Dealish trade union-ism. Thus SDF supported Franklin Roosevelt and New York governor Herbert Lehman rather than SP candidates; and they left the weakened Party to Thomas, the Militants, and rank-and-file loyalists, a total of about 12,000.

The Socialist Party had divided along lines not very different from those apparent at the 1901 Unity Convention—namely, generational, tactical, and ideological differences, and the struggle for power emerg-ing out of them. Possibly doctrinal conflict had primacy. But, of those who contested the 1934 Declaration, Thomas and the Militants were younger than their antagonists and the struggle was in part precipitated by the fiercely proprietary spirit of the Old Guardists, who were deter-mined to protect their bureaucratic turf. Further, for those involved, this 1934 contest was laced with the awareness that capitalism was doomed. The Depression had been a tocsin for them. Buoyed by the possibility of a social eruption, they thought their decisions would di-rectly affect the course of history.

If factionalism comparable to that of its founding days riddled the Party, there were also marked dissimilarities. Debs suggested one. He had emerged from the labor movement and his main strength remained there; Princeton-educated Thomas, on the other hand, attracted an educated middle-class sensitized to social inequities. The Party itself had taken on Thomas' orientation and few farmer-socialists—such as those once emerging in Oklahoma and Wisconsin—now remained.

Moreover, the grass-roots support for socialism within trade unions from roughly 1880 to the 1920s, especially among miners, machinists, brewery workers, and shoe operatives, had also evaporated.

Paradoxically, the SP's growing middle-class outlook did not discourage a temporarily leftward movement after the Old Guard departed. The program that had attracted voters in 1932—that is, meliorative reform within the capitalist system—increasingly dominated Party circles. Government intervention itself was encouraging, socialists concluded, since it seemed to be a step in the right direction.

The consequences of this immediatist and parliamentarian orientation come as no surprise. First, the Party's theoretical poverty continued; not one major or original theoretician emerged in the 1930s, except perhaps Lewis Corey. Second, emphasis on the ballot box and economic reform produced a mutinous state of affairs. The Party seemed united behind Thomas' presidential campaign of 1936, which produced a modest resurgence of socialist fortunes, but the unity was more apparent than real. Internal divisiveness remained. Indeed, the admission of splinter-group Communists—the Trotskyite, Lovestoneite, and Gitlow factions—sharpened the struggle for control of the Party and its local units. Even the Militants did not speak with a single voice. Some of them were eager to work with the American Labor Party (ALP), a New York State-based third party founded in 1936 by unionists who wished to support Roosevelt but not on the Democratic ticket. But others, adherents to revolutionary socialism, formed a new group, Clarity. It included Trotskyites, expelled CP'ers, followers of Lovestone, Zam, or Gitlow—all past masters of Byzantine politics and hairsplitting doctrinal debate which they had refined to a sharp theological edge. With such recruits, as Bernard Johnpoll concludes, it was impossible for the Socialist Party to remain cohesive and effective.

Most Trotskyites did not join Clarity, though sharing its suspicions of ALP'ers and equally hostile to reformist politics. Clarity members duly noted that the ALP included some strange bedfellows: Old Guardists, former Militants, socialist advocates of middle-class reforms, Communists (then in a Popular Front period), pro-New Deal trade unionists. Being leftists, they would have nothing to do with the New

Deal or reformist capitalism and urged the SP to run independent political campaigns on the hallowed grounds of socialist integrity.

Trotskyites were influential far beyond their numbers; indeed, they
had their greatest impact on the American intellectual community in
these years. For they were the magnetic core for those disillusioned
with Russian Communism, a sharply mounting number, and for those
who found Trotsky himself, tried and convicted of treason in absentia,
the symbolic victim of Soviet repression. The Trotskyite and Clarity
groups of socialists were both concerned with the Lovestoneite charge
that the SP was a mass reformist party and that it blocked revolutionary activity, and the deepest Party divisions—much as in the CP—
turned on this issue. But they were divided over some critical questions—such as Trotskyite allegiance to the Fourth International, publication of their own journal, and refusal to follow official Party policy,
a condition of their initial entry. And it would eventually be the Clarity bloc, collaborating with the Militants, which successfully pressed
the Party's purge of Trotskyites in 1937.

Thus the once-messianic Party seeking the "truly human" promised
land became fitfully accommodationist over the years. Since its founding, it had cooperated with those seeking a shorter work week, old-age
insurance, federal and state unemployment insurance, and public
works. Daniel Bell notwithstanding, the Party was aware of the world
in which it lived, and perceived it in immediatist and collaborationist
terms. This perception, it needs reiteration, did not necessarily mean
that different tactics would have substantially altered things. Even if
the Party had not abandoned the relative militancy of the 1920s and
moved into the New Deal orbit, the results would have been much the
same. Qualitative change would require, among other factors, a sharpening of the irreducible structural antagonisms between capital and
labor, a diminished capacity to produce consumer goods, the decreasing cooptation of trade-union leaders and political representatives, a
movement away from voluntarism and the ideology of self-help and
from the pervasive ideological and structural privatization accompany-
ing them.

Socialists, paradoxically, flailed away at the New Deal even while
cooperating with it. It was, they charged, a "capitalist" scheme, a

harbinger of imperialism and of the "fascist state," like Mussolini's in Italy. Roosevelt's domestic policies, Thomas declared, simply adopted some of the "immediatist" demands of the SP platform; and, he continued, "the essential thing about the Socialist platform has always been its purposes and its goal rather than its immediate demands."

The Party's hallowed reliance upon labor was now decisively undermined—and by labor itself, as union leaders turned to Roosevelt as their savior. That Roosevelt's programs were dedicated to reviving capitalism seemed unimportant. His provisions for social security, recognition of labor's right to bargain collectively, efforts to get people back to work, to raise living standards, to help the hungry, were what counted. They would not bring full employment, but they eliminated the worst aspects of the Depression for the work force. Consequently, they also contributed to a declining class consciousness and shaped Roosevelt as the champion of the common man. Understandably there was meager labor support for socialism in the 1930s: the AFL failed to endorse socialists in 1932, AFL'ers did not vote the SP ticket, David Dubinsky and many ILGWU members defected, most of the Amalgamated Clothing Workers' socialist officials did the same, and needle-trade unionists as well as leaders of the Steel Workers Organizing Committee (SWOC) and John L. Lewis' miners flocked to the Democratic colors. That mine owners opposed Roosevelt was reason enough for their employees to support him. Trotsky, it would seem, had been justified when warning that "the danger—the terrible danger—is adapting to the pro-Rooseveltian trade-unionists."

The Party's dilemma was clear enough. The New Deal had massive appeal for labor. SP leadership might perversely dismiss the CCC's "proposed labor camps" and equate the NRA with "state capitalism," providing no "basis for permanent protection against the evils of capitalism." But hungry workers, poverty-stricken farmers, unemployed youth were not convinced. Moderate and right-wing socialists—as well as the entire Old Guard, much of whom was now in the Social Democratic Federation—viewed the reformist New Deal as an important step forward, preparing the way for socialism. Roosevelt thus produced "vast ideological confusion" among radical groups, as Laslett has concluded, and "left socialist principles in a state of utter chaos." His very electoral successes seemed to be in inverse propor-

tion to the Party's decline. But even before his emergence, even before the early 1930s when socialism peaked, defections to liberalism,
specifically to the Democratic Party, had become common. By 1931,
prominent members like Upton Sinclair and Paul Blanshard had grown
impatient with the SP's isolation and impotence. In California, for instance, the state's socialists joined Sinclair's EPIC; and his defiance of
cease-and-desist orders from the Party resulted in expulsion and a shattered state organization.

By 1936, the swing toward Roosevelt was plain even to the most astigmatic socialists and it produced angry and despairing reactions. The
Party's National Executive Committee criticized the President's infla-
tionary policies, while Thomas attacked his civil rights and civil liberties record. Labor, he insisted, must remain in its "house of bondage"
if it was satisfied with the pastiche of New Deal reforms; and he vocif-
erously denied that Roosevelt, by such reforms, could stabilize and
save capitalism. While not condemning the New Deal as outright Fascism, which the CP did at the outset, Thomas saw parallels between
Fascism and "state capitalism," as he derisively labeled it. He had
serious reservations about the NRA, with its anti-union tendencies,
found the farm tenantry program inadequate, criticized the social security, public housing, and unemployment and relief measures of the
Administration. But his most vehement attacks were reserved for those
socialists and liberals who flocked to Roosevelt's banner.

The 1936 election results were disastrous for socialists and a portent
of worse things to come. Thomas' vote had slipped under 200,000,
plummeting in every city and state. In the Reading stronghold, for instance, only a third of the registered socialists cast ballots for Thomas.
By 1938, SP membership had dropped to 7,000, a third of the 1934
total; and it was reduced to 2,000 by 1941. (It would not exceed this
last figure over the next three decades.) And Thomas, in sum, was
partly right in explaining the 1936 results: "What cut the ground
pretty completely out from under us was this. It was Roosevelt in a
word." But if the New Deal undermined a deeply divided Party,
Thomas failed to admit that revolutionary theory was hollow at the
core, that the SP no longer offered a genuine alternative, that it deserved what happened to it after 1936 when it became naked to the
class enemy.

Socialism, Daniel Bell concluded, failed because of grave strategic mistakes. Like Thomas', his diagnosis is only partly right. That Bell's claims are incomplete becomes evident when we ask whether a different strategy would have produced a happier outcome for the Party— or, for that matter, whether even the absence of internal feuding would have done so. Clearly, it would seem, the answer on both counts is no. In explaining socialism's failure, then, one must look to outside forces—to the lack of class consciousness in the work force, the high degree of mobility, the identification of socialism and Communism in the public mind, the system's capacity for accommodation.

Consequently, we may assume, even a complete victory for Clarity, or for Trotskyites, would not have much altered the national scene. Thomas' anti-New Deal shafts may have been more doctrinally consistent than the pro-Roosevelt columns of *The New Leader,* but the clearcut emergence of a revolutionary bloc within either of the major radical parties would have gone unnoticed nationally unless the working class was ready for socialism.

However, had such a revolutionary potential existed, then surely it would not have been so readily dissipated by social and economic reforms or, as Tom Bottomore contends, by the new optimism Roosevelt engendered, a reawakened populist sentiment which had lain dormant for a generation; and then possibly the New Deal would not have been able to bite so deeply into socialist strength. But its reform programs *were* able to cut the ground out from under the SP, much as Wilsonian liberalism did some decades earlier. That two Presidents made consecutive contributions to the Party's irrelevance only partially and superficially explains the downhill slide; or why severe economic depression did not halt it and present socialists with their golden opportunity.

One thing appears indisputable. Economic deprivation did not rouse the exploited and revolutionize consciousness. Of course, some increase in radicalism occurred. Many workers were even prepared to accept militant rhetoric and tactics—but only a handful would follow through to radical ends. There was no ground swell of socialist or revolutionary thought; there was no substantial number, or even insubstantial number, willing to challenge the capitalist system. Rather than attributing their woes to this system, workers responded to the Depression in a personal way; they blamed their unemployment on themselves, on their own incapacity to find work. Those most affected may have been disoriented and demoralized, but they did not fault the system. Rather, they internalized their frustrations, channeling them inward, and believed their demands could be met within the context of capitalism. These demands were recognized by socialists, who were sensitive to human needs; and the New Deal helped implement them—within the established power structure.

Understandably, given labor's response, the American workers did not have a unified response or solidarity of attitude. To apply for relief was debasing, a confession of personal failure rather than a reflection upon the failure of capitalism. Those who had ability, so every source told them, could find work. And naturally enough, as Richard Sennett and Jonathan Cobb have shrewdly observed of the work force today, if they felt inferior it follows that their superiors had a right to an unequal share of the resources of society. So stigmatized by personal inadequacy, workers rarely questioned the system itself or found its values at variance with their own. Nearly fifteen million were unemployed in the darkest days of the Depression, and another thirty million had frightening job insecurity; and it is difficult to comprehend why their response was not one of seething and generalized social discontent. But, except for small pockets of protest, such was the case. And even such discontent, as observed, did not extend to a critique of capitalism and, beyond, to a socialist solution.

There were signs to the contrary: the diffused attack on "economic royalists," the interest generated by Marxist thought, the increasing militance of labor, the flood of books and articles by liberal intellectuals which focused on the inequities of wealth and power in American society, the restless and angry students—at least those at the better colleges. But distinctions must be made between ephemeral militancy and ad hoc means, and sustained radical thought and revolutionary goals. Labor unions were prepared to follow SP activists, even employ their vocabulary, but few subscribed to their proclaimed ends. None of this is especially surprising; the AFL's pragmatic temper and its bread-and-butter unionism remained the acceptable model for America's work force.

This work force, whether native-born or immigrant, was powerfully affected by conformist social strains and dominant values. There was the ideology of "Americanism" for one. A mix of socially sanctioned canons, it included an emphasis upon occupational mobility and material accumulation, both militating against a class orientation, as well as a belief in hard work, which, for the gifted and industrious, opened the frontiers of economic opportunity even in Depression America.

Hence a disorienting sense of personal humiliation, rather than hunger marches, amounted to an oblique and unmerited tribute to capitalism. But why this faith? Why have political parties hostile to socialism or even to labor been so regularly legitimated by working-class votes? Why have the dominant interests been able, within the democratic political process and by peaceful means, to continue economic and political dominance? These questions are perhaps best answered by referring to earlier observations about the successful "engineering of consent," which relates to Marx's comments in *The German Ideology*. "The ideas of the ruling class," he wrote, "are in every epoch the ruling ideas" because "the class which is the ruling material force in society is at the same time its ruling intellectual force. The class which has the means of material production at its disposal has control at the same time over the means of mental production." Paul Lazarsfeld and Robert Merton have written about one form of "mental production," namely, the manipulation of mass publics through propaganda, "through the mass media of communication. . . . These media have taken on the job of rendering mass publics conformative to the social and economic status quo."

There are other, more sophisticated forms of "mental production." Refining Marx's proposition, Gramsci, in Gwynn Williams' summary, has described how popular consent may be "engineered" by "an order in which a certain way of life and thought is dominant, in which one concept of reality is diffused throughout society in all its institutional and private manifestations, informing . . . all taste, morality, customs, religious and political principles, and all social relations, particularly in their intellectual and moral connotation." In no sense, as the introduction cautions, is this "one concept of reality" static and immutable. Emergent cultural values can eventually be incorporated into dominant means and practices, thereby changing and remaking the latter. Hence, while the central social-economic formations do not alter, hegemonic values are always in process.

America's "chief power groups," by controlling these subtle and pervasive "means of mental production," have been spectacularly successful in legitimating capitalism. Their dominant values have drawn all but the most radicalized into the myth of a shared consciousness—that is, a sensibility held in common with middle- and upper-class Americans, and dictated, however obliquely, by these classes. Thus a dominant social-economic elite fastened its complex amalgam of assumptions, ideas, interests, and attitudes—that is, its pervasive world view—upon a middle and a working class. It convinced them by both overt and subliminal means that there was another source of their misery, and that it worked in behalf of commonly shared values. Consequently, workers were easily dissuaded from holding dissident ideas. And dissidents, whether in the factory or in the academy (Robert L. Heilbroner has written), all sought "to accommodate their proposals for social change to the limits of adaptability of the prevailing business order. There is no attempt to press for goals that might exceed the powers of adjustment of that order. Indeed, all these groups recoil from such a test." Hence no one had to be coerced. No political and no overt means were required. Labor in the 1930s responded to deprivation and social-economic injustice with consent. Its ideas, culture, life style, what it wanted from life was confined within the context of capitalist society. John Cammett seems relevant here. "In a general sense," he writes, "hegemony refers to the 'spontaneous' loyalty that any dominant social group obtains from the masses by virtue of its social and intellectual prestige and its supposedly superior function in the world of production."

This loyalty, this dominance of elite assumptions, is demonstrated by Roper's study of public opinion about social class. When asked, "What word would you use to name the class . . . you belong to?" a fourth of those polled in the 1930s replied that they did not know; and to another question, nearly 90 percent affirmed itself middle class. So did over 70 percent of those whose incomes were such that they were in the "poor" category. And less than 8 percent were self-designated "lower" class. Such responses are a tribute to the success with which the mechanism of ideological hegemony has been hidden.

Jerome Frank did not believe institutional change was possible in the 1930s, not "until we have . . . a previous revolution in the attitude and vision of the American people." Such a "revolution" was simply unrealistic at the time. Certainly the Socialist Party was unprepared to make it, riddled and splintered as it was. Nowhere was its lack of a unified world view—one which might challenge the cultural hegemony of capitalism—more desolately apparent than in its responses to reform, to trade unions, and to United States foreign policy.

Overseas events inevitably shaped the course of American radicalism in the interwar years. Socialists did not, like CP'ers, give mindless deference to the U.S.S.R. True enough, especially among youthful recruits, unscarred by the earlier factionalism, there was renewed sympathy for the Soviet Union. But Old Guard socialists such as Oneal accented Russia's repression of dissent and the forced collectivism, including the murderous elimination of the kulaks, and they looked upon the pro-Soviet socialists as naïve, dupes, and possibly agents of the CPUSA. As they turned toward the New Deal, their anti-Sovietism hardened and, becoming pathological, distorted their perception of the realities about them. They became increasingly susceptible to any anti-Communist critique.

Events in Spain, unlike those in the U.S.S.R., did not initially produce intra-Party divisions. To the contrary, it would appear that all radicals could unite in their response to the military uprising of June 1936—which produced the civil war that, until it ended in 1939, tore the country apart. Writing of this war, literary critic Malcolm Cowley stated that "people of my sort were more deeply stirred" by it "than by any other international event since the World War and the Russian Revolution." It was, Eric Hobsbawm recalled, a marvelous drama, an epic of heroism, the *Iliad* of those who were young in the 1930s. There was a lack of moral ambivalence about it, an absence of the customary controversy that swirled around most left-wing causes in the mid-1930s. On one side were the peasants, poets, and workers; on the other, the generals, bishops, and landowners. The former, the Loyalists, were invariably portrayed as defenders of reason, liberty, and democratic government arrayed against the forces of darkness—feudalism, clericalism, and brutal military power. On one side, too, stood the U.S.S.R., giving military and economic aid to the Republic; on the other, those who would destroy democracy in Spain. The Loyalist cause seemed to represent the last chance to halt the spread of

Fascism. Its supporters were driven by an ardor and idealism so generous that it is nearly impossible to recapture. Certainly no crusade since that against slavery so caught the imagination and moral sense of writers and intellectuals, liberals and radicals.

The moral reductivism of the Loyalist cause is reflected in the comments of Clarence Hathaway, *Daily Worker* editor. "The issue in Spain today," he declared, "is the issue of democracy versus fascism." This simple political equation had virtually unanimous approval from the left. The struggle of the Loyalists seemed like a clash of the powerless against the murderous rich. It was the one fixed light in a darkening Europe. It was, for SP'ers, the single most important test of Party unity and Roosevelt's sincerity. Roosevelt's trade measures, especially the January 1937 embargo, passed by joint resolution of Congress, became the target of an intense and continuous barrage. It prohibited the export of munitions "for the use of either of the opposing forces in Spain," which had the effect of helping Franco, who received massive support from Germany and Italy.

Socialists, however, were not in accord on other Civil War-related issues. The official Party line endorsed Premier Largo Caballero's socialist regime, a Popular Front coalition that enjoyed widespread support. But all coalitions, Trotskyites and Clarity believed, only strengthened capitalism, as well as Fascism, each a variation on the same theme. Thus Clarity leader Gus Tyler complained that Communists supported Caballero's "people's government"—which was bad enough—and that this coalition had "de-Bolshevized" the Spanish left. The reaction of one writer in the *American Socialist Monthly* was typical: Spain's Popular Front was "pusillanimous," and, he concluded, "liberals, democrats, people's fronts, all alike will fall before the onrush of fascism, unless that rush is checked by the revolutionary working class."

Like the CP, socialists also solicited funds for Republican Spain and sought to recruit volunteers—for the Party's Eugene V. Debs Brigade. Such a military force, the *Call* declared, "is our small fighting contribution to our class comrades across the seas." Joining the Militants, Thomas affirmed that Franco must not be allowed to triumph. "Any further great success of fascism is more likely to mean a long night for Europe and the world."

Thomas' reluctant shift from nonviolent means reflected that of many pacifists who were socialists and who retained an internationalist outlook. They were all pulled between Christian ethics and an increasingly desperate global scene where something other than nonviolence seemed highly appropriate. Thus Thomas, reflecting this pull of antagonistic forces, would work ceaselessly "to change President Roosevelt's version of the hypocritical Anglo-French nonintervention" policy since it "was indisputably an aid to fascist aggression" in Spain. But he also organized in March 1938 the Keep America Out of War (KAOW) conference. It included many radical and pacifist groups (except Communists, who were barred) and endorsed opposition to conscription and even to collective security since "that would lead to war."

Thomas nonetheless slipped away from absolute pacifism. He rejected the contentions of Trotskyites, Clarity, and FOR socialists that the Civil War was simply a conflict between "two groups of European nations which are in effect using the Spanish masses as pawns." He disregarded the plea of John Haynes Holmes "to save the Party" by returning to an uncompromising pacifism—and would place an arms embargo on the aggressors but not on their victims.

Thomas' defection did not leave him without allies. He was joined by the Party's internationalist bloc, which spoke through two major socialist organs, *The New Leader* and the *American Socialist Quarterly*. The latter, socialism's official voice, reflected its readers' ambivalence toward peace workers, though disavowing the "sentimental pacifist." *The New Leader* was the Party's most articulate internationalist journal. Unlike Thomas, who vacillated, it firmly rejected both pacifism and isolationism. Readily contemplating the use of force against Fascism, it warned that "pacifist submission to fascist aggression [would be] suicide." Its position, then, did not differ substantively from that of many liberal and Communist periodicals: capitalism was responsible for the rise of Nazism and Japanese aggression; and the English Tories were aligned with Hitlerism owing to common class interests.

Perhaps the most divisive of all issues for SP'ers was the Popular Front of 1935–39. Written by Hungarian Communist George Dimitrov at the Seventh Congress of the Comintern, the proclamation affirming it called for an "anti-fascist People's Front," a broad common effort to defeat Fascism—which the U.S.S.R. finally saw as the immediate threat it was. Those parties which entered into the fraternal struggle, the CPUSA pledged, would retain their right of criticism and their structural identity. But major segments of the Socialist Party nonetheless greeted efforts at inter-radical cooperation with undisguised hostility. Any collaboration with the CP, Old Guardists insisted, was immoral and possibly catastrophic, and all discussion toward this end should cease immediately. *The New Leader* also rebuffed the CP's invitation, while the increasingly influential *Partisan Review* charged that the Popular Front betrayed both political and cultural radicalism.

Thomas and the Militants, however, were prepared to consider some joint effort owing to their fear of Fascism. Though suspicious of Communist motives, they would join in ad hoc measures such as civil rights cases and hunger marches, and consequently they welcomed the invitation of Earl Browder, CPUSA general secretary, for a Madison Square Garden debate in 1935. Browder greased the wheels by suggesting that all gate receipts should go to the *Call* and the Socialist Party. What Communists wished, he stated, was the immediate implementation of a program of joint struggle for "the victory of the united front . . . against war and fascism, and victory of the mass movement for a Farmer-Labor Party in the United States."

Thomas would take the CP at its word. His personal independence, however, was a constant irritant to Communists. He criticized Stalin's "kind of terrorism," doubted the veracity of the Russian purge-trial confessions, joined the Committee for the Defense of Trotsky. He invariably made socialist participation in Popular Front organizations conditional. But no matter how Thomas qualified proposals for cooperation, there were those on the Party's NEC who found cause for rejection—because, as one of them declared, the "Socialist Party cannot afford to have anything to do with the Communist Party until it ceases to take orders from Moscow." *The New Leader* concurred. The CP's rapprochement with Roosevelt simply confirmed socialist suspicions. Trotskyites and Clarity members remained unalterably opposed to reformism as well as collective security—the latter being a Popular Front mandate which, it was charged, was designed to support Stalinist Russia. The Popular Front, Clarity continued to assert, was only one more manifestation of liberal reform. Gus Tyler claimed that Communists, by endorsing a government of "all anti-Fascist parties," had abandoned "a revolutionary position on the capture of state power." Others on the socialist left joined him in arguing that capitalism and war were inseparably enmeshed and that compromise with "bourgeois democracy" was inadmissible.

With the Third Period of the Communist Party, to return briefly to the late 1920s, an insurrectionary rhetoric and vision had priority, but militant, issues-oriented trade unionism and social-democratic tendencies were frequently practiced. Notwithstanding the CP's ultra-left sectarianism, its Central Committee in March 1933 admitted the possibility of cooperative efforts by modifying policy vis-à-vis dual unionism and socialists. The Committee was now prepared "to withhold all attacks upon Socialists [and the] A.F. of L." in the interest of a "united struggle." By mid-1934, this approach, now an unabashedly "united front from above," had become official policy. The SP's National Executive Committee was informed that "one does not have to agree with the platform of the Communist Party . . . [or] accept the Communist Party position regarding the ultimate necessity for the revolutionary seizure of power" in order to cooperate in agitating for "immediate demands." And in 1935, just before the Popular Front was formally adopted, a *Daily Worker* editorial exhorted Party members to "break the dead hand of sectarianism that has held us back in the past." It is necessary to do so in order to mobilize the broadest possible coalition of all "progressive forces against fascism."

Thus the Party had forsaken the Third Period's revolutionary perspectives even before 1935. Its official abandonment reflected the CP's conclusion that such policies were a liability in union organizing drives as well as an impediment to collective security, so needed by the U.S.S.R., and to cooperative efforts against Fascism. Whether Fascism was or was not an ephemeral stage of capitalism in decline, it was now depicted as an immediate threat. Consequently, a broad anti-Fascist coalition was essential, and the CP proclaimed a moratorium on doctrinal toughness and the spread of revolutionary dogma.

Readily abandoning ideology in order to fight Fascism, Communists turned to collaboration with liberals and radicals of every persuasion. Browder declared: "We will fight together with all those in the United Front, for a majority in all elective bodies, local, state, and national." Elsewhere he stated that the Party "relegated its revolutionary socialist goals to the ritual of chapel and Sundays." Such goals could be postponed. The Popular Front "is not a program of revolutionary overthrow of capitalism. It can be realized within the framework of the present economic system. . . ."

"We of the Communist Party," Browder affirmed, "are prepared to cooperate with everybody who will help win that higher standard of living." In so doing, Communists "ceased to be rebels, alienated and in resistance to American society," George Charney recalls; "instead they behaved like men anxious to fit in and conform." They did so happily, since such tactics promised an end to political isolation. They would enable Party spokesmen to declare with conviction that Communism is "twentieth century Americanism." CP'ers displayed a growing awareness of their national heritage. The *New Masses* eagerly identified with the heroes of history. Jefferson, Lincoln, and Paine were enshrined in the pantheon of American Communism, sharing equal time with Marx, Engels, and Lenin. Browder's lineage was proudly noted: Kansas-born, with colonial Virginia antecedents. And certainly his speeches sounded closer to Wilson and Roosevelt than to the Bolsheviks. Young Communists made their own contribution. They celebrated baseball, Hollywood films, and Paul Revere's ride; and they proudly observed, "The DAR forgets but the YCL remembers."

Thus the Popular Front became more than a temporary pause in the class struggle, an expedient needed for the U.S.S.R., a tactic buying time for it to prepare militarily for the expected German onslaught. But it was that as well. Collective security—the alliance of "anti-Fascist powers"—became the strategic centerpiece. The "social fascists" of 1934 became the "progressive forces" of 1935, and their cooperation energetically solicited. Russia, of course, was automatically praised, but so, too, were the virtues of democracy and the New Deal. And now as well, national third parties and dual unions were opposed, thereby depriving Party leaders of a bargaining chip in dealing with Democrats and rendering them unable to wring concessions from the

Administration. Finally, the Front fed those inherent strains in American Communism that contributed to its debilitation.

At first, however, the Popular Front had promising results. CP membership doubled—to about 55,000 in 1938. Some bitter anti-Communists were temporarily converted. Herbert Zam for one. A former Lovestoneite and an SP'er, he argued that one did not have to desert socialist principles in order to work for the defeat of Fascism. Other Lovestoneites joined him in urging Communist-socialist unity toward the end of an unconditional defense of the U.S.S.R. against Fascism.

In such manner, the Popular Front sharpened inherent tendencies, and encouraged those who would declare a moratorium on the war for structural change. Palmiro Togliatti, the Italian Party chief in the 1940s, noted in a series of postwar articles that Communists must incessantly struggle against bourgeois ideology and unremittingly work for the conquest of state power; anything less would produce reformism rather than revolutionary social change. Choosing the former route, America's Communists turned to liberal democrats. Means were substituted for revolutionary goals, and thus the CP surrendered its identity as an independent political force. The old vacillations, never wholly absent, between militancy and opportunism, revolutionary idealism and a desire for acceptance, reappeared, and with predictable outcome. Gone was the old insistence that the capitalist state apparatus had to be dismantled, the hallowed belief in working-class immiserization, the distinctions among pacifism, liberalism, Marxism. Rather than reaffirming the class-war thesis, the *New Masses* now declared that the "dominant finance capitalist groups [were] on one side," while "the overwhelming majority of workers, farmers, and small business and professional people [were] on the other"—which was hardly what Marx had in mind. Naturally enough, the Party even considered converting the Democratic Party into a Popular Front movement; and the middle class, as Richard Pells observes, became a "vigorous" partner in this struggle against war and Fascism.

The Popular Front produced a marked shift in Party trade-union policy. Before the Third Period, CP'ers had sought to infiltrate trade unions—by "boring from within." William Z. Foster, a long-time opponent of dual unionism, was primarily responsible for the Trade

Union Educational League (TUEL). Founded in 1919, and supported by the CP after 1922, it was the vehicle by which militant CP unionists would work within existing unions, such as those crafts affiliated with the AFL.

But League members were being expelled from the AFL in mounting numbers by 1924, as prosperity brought increased confidence to AFL leadership. What remained of TUEL within the AFL gradually dwindled into a powerless propaganda voice. Foster, however, remained stubbornly loyal to "boring" and did not believe "the AFL and big independent unions" were "hopeless." So he asserted as late as 1927, and the Party officially endorsed his views.

Party tactics, however, were flexible. At times dual unionism seemed the answer—as in the needle trades; or in the mines, when the established AFL unions were so repressive that Communists could not function effectively; or in Bedford, Massachusetts, where the Party encouraged unskilled textile operatives, most of them Portuguese, to join a militant, Communist-guided union rather than the passive, craft-conscious AFL.

The Third Period dictated a return to dual unionism. "Further appeals to the [AFL] bureaucracy," resolved the Profitern (the Red International of Labor Unions), ". . . is useless and wrong." Foster was now directed by Moscow to guide the dual-union strategy, the first since the IWW. Following hard on this ukase came the National Miners Union, the National Textile Workers Union, and others. TUEL changed its name to the Trade Union Unity League (TUUL), and it was the Party's prime vehicle for dual unionism, especially in the industrial unions, then largely ignored by the AFL.

But TUUL was never very important and the dual unions in mining, textiles, and shoe manufacturing were disappointments. Not that TUUL organizers lacked energy or courage. Indeed, they were repeatedly beaten and jailed, even murdered. They worked endless hours for subsistence wages and displayed passion and self-sacrifice beyond the call of duty. And out of their strikes, even when defeated, emerged a corps of labor militants. They were trained in basic trade-union practices, joined left-wing theory to sound union practices, and went on to become important CIO organizers.

Most of the TUUL-sponsored strikes did fail, usually owing to labor's fear of loss of employment in these Depression years. And most workers, when they moved toward union membership before the CIO appeared, sought entry in the AFL. All the more reason, Party leaders realized, to return to "boring." Class struggle thus yielded to the imperatives of the hour—to work within existing unions and to seek immediate demands.

Thus TUUL officially died in March 1935, when it became apparent that few independent unions could remain viable. Communists now called for penetration and capture of existing unions and they would eventually turn to the emergent CIO. Before this development, however, the Party's major effort was among the jobless. CP-led Unemployment Councils organized demonstrations for jobs and pressed local relief measures upon urban government. They did so almost without plan, simply by drifting with social needs and events, by admittedly following "the line of least resistance." But they did so effectively. One hundred thousand Detroit workers, for instance, protested unemployment and marched under Party and Council banners. Indeed, Detroit had possibly the nation's most active Communist district. One YCL demonstration there drew 10,000, while several others attracted 5,000 or more.

By these Unemployment Councils, Party members sought to arouse labor militancy. The unemployed were grateful, but had no real interest in the Party or the Third Period analyses of capitalism. And the Councils, not catalyzing class consciousness, evolved into reform bodies which fought for jobs and against evictions; that is, they became concerned with means and immediate ends.

America's industrial work force, even before the mid-1930s, began to seek control over production and to eliminate the punitive powers of business. Much like the reaction to Taylorism earlier, labor turned to direct action and workplace militancy which, in 1934, took the form of wildcat strikes—among Minneapolis teamsters, Akron rubber workers, Detroit auto workers. Grievances and negotiations again originated at the shop level; workers formed new unions; and management was confronted with the loss of discipline and of many assumed "rights"—to hire and fire, to discipline and promote, to establish pay scales and hours of work without interference.

The Party, which had announced a *prole-kult,* proclaimed itself the vanguard of the proletariat, and prided itself on sensitivity to labor's demands, failed to recognize that these were the first gusts of the storm and that a new labor federation was emerging. Even three years later, when a wave of strikes swept the country, the Party's response was uncertain. The strikers, opposing the cautious and conservative Federation leadership, fought for militant and democratic unionism, and began forming industrial unions outside AFL jurisdiction at about the time that Moscow dictated a return to Federation "boring." Hence the AFL connection partly explains the Party's belated recognition of rising labor militancy and of the new CIO. Whatever the reason, CP leadership seemed insensitive to rank-and-file restlessness.

On the shop level, however, Communist trade unionists correctly assessed the situation, took the initiative, and joined in local organizing drives. Party leadership only began to fall into line in late 1935, when they tardily recognized what was implied in the resignation of mine chieftain John L. Lewis from the AFL.

Thereafter they streamed into the fledgling CIO and had an influence beyond their numbers in some industrial unions. In auto and steel, for instance, the foreign-born Party worker, often coming out of TUUL, made a great impact upon non-Communists of his ethnic group. Moreover, Party rank-and-filers—much like socialists and Trotskyites in the local work force—frequently commanded the respect and personal loyalty of other shop labor; and sometimes non-Communists might be drawn to the Party because of the self-discipline and high ideals of its members. But they were largely untouched by Communist doctrine; and certainly the nation's institutions routinely continued, partly because CP'ers recognized their legitimacy.

SP unionists, resenting Communist organizers and influence, stressed their dependence upon Moscow. So did the Trotskyites—only more virulently. Seeking to build anti-Soviet sentiment, first as members of the SP and then as members of the Socialist Workers Party (SWP), Trotskyites attacked the "degenerated workers' state" in Russia, condemned Stalinist officials in the United Auto Workers (UAW), and even supported those union officials who had made "bureaucratic missteps" but—priorities had to be honored!—were opposed to Stalinists. Scarcely less hostile, AFL leaders were also vehemently anti-Communist—if only because, as Federation chieftain

William Green charged, the CP's "avowed purpose" was "to destroy" his organization. Although aware of such enmity, the Party, as late as 1934, only tentatively opposed Federation efforts to brake labor militancy; and it had not yet cast off the AFL or the image of it as central to America's labor movement. Such convictions flowed from a gross self-delusion as to Federation intentions and its own influence within the Federation. Before 1935, these practices were contrary to Third Period dicta; thereafter they were astigmatic.

CP shop-level policies, however, did not alter substantively during the Depression. They continued to have militant, sometimes revolutionary overtones. They did so especially within the context of the CIO, which emerged in November 1935—to fill the vacuum created by AFL reluctance to organize the great mass-production industries. CP'ers had been seeking for years to obtain influence in such industries as transport, electric, auto, and shipping, and these emerged as prime targets of CIO organizers. The CIO needed experienced union leaders and naturally drew upon Communists (and socialists), while the Party in turn took the initiative and assigned its members to factory work, to organizing, to establishing a political base within the mass-production industries.

Thus Communists proposed mass picketing, rank-and-file control of strike actions, black-white labor solidarity—all toward the end of intensifying the class struggle. They sponsored daily mass meetings, anti-racist demands, abolition of discrimination in wage and promotion practices for women and blacks; and they took up the case of black labor more effectively than any other group. The Depression, with its astronomically high unemployment rate for Negroes and the notorious job discrimination against them, finally awakened CP leadership, gradually to be sure, to the possibility of a burgeoning black membership. By the early 1930s, the CP was working diligently in black ghettos and emphasizing immediate issues like housing, jobs, unemployment relief (rather than abstractions like "self-determination"). It filled a vacuum, for Communists lacked an effective organizational competition; and it won a modest respect among some black workers, sharecroppers, and intellectuals.

The CP's union activities were designed to heighten labor unity and ensure mass participation in strike actions. They would have another effect, inadvertently triggering AFL fears and a rising anti-Communism. That the auto strikes were led by the Auto Workers Union (AWU), a dual union, rather than by the Federation, furthered AFL antagonism to the Party and to Communism.

A postscript is useful. In this Third Period, when many radical historians find a marked Communist sectarianism, the Party-dominated AWU worked actively to create coalitions with elected strike committees in which AWU members were a distinct minority. It is one of numerous instances of Front activities in pre-Front days, another example of how doctrine and rhetoric took a distinct backseat to social-economic necessities.

Party unionists also led rank-and-file local caucuses in opposition to ineffective union leadership. The least democratic unions were invariably and paradoxically unions without Communists. Those controlled or influenced by Party members were usually aggressive toward employers and internally democratic—with monthly membership meetings, annual conventions, regular elections of all officers. Cynics might argue that they most consistently upheld democratic rights in unions where they held no power. Perhaps. But militancy and democratic organization were major emphases of the Party in virtually all Popular Front groups. And even in unions which they controlled, like that of the fur and office workers, Communists were usually forthright when democratic practices were at issue.

The Communists won power and respect in the CIO, and that they deserved it is indisputable. For they were ready to undertake the unpleasant chores—to hand out leaflets in blizzards, to expose their union and Party affiliations in non-union shops, to stand against armed vigilantes hired by anti-union management. They were the best organized, best disciplined, most effective radical sector in the CIO—and most shop workers were willing to accept their efforts to improve conditions. Understandably, then, at their peak of power, Communist-dominated unions in the CIO represented about a fourth of all CIO workers.

The Popular Front emphasis upon collaboration with liberals and union leadership precluded revolutionary indoctrination of the work force. But the slackening concern with ideology, both before and after 1935, also had other causes. First of all, new Party recruits came from middle-class and native-born ranks, and while paying obeisance to the rhetoric of proletarian vanguardism, these members had an essentially reformist perspective. Second, Trotsky's fears had materialized: trade-union preoccupations gradually moved many CP'ers away from what Trotsky called "their historic class interests." His predictions were reflected in a Party assessment of its trade-union work: "Some splendid trade union members have joined our party but do not see the party except as a necessary force to help them organize the trade union. Very many workers have joined the party because of their support for our immediate program."

The Popular Front emphasis on Party trade-union practices also offered a heady (though transitory) prospect of labor's acceptance as well as public acceptance. Certainly it seemed to promise a working alliance with the CIO's national leadership, reason enough to mute socialist rhetoric, neglect revolutionary goals, ignore working-class needs and demands on occasion.

A digression of some importance may be illuminating. Rank-and-file militancy was frequently thwarted by trade-union leadership, for they had intrinsically different goals. Witness, for example, the fears of the Steel Workers Organizing Committee that if the militancy of local union officials and members was not curbed, peaceful union-management relations would be impossible to establish. The early UAW was even more radical and aggressive, but its officers always recognized the need to accommodate to management and to government. They were of course painfully aware that stability and formal authority ran counter to shop-floor activism, but the latter had to be curbed before it led to wildcatting, which would be in violation of contract. In this way Trotsky's warning of the "terrible danger" of being "pro-Rooseveltian trade unionists" was fulfilled. Communist cadres, seeking to perpetuate collaboration at the top—with the CIO leadership and the Democratic Party—surrendered larger socialist ends, lost their Party identity, and became trade-union bureaucrats instead. Like Foster, they invariably bowed to expediency. Their union work, one 1939 directive disclosed, "changed radically to correspond to the present period [of unity]. . . . The Party . . . has liquidated its Communist fractions, discontinued its shop papers, and is now modifying its system of industrial branches."

Communists, Foster affirmed, were involved in "building the highest type of trade union leadership" and in organizing unions rather than, as Weinstein observes, in organizing a socialist consciousness among workers. They were, therefore, tacking in a direction taken by the SP over the years. Again Gramsci is instructive. Discarding the notion that trade unions could be organs of revolutionary struggle, he noted how labor bureaucrats were isolated from the rank and file—how this condition legitimized unions in the eyes of businessmen and made possible those union-initiated reforms which occurred under capitalism; in effect made possible the perpetuation of hegemonic values and of the system itself.

Subordinating themselves to CIO leadership, Party members, so Browder insisted, should undertake no action which might disrupt their alliance at the top. By 1939, the Party ceased building a strong independent base in most unions and enervated the militant radical bloc it had relied upon. These were acts of self-immolation in 1939. CIO leaders only waited for an opportunity to abandon their former allies. When the time came, even the CP's closest friends in the CIO—in the maritime and transport workers unions—turned away from them. Being practical men, CIO leaders recognized that the moment had come for them to demonstrate impeccable anti-Communist credentials, and they savagely and completely repudiated their old comrades. But these events carry us down to 1949. Enough now to note that the Party abandoned the struggle for socialism, supported the New Deal, and tried not at all to challenge or distinguish itself from liberalism.

To account for the failure of the Party, and of all radical parties, there is a final observation that needs reiteration. The CIO, for all its militancy, never expressed a class politics. Much in the AFL's fashion, it grew increasingly job-oriented, even in the 1930s; and, entrenched in power, it tended toward the traditional "business unionism"—which would encourage CIO bureaucrats to be guided by the same standards governing the business community. Understandably, then, the CIO largely served to integrate labor into the existing system, to direct militancy into relatively innocuous channels—with the encouragement of liberal capitalists and government officials.

These new union leaders intuitively recognized that labor's very idea of work had been shifting over a half century; and most sharply in the 1920s, when consumerism became more than ever a national value and characteristic. Owing in part to consumerism, and in part to the breakdown of craft, with the development of specialized and repetitive labor, work and the workplace were no longer central to the life of the operative. Labor had become a way of acquiring income, a necessary evil. And those who performed it wished to escape from it and from the working-class community which identified them with the work force. Even before the 1940s, when the trend became pronounced, they had begun to move into small suburban homes and private, low-cost housing—where, unlike the earlier cohesiveness, their neighbors had no shared work experiences, ethnic ties, or even patterns of sociability. The gradual breakdown of the old working-class communities and the trend to suburbia is most significant. Most people, after all, visualize the class structure of their society from the perspective of their own milieu. Their perception reflects their experiences in the small society in which they lived out their daily lives. Given these shifting primarily social experiences, the labor force, more than ever wage- and consumer-oriented, increasingly felt no sense of definite social location or class and status membership. The worker looked to the unions, to the CIO as well as to the AFL, as bodies devoted to bettering his own economic position, rather than to organizations fostering political or social upheaval.

Liberal businessmen and liberal Democrats, much like the CIO leadership, instinctively recognized these unfolding changes. To assist the working class, they all believed, was to assist the consumer and the national economy as well. The flexibility of capitalism was no con man's trick; rather it was an integral characteristic of the system, manifest in its ability to maintain order and prevent a revolutionary situation from developing. For instance, when Michigan governor Frank Murphy refused to bring in the state's National Guard during the General Motors sitdown strike, the importance of a favorable governmental climate became obvious: not only did GM yield, but labor antagonism was limited to ad hoc issues and went no further. So, too, when SWOC locals in Pennsylvania in the mid-1930s initiated a labor-liberal coalition ticket that won local political office, such social-democratic practices served to legitimize the existing political process, the government itself, and hegemonic dominance as well. So at first Little Steel bitterly resisted union drives, but management eventually adapted. Of course, not all corporations displayed such resilience. Faced by the loss of traditional "rights"—to hire and fire, to promote and demote, to unilaterally set pay rates and hours of work—many employers resisted. Such businessmen, usually in smaller and non-monopolistic industries, displayed enormous hostility toward union drives and demands. They must be considered—even though we are here commenting upon corporate liberalism. In any case, a significant sector of the business community "became smart." It learned that by recognizing national union leadership and the collective bargaining agreement, business could rationalize industrial relations, bypass local shop leadership, undermine shop-floor militancy, and discipline the labor force. It learned "how to adapt, co-opt and engulf the union and make it part of the establishment."

Roosevelt's administration intervened in economic life on a massive scale. It combined with union officials and liberal banking-business elements—with the Communist Party looking on approvingly—in order to contain antagonisms, and to do so cheaply and effectively. The price was not sweatshops or abominably low wages and long hours, at least the unions had seen to that: they had taught, and liberal capitalists had listened, that this was not the 1860s or the 1880s, and that it was possible to pay decent wages and provide decent hours of labor and still make enormous profits. In this way potentially anti-government actions, even non-ideological protest, were bought off (by such measures as the WPA and the Wagner Act), and the elites maintained control. No class can rule for long without successfully presenting itself as the guardian of, or as working in the interests of, the values and sentiments of the ruled. The coalition of labor, banking, business, and government that emerged in a hungry and depressed America was spectacularly effective in conveying this proposition.

Hence the widespread spontaneous strikes produced no revolutionary activism, economic militancy failed to evolve into political radicalism, and the struggle which began with the rubber and auto workers did not lead to socialist consciousness. Whether it would have if a revolutionary socialist sector existed is moot; except for a few sectaries, no insurrectionary groups had appeared. It is significant that this labor-business-government coalition was not unprecedented, that an issues-oriented labor movement was pulled into the Democratic Party without protesting too much, that this coalition maintained labor's dependence upon state welfare measures. "The tragedy of justified revolt," Roger Baldwin understandably lamented in 1935, "is that it can be bought off so cheap"—by farm subsidies, relief payments, PWA projects. The strike wave that periodically swept the nation in the mid-1930s, he pointed out, did not represent an assault on liberal capitalism but was an effort to enforce its premises.

7 American Radicalism in the Twilight of Peace

THE POPULAR FRONT, we have seen, owed its existence to a number of factors. First, there was Russia's belated recognition that Nazism was no passing stage and alliances were necessary in order to thwart this threat to a socialist republic, surely the most important of reasons. Second, Roosevelt was proving to be the savior of American capitalism, which was also displaying a remarkable durability. Third, the Depression was not raising the class consciousness of the work force, something it was supposed to do with the help of the CPUSA.

Like the SP as well as all radicals and liberals, the Communist Party had been profoundly affected by events overseas. Dictatorships were on the rise and threatening the fragile peace. Mussolini became Il Duce in 1922 and invaded Ethiopia in 1935. By 1933, Hitler was allowed to take office as Chancellor; and, owing to economic discontent and repressive emergency legislation, death came suddenly to German democracy. He had outlawed trade unions and destroyed radical parties, including the Socialist and the Communist, which, like Moscow, had understood him to be a temporary actor on the national stage. Jews were openly assaulted, their shops boycotted, and an anti-Semitic campaign steadily mounted in intensity. German troops marched into the Saar in 1935, following a plebiscite. Three years later, Hitler bullied Austrian Chancellor Kurt von Schuschnigg into resigning and German forces swarmed into Austria. In the Far East, meanwhile, the Sino-Japanese conflict reopened in January 1931, followed by the Mukden incident in southern Manchuria, the Japanese drive to the Great Wall, and the attack upon Shanghai, occupied on March 2, 1932, after a murderous siege.

Such realities prompted Soviet leaders to adopt "collective security." America's Communists followed suit. For them, uncritical devotion to the U.S.S.R. remained the litmus test of true radicalism. Such devotion had been the major source of Party status and strength, though paradoxically, it also contained a fatal flaw. For the enormous emotional investment in Russia distorted a rational assessment of the regime, and made a critical approach toward it impossible. Soviet efforts to build an anti-Axis coalition required unswerving membership support. And it followed that Roosevelt's neutrality policy, according to the *Daily Worker,* would "serve only to lull the American people into a false sense of security."

Isolationism became the gravamen of the Party's complaint. "Keep out of war" slogans, it warned, were being used alike by "warmongers like Hearst and adherents of the status quo like Roosevelt." Repeatedly emphasizing "the peace role of the Soviet Union," Communist leaders clamored for greater Russian-American cooperation to prevent war, focusing on a trade agreement as part of a united diplomatic front against Hitlerism.

As late as May 1939, in a report to the Party's National Executive Committee, Browder urged the repeal of the Neutrality Act, and believed that contrary policies were aligning the United States with German and Italian interests. The possibility of another alignment, that of England and France with Germany, was a recurrent Party nightmare; and it evoked continuous admonitions—to the effect that Great Britain might "appease" Hitler on the Polish question and that the U.S.S.R. alone "warned the world weeks and months ago of a new Anglo-French Munich intrigue." The CP, it followed, found newly discovered virtues in a group of liberals and congressmen who had long argued that America's neutrality measures should include a proviso denying aggressors access to American-made munitions. It had warm words for Roosevelt's "Quarantine Speech" of 1937 and for a congressional measure which would ban arms shipments to Germany and Italy.

The Popular Front, we have seen, muted the Third Period appeal "for a Soviet America" and provided sotto voce support for the belief of the proscribed Eduard Bernstein, the doyen of social democracy, that "the movement is everything—the ends are nothing." Though continuing to speak of a "decaying capitalism," CP'ers made common bond with liberals, pacifists, and Democrats. Their 1938 Party platform included the obligatory pledge to socialism as "the highest form of democracy," but also declared: "Today the issue is not socialism or capitalism—the issue is democracy or fascism." How different from the earlier days!—when Communists greeted the New Deal with suspicion and disapproval. Now the Party declared that Communists were "as devoted as any other group . . . to the principles and institutions of democracy"; and Roosevelt stood "on the same plane with Jefferson, Jackson, and Lincoln."

CP'ers thought they had sufficient cause for such sudden and marked reversals of policy. Roosevelt's welfare measures, Browder stated, had obscured "a clear posing of issues," but CP'ers implausibly concluded that the inherent contradictions in capitalism had been accelerated and that the inevitable struggle for a new society was only briefly postponed. If the Party fought for immediate demands, they reasoned, the masses would accept it in the struggle for total social change. Thus they proposed redress of grievances while believing the system beyond repair. Thus they straddled; they endorsed Max Weber's "ethic of responsibility," which offered practical work toward immediate ends, while being comforted by insistence upon an "ethic of ultimate ends." And they rationalized their position by concluding that the system could not withstand even these middle-class reform pressures. That such thinking is unconvincing and exiguous seems obvious. That it led ineluctably to the conviction that the system was not inherently an enemy of the masses and could be made to serve them is perhaps more significant.

To middle-class writers, artists, and professionals who were Party members or fellow travelers, the new line made it possible to be simultaneously part of a socialist vanguard and of the "American spirit." They were no longer isolated and outside society. Thus they drew away from radical change and toward recovery, and channeled their creative energies into a rediscovery of the nation's past. They traced the democratic heritage and celebrated the struggle of the "people," temporarily shelved any thoughts of a revolutionary crusade, worked rather to defend the U.S.S.R. against Fascism, and had the comforting belief that an authentic national purpose motivated them as well—to save American democracy. No problem of acceptance of the new line existed for the Party member—except for those few skeptics who were silenced or purged. The professional, as one untroubled Comintern member declared, "gives his whole life to the fight for the interests of his class. A professional revolutionist is ready to go [physically and intellectually] wherever the Party decides to send him."

Collaboration existed during the Third Period, but never on so systematic or extensive a scale as after 1935. Front organizations became respectable and prominent—and many who were not Communists tolerated or joined them. The American League Against War and Fascism, formed in 1933, was the premier Front group. Typically, it accepted both individual and group affiliation, with the latter permitting League officials to claim a total paper membership of over seven million; individual members numbered about two million. Among them were liberals, radicals, students, even AFL'ers. By 1937, the League had been pledged to collective security and changed its name to the American League for Peace and Democracy. So completely were anti-capitalist traces erased that Harold Ickes and Robert Jackson, two prominent New Dealers, endorsed its goals in 1939. It had a good press, influence among congressmen and unionists, attracted mayors and ministers to the speaker's platform, as well as Browder, in what was a notable collaboration of Communists and Christian pacifists.

The National Negro Congress (NNC), established in February 1936, reflected the entry of a modest number of black workers and intellectuals into the Party. Most of its membership was non-Communist, to be sure, but the CP considered the Congress a valuable asset. It bridged the black and white worlds and enabled the Party to recruit and proselytize in the NAACP and among black unionists. Such efforts were singularly unrewarding, for the Party slogans of "Black Belt" and "self-determination" had no great appeal: black CP'ers comprised less than 8 percent of the rank and file. Communists actually won control of the NNC in 1937, which was consistent with the Comintern directive at the Seventh World Congress; namely, that Party members seek leadership positions in Front organizations—so that they could guide the working-class revolution when the time came. The Congress gradually evolved into a sectarian organization, with black Communist activists like James Ford seeking to transform it into an "expression of anti-war and anti-imperialist struggle"; by 1940 they had succeeded.

The International Labor Defense (ILD), the Party's legal arm, claimed about 300,000 members. Proclaiming itself "non-partisan," it rallied opposition to German pogroms, Japanese anti-labor measures, the imprisonment of "more than 34,000 Austrian people—trade unionists, Catholics, Jews, all who oppose fascism."

Like the ILD, the League of Professional Groups was a Front organization founded before the Popular Front was proclaimed. Its purpose was to campaign among writers, scientists, artists, and teachers for the Party's presidential ticket of Foster and Ford. It did effective work, with a distinguished galaxy of professionals endorsing these candidates.

The League's success tells us something about culture radicals in these years and about their influence upon cultural institutions like literary magazines and theater groups. A substantial number of intellectuals and creative people were touched by radical thought, naturally enough since the Depression had produced a crisis of faith for their value system. It confirmed the sense that things had gotten out of control, as Lippmann concluded in his sadly neglected *American Inquisitors,* that men were no longer able to order events but, rather, were governed by powers remote from them. The mood, surprisingly, was not one of hopelessness and impending doom. Instead there was a feeling that the old order was changing, that American exceptionalism was an obsolete proposition.

A tone of urgency dominated the thinking of many writers and intellectuals. There was no middle of the road: only the alternative between a dying capitalism and a brave new world struggling to be born. But there was a choice; and, consequently, they were anything but despairing. Intellectuals, they believed, could once more take an honored place as social engineers and help prepare the masses for a sweeping social change. Recalling 1937, Rahv and Phillips stated, "Writers felt that they were at the dawn of a golden age."

No wonder that some culture radicals actually turned Communist or that many felt drawn to the Party and its causes. We felt close to men, Granville Hicks recalled of his own CP experience, who were "touching history at its vital center." Literary critic Alfred Kazin reminisced, "The unmistakable and surging march of history might yet pass through me. There seemed to be no division between my effort at personal liberation and the apparent effort of humanity to deliver itself." Scholar Newton Arvin was willing to cast his lot with "these grim fighters in about the most dreadful and desperate struggle . . . in all history." Commitments of this sort, so overwhelmingly emotional in nature, brought sudden disenchantment at times. So that the Party's defection rate remained very high, especially after 1936; indeed it was higher than in the 1920s, when relatively few men of letters followed Dos Passos and Eastman and were categorized as "class enemies"; by the late 1930s, virtually everyone who had once contributed to the *New Masses* (founded in 1926, as the successor, in a limited way, to the old *Masses*) could be so classified.

Such commitment, however, compensated for any feelings of doubt, for the novitiate at least. The CPUSA was so much more than a political party or an ideological cause; rather, it was something special in history—a fraternal order, a mission, a religion, a proselytizing church. Hence it provided unique social and psychological advantages which often took precedence over its body of theory. George Soule remembered that "warm and active bond with our fellows," referring to those (non-Party and Party workers in this instance) who labored for a new moral and economic order. Whatever their faults, and the prestigious Edmund Wilson itemized them, Communists had a sense of solidarity and purpose which one could not help but admire, especially in the midst of the Depression's social and economic wreckage. "They are a people willing to die for a religion," Wilson conceded. To him, to such writers and critics as Arvin, Steffens, Malcolm Cowley, Erskine Caldwell—some fifty-two in all who signed a petition for Foster and Ford—the Communist Party's candidates in 1932 were vastly superior to those fielded by the two major parties. Democrats and Republicans, they agreed, wished to patch up the system; the Socialist Party sought respectability and election victories; only the CP had an unwavering commitment to social and cultural transformation.

Marxism was the ideology forecasting this change and it was claimed as the special property of the Communist Party. The most interesting and creative socialist thought, however, came from non-Communist intellectuals, from such unattached radicals as Calverton, Lewis Corey, Dwight Macdonald, and Philip Rahv. Their critical work maintained a high analytical level and, though sometimes polemical and shrill, was most clearly linked to traditional Marxist exegesis.

Such men were exceptions. For Marx's emphasis upon the historic inevitability of revolution had diminishing importance for Party members and left intellectuals alike in the thirties. Communists may have claimed Marxism as their own, but it was merely a ceremonial claim after the Popular Front had been announced. There were, however, few times in CP history when Marxist theory was applied in a serious and sustained analysis of American society. And even the non-Communist intellectual, with those exceptions noted above, made only infrequent and incomplete stabs at such analyses. Usually, CP'ers and leftists settled for that feeling of commitment to larger humane values and a restored purpose to their lives, that feeling of moral certainty which Marxism almost always ignites. So that the body of beliefs known as "Marxist" provided a sense of historical direction and an organic vision of life even more than it did a tool of class analysis.

For Communist students and middle-class left intellectuals, Marxism offered an analytical system which predicted the contemporary crisis of capitalism, persuading them that these crises were recurrent and in the nature of their system. For non-Communists, such as the culture radicals, Daniel Aaron has written that "it seemed a science as well as an ethic, because it explained and foretold as well as inspired." To them, Howe stated, it provided a unity of self and society, art and life, thought and practice—where before these had been compartmentalized. Hence the stress upon the whole man as well as on a code of personal conduct and commitment, rather than Marxism's theory of capitalist crises, provided the major appeal. Non-Communists like Dewey and Robert Lynd would translate Marx into the vernacular. They were drawn, much like the *New Republic*'s liberal planners, to Marxism, but did not accept it without qualification. Indeed, they brought their own gloss; they championed the principle of social democracy rather than violent insurrection, and wished somehow to "Americanize" Marxism—and how accommodating was the Party!

For most unattached intellectuals, radical protest was effortlessly transformed into an act of "democratic affirmation"—and the "progressive" artist thereby testified to his "solidarity" with labor and the "people." Popular Front groups were ideal vehicles for such actions. They were rarely criticized—to do so would weaken the U.S.S.R.! Nor were events in Russia rigorously scrutinized. The result, predictably, was a loss of intellectual vigor, the attrition of critical faculties, the acceptance of a self-deceptive and simplistic black-white, either-or moralism.

Since the Party above all others was the voice of Marx, writers and artists and critics sympathetically followed its activities, even if they did not join. Unlike capitalism, "dying at the end of its blind alley," unlike *New Republic* liberalism with its inherent sense of failure, the CP seemed to possess a positive vision of mankind just coming to maturity. Calverton said it: "The individual derives his meaning . . . in relation to society, and not through himself." So much for liberalism. And writers and critics, given Marxism as their theoretical guide, were forward-looking about the future despite the shattering impact of the Depression. Few of them could care if the CP stage-managed the American Writers Congress—which was hosted by the League of American Writers, a typical Front group composed largely of non-Communists. Organized in 1935, the League had veered toward Van Wyck Brooks's effort to re-create a cultural nationalism, and its speakers—Hicks, Cowley, Joseph Freeman, *et al.*—emphasized the defense of "democratic" literature and rallied writers to the "unending campaign against the enemies of democracy."

It was natural, then, for many of these culture workers to make a large emotional investment in the cause of the proletariat and in the political organizations which claimed to serve it. Natural, too, to write proletarian novels; or to paint in the genre of socialist realism, with canvases depicting heroic labor or labor struggles; or to glorify the factory operatives and those who work with their hands. "Always the workers speak better, more directly, than the intellectuals," declared Sherwood Anderson; and the obviously anti-intellectual overtones of such comments—ironically coming from those who were men of the word and who used their minds—were widely shared. Culture radicals like Anderson and Eastman felt a barely concealed sense of shame for being writers. They dismissed their own work as less humanly relevant and less rich than that of the proletariat and, as Christopher Lasch has concluded, they questioned the value of intellectual speculation and rational endeavor. Their self-deceptions were such that they frequently squandered their gifts in an effort to cross over to the working class.

The complex story of 1930s radicalism is incomplete without a review of the role of pacifists and students. About the former we can be brief, having already commented upon their willingness to join Popular Front groups. Harry Ward, for example, would head the American League for Peace and Democracy, and its journal, *The Fight,* frequently expressed pacifist sentiments. Many members of FOR, WRL, and the Women's International League for Peace and Freedom (WILPF) attended the United States Congress Against War and Fascism in September 1933. There are countless instances that suggest the interlocking character of liberal, pacifist, and radical thought in this decade.

Students should also be included, since a substantial number wanted peace at all costs. Their radicalism and pacifism were barely noticed in the 1920s. What flourished then was the "collegiate" mentality—of football, fraternities, dances, noncontroversial debaté. But issues of war and peace were not entirely neglected; they were simply centered upon the question of America's entry into the League of Nations. Furthermore, for every ten undergraduates who urged participation, there were a thousand who marched to colors in the campus ROTC. When, in the early 1930s, a growing number of students awoke to the dangers of war, they were confronted by this powerful vehicle of patriotism and national honor. The early student congresses, as we will see, all resolved to fight unto death against the ROTC and it became "the *bête noire* of students opposed to war and militarism."

Of that minority of undergraduates who reacted negatively to the ROTC and then to the threat of war, pacifists bulked large. Brown

University's *Daily Herald* polled over 20,000 students at sixty-five colleges in 1933 and found that the largest number, nearly 8,000, pledged themselves to absolute pacifism, another 7,221 would bear arms only in event of invasion, and barely 6,000 were willing to serve in any war that involved the United States.

The shock waves of the Depression must not be forgotten. They came slowly to the campus, but became a primary undergraduate concern. Poverty alone, however, could not have radicalized students. Those driven leftward had a sense that society was adrift, that their political leaders were untrustworthy, that their saints had feet of clay, that no large moral purpose touched the world of American politics.

The original radical student group, the ISS, had been founded in 1905 by those two literary firebrands Jack London and Upton Sinclair. Its prewar successor, the League for Industrial Democracy (LID) remained small, obscure, and quiescent, controlled by such undergraduate leaders as Harry Laidler and including the likes of Dewey and Thomas among the leadership. Mushrooming in the first years of the Depression, LID was soon established on the major university campuses. The student wing (SLID) was organized in December 1932. It ran the Thomas for President campus clubs in 1932 and retained intimate ties to the Socialist Party, though maintaining its outward independence.

The Young People's Socialist League (YPSL) was numerically more important and more unequivocally socialist, being the SP's youth arm. Known popularly as the "Yipsels," it assisted SLID chapters, especially on large urban campuses, such as in New York City, and tended to dominate them. Not only were they more militant than SLID; Yipsels were more so than the SP itself and before long were infected by factionalism. Some New York Yipsels even declared for the dictatorship of the proletariat and urged the Socialist Party to abandon reformist and electoral activity. It was not a position which would endear them to mainstream socialists.

Communist students had their own organization, the Young Communist League (YCL). It, too, indulged in the rigors and fantasies of the Third Period—and it made substantial gains in those schools that had a liberal or radical tradition. YCL'ers never comprised more than a small minority of undergraduates, but by virtue of their devotion, energy, and courage, they made an impact. Intelligent and selfless, they possessed a sense of purpose that touched the lives of many youthful liberals and non-Communists. Often coming out of socialist homes, they were prepared for ostracism, and thrived on it; they were frequently provincial in taste and outlook; and they were among the best and the brightest of their generation. The YCL began to grow in numbers and influence in the early 1930s owing to the Depression— and more: to their own passionate conviction, whether the issue was Harlan County labor violence or the Sino-Japanese conflict.

Then there was the National Student League (NSL), the creation of YCL'ers and of student militants who had fled LID. From its founding in 1931, League Communists parroted the Party's opaque language about "social fascism," but nonetheless worked with SLID on specific programs. Thus the NSL ceaselessly courted socialist students and charged LID with being dominated by thoroughly middle-class, non-student officials, which LID countered by labeling the League a "Communist organization."

SLID and NSL members nonetheless cooperated on ad hoc issues, such as sending a student delegation to the Kentucky mine country. They drew closer to an alliance after the NSL endorsed the World Congress Against War, which appealed to *all* students "to carry on a fight against war." "United Against Fascism," explained the NSL's *Student Review* in March 1933; and followed it with the directive that League members participate as well as lead "in demonstrations and anti-fascist activities of all revolutionary political and trade union organizations." Elsewhere it declared: "One must maintain unity of action with the Student League for Industrial Democracy, and the student councils of the Y.M.C.A. and the Y.W.C.A."

The student left's ecumenism was established with the 1932 Chicago Congress. Initiated by the NSL, its delegates were a diverse lot, including Republicans, Democrats, socialists, Communists, pacifists, spokesmen for campus liberalism and for literary societies—a mixed host aroused by the troubled state of the economy and of the planet. Local antiwar conferences of later that year and in 1933 followed the Chicago formula—in that even students from conservative campuses, such as MIT, elected delegates who represented undergraduates from Fraternity Row as well as the YCL.

Conflict between NSL blocs also crystallized around the Oxford Pledge. Originally a resolution passed by the Oxford Union in February 1933, the Pledge bound its English signatories not to fight for King and country. As adapted by America's socialist and Communist students, it became a refusal "to support the United States government in any war it may conduct." Conflict swirled around it after the CP, and the YCL, shifting tactics, endorsed collective security and thus advocated United States participation in any conflict in which Russia was "allied with capitalist states against fascism." From Christmas 1935, student Communists interpreted the Pledge as hostile to a possible American-Soviet alliance against Hitlerism, and the issue was joined. For socialist, liberal, and pacifist-minded undergraduates, on the other hand, it was a rallying point. But YCL'ers eventually carried their position and beat down pro-Pledge socialist students at the 1937 convention of the American Student Union (ASU). The Pledge issue, however, would continue to strain Communist-socialist cooperative efforts on campuses everywhere.

By 1936 and the ASU Christmas convention, student Communists had extended themselves even further in the cause of unity; they temporarily abandoned their fight against the Pledge. Their position shifted again, however, as the New Deal moved toward open intervention abroad; and, to repeat, after Roosevelt's 1937 Quarantine speech—which seemed to signal approval of collective security—the Pledge was finally repudiated. The student movement then turned respectable. The ASU was officially endorsed by the Administration and its 1937 convention heard greetings from Roosevelt, the Democratic National Committee, and Mayor Fiorello La Guardia of New York City.

Of course, the ASU gave unqualified backing to Loyalist Spain. Thus it proposed to "fast that Spain may eat." Virtually all liberal and radical undergraduates felt the same way, for the Loyalist cause had overwhelming appeal. One reason is obvious: the conviction that general war would be less likely if England and France sent supplies to the legitimate Spanish government. Then there was the assurance that the Loyalist cause was the cause of democracy. Thus those students and others who volunteered for the Lincoln Brigade frequently maintained that they enlisted in the democratic struggle against Fascism; or, as a veteran of the war declared, because they felt that the cause of Spain was "the cause of all progressive mankind."

For the most part, radical student sentiment was a mix—of genuine pacifism, deeply felt grass-roots socialism, and a desire to shock or rebel against middle-class parents and society. Student demonstrations did indeed catch the public eye. When gas masks were distributed in classrooms, or toy medals presented to interventionist-minded instructors, or demonstrations were conspicuously loud and well attended, the nation took notice.

The American Youth Congress, founded by youthful liberals and leftists, was a major Popular Front group, though its life began before the Third Period ended. An umbrella organization for a large number of affiliates, including Christian youth groups, representing nearly five million members by 1939, it was a notable example of effective socialist-Communist collaboration. Such an alliance is the more impressive when one recalls that the CP opposed all non-Communist-led socialist and trade-union groups. Yet the AYC was controlled by SLID and YCL members, until July 1937, when Communist youth leaders took over the reins and passed a full collective security program. It included a resolution of support for "China's heroic youth," while a YPSL amendment expressing socialist concern lest this resolution involve the United States and Japan in war went down to defeat. The Yipsels eventually created a new organization, the Youth Committee Against War, which would stand firm on the Oxford Pledge and oppose collective security.

Student militancy began to mount after 1933. The Strike Against War of that year prompted demonstrations on many campuses, perhaps the most notable being at Columbia University and at Vassar College, where some 500 coeds, a majority of its undergraduates, chanted, "No more battleships. We want schools." The April 1934 antiwar strike was most effective in the radical student strongholds—the campuses in New York, the University of Wisconsin, the University of Chicago, and UCLA—and a disproportionate number of the 500,000 to 1,000,000 protesting students came from them.

The 1934 strike was a collaborative display. Few of its participants believed that they were thus demonstrating their hostility to the existing order. Most were liberal students who applauded earlier anti-

ROTC parades and antiwar mobilizations. But YCL'ers were there in force, Third Period dicta notwithstanding. They would join SLID in other mass demonstrations—protests which had the blessing of all segments of the student population, football players and YCL'ers alike, and which attracted hundreds of thousands of undergraduates. Pacifists among them could certainly subscribe to slogans urging "the struggle against war." And undergraduate liberals and radicals alike readily agreed with their adult counterparts that the U.S.S.R. was devoted to peace and to building "a workers' fatherland."

Until Russia's great purge trials of 1936–38, it was possible for radicals, liberals, and left intellectuals to ignore earlier judicial proceedings, such as the 1928 Shakhty trial or the Metro-Vickers affair of 1933. They could close their eyes to such events, discount reports of restrictions imposed upon Soviet culture workers, of imprisonment or worse for critics and dissenters. They could close ranks in the face of overriding necessities. If one were convinced that Communists alone were true fighters against Fascism, as many believed, then any question of Soviet motives might breach the Popular Front or detract from collective security, and could thus be interpreted as tacit support for the common enemy.

The reported assassination of Sergei Kirov, a prominent Russian official, became the first real test of political and emotional loyalties. Sixty-seven suspects were tried by secret courts in August 1936, without the right of appeal or of counsel, and summarily executed. Reverberations could be heard for months among liberals and radicals, but most rationalized the affair, which is understandable. Conversion to radicalism had been the grand adventure of their lives. It was virtually impossible for them to cope so abruptly with the fact that the anti-Fascist forces might themselves be impure.

But a new wave of trials began in 1937 and now thousands of former Bolsheviks, many of them heroes of the Revolution, were being charged as traitors or German agents. Their trials continued over two years and raised questions about Russia's judicial system, the nature of revolutions, the Soviet Union itself. Since lifelong attachments are not easily altered or discarded, the first reports of arrests brought skepticism rather than sudden estrangement. Only a handful of left intellectuals expressed serious misgivings. Edmund Wilson, for one, in an April 29, 1936, article, in *The New Republic,* was openly doubtful about Soviet achievements, and within the year confided that he "went dead" at news of the trials. Few others joined him—for the moment.

But the bad blood which always existed between radical groups became more apparent. The issue of Stalinism was evolving into a most durable obsession, with liberals sniping at liberals, radicals at liberals, pacifists at radicals, and so forth. *The Nation* and *The New Republic* still urged readers to accept the official verdict of the trials, though both would soon denounce the proceedings. Socialists, however, were more aware that something monstrous was happening. The trials eliminated their last lingering sympathy for the Soviet Union. Thomas, for example, became highly critical after 1937. The *Modern Monthly* rallied every shade of independent opinion on the left—with editor V. F. Calverton sickened and outraged by Stalin's excesses, finding them a betrayal of the October Revolution. The *New International,* a theoretical organ of Trotskyism, savagely tore into "Stalin's Public Trials"—in which "history, facts, dates, evidence are as of little moment as human lives and human dignity." But the *New Masses,* by now at the other end of the ideological spectrum, branded such critics miscreants who would literally sabotage the Soviet state.

Many liberals and radicals, after considerable agonizing, continued to dismiss the charges against Soviet Russia. But when the entire elite of old Bolsheviks was brought to the dock, liberals were caught in a cross fire between Moscow's critics and defenders. Their journals had long staked out familiar grounds: Russia was a democratic state, as its constitution indicated. *The Nation* editorially labored to portray things in a light favorable to Moscow, found it hard to believe that the defendants had been framed, and pleaded for a "suspension of judgment" until the facts were known. Echoing its famous Kremlin watcher, columnist Walter Duranty, *The New Republic* worried that Russia might now be presented unfavorably. And Louis Fischer told its readers about Soviet democracy, assuring them that those who did not believe in it were "either ignorant or malicious." Too bad that sixteen old Bolsheviks had been executed. The U.S.S.R. remains a "workers' state," as Alfred Kazin reconstructed radical opinion. Stained only with the unaccountable sins of its leadership, it "still represented the irreversible movement of human progress."

But continuing purges forced liberals and intellectuals to face the realities of Soviet life. And by 1937 their grand political amour with Russia had started to sour, with a growing number joining that handful of former Communists who had been living in political purgatory for a decade or more. These desertions were braked, however, by the Munich agreement and the German occupation of Czechoslovakia's Sudetenland, with only the U.S.S.R. supporting that little democracy. Non-Communists reacted angrily. *The New Leader* warned against the danger of appeasement and found ample evidence that Hitler not only intended "to rule all Europe . . . but the rest of the world as well."

The climax to this ripening conflict among leftists and liberals came on August 22, 1939, with the Russian-German non-aggression pact. For many radicals, Russia's standing had been enhanced by Munich— if only by virtue of her exclusion from a gathering which betrayed Czechoslovakia. But the purges tarnished her image and the Pact completed the denigration. It was a profound spiritual shock. Unlike the trials, which many liberals could accept, half believing the Party's explanation that the defendants were guilty as charged—they so wanted to believe!—the Pact was indefensible.

Of course, there were those who tried a defense. Communists predictably did so. The August 1939 Pact hit them like a bombshell, producing a literally overnight switch from support of anti-Fascist liberalism to attacks upon it, from collective security to isolationism. The *Daily Worker,* following twenty-four hours of embarrassed silence, reacted pitiably; and three weeks later it published the now famous open letter from Browder and Foster to Roosevelt which, reversing policy, pledged firm opposition to "American involvement in the war, or in the rivalries and antagonisms which have led much of Europe into chaos."

Communists thus once again cynically subordinated consistent policy to Soviet needs and maneuvers. They moved from an anti-Hitler position, alienating thousands of fellow travelers and members in the process. Such abrupt and wrenching Party reversals certainly did not constitute its finest hour; and there is something foolhardy and yet, writes Hobsbawm (about English and French Communists in 1939), "something heroic" about what happened. His remarks are partly applicable to the CPUSA:

> Nationalism, political calculation, even common sense, pulled one way, yet they unhesitatingly chose to put the interests of the international movement first. As it happens, they were tragically and absurdly wrong. But their error . . . should not lead us to ridicule the spirit of their action. This is how the socialists [in England and France] should have acted in 1914 and did not: carrying out the decisions of their International. This is how the communists did act when another world war broke out. It was not their fault that the International should have told them to do something else.

So however dumbfounded hard-core Communists may have been, indeed however much on the defensive, they assumed an aggressive rhetorical stance. They may have inwardly winced at Molotov's description of Fascism as merely "a matter of taste," but they justified Russian actions as necessitated by Anglo-French policies, especially by appeasement of Hitler in the hope, so they understood, that he would turn eastward. For them, Russia seemed to be the one nation in which a revolutionary socialism was operational and its safety remained a hallowed mandate. The Pact would "directly strengthen the anti-Fascist struggle for peace." In this same shallow and morally obtuse vein, V. J. Jerome, the Party's cultural commissar, categorically declared: "The Soviet-German Non-Aggression Pact drew an entire sixth of the earth out of the war. . . . It thus promoted the interests of all peace-loving people." Party leaders now unembarrassedly launched a peace campaign, and its twin slogans were "The Yanks Are Not Coming" and "Hands Off," the latter being the 1919 admonition directed against Wilson's intervention in Russia. They embraced isolationism, scorned opposition to the Pact as "petit bourgeois," began a "perpetual peace vigil" around the White House, and led a series of crippling strikes against aircraft and tank factories. Earl Browder, a marvel of invertebrate accommodation, no longer pleaded for a common front against a common enemy. He now proposed neutrality in a conflict which, as he had come to understand it, was between rival imperialisms. Elizabeth Gurley Flynn's pamphlet *I Didn't Raise My Boy to Be a Soldier—for Wall Street* succinctly stated Communist views. CP'ers naturally opposed conscription, the overage destroyer deal, and Roosevelt's March 1941 Lend-Lease measure. The last was explained away by *Communist* as the product of "idealistic demagoguery" that had deceived the masses. By it the "administration has entered into a compact to aid the British ruling class to retain control of a slave empire in half of Africa, to continue to rule three hundred and fifty million Indians against their will." There were countless other instances of how CP'ers altered tactics and with humorless effrontery invoked dialectics as the theoretical justification for admitted policy contradictions.

Liberals and culture radicals, however, were now ready to challenge the most sacred of Communist assumptions, and even those with heretofore unimpeachable credentials joined a growing number of ex-Communists in their painful journey into anti-Communism. Traumatized by the Pact, Communist sympathizers and the literary left, as well as CP'ers, began to desert the colors. Louis Fischer, the *Nation* reporter whose "beat" was Moscow, finally went "public" and voiced long-suppressed doubts. Literary critic Granville Hicks was typical of those who left the Party at this time. "The masquerade is over," proclaimed Heywood Broun, the nationally known journalist. Another newspaperman, James Wechsler, having recently emerged from the student left, wrote of the campus radical as being "confronted with the necessity of evaluating his own position, rediscovering some organizational ties, or fleeing into lonely isolation." And he plaintively asked, "Where does he go from here?" One thing was sure: liberals, men who had praised the Soviet experiment and made it one of the great events of their lives, could not now accept the Russian fall into *Machtpolitik*. That the U.S.S.R., according to the Party, acted for reasons of national security, was not enough. More had been expected of her.

Russia's invasion of Finland brought on yet another crisis. Undertaken in September 1939, it came after Finland refused to yield strategic border points sought by Russia in order to bolster Leningrad's defenses. It was yet another event adding to the sense of personal betrayal, to a bitter sense of loss that not even the Grand Alliance forged in World War II could ameliorate.

Only shock waves of great intensity could have shaken the

religious-like commitment to a Marxist vision of society. The Pact was that. It produced heretics. So Hicks, originally trained for the ministry, now sought salvation elsewhere. So Louis Budenz, the *Daily Worker* editor, was among those who crossed over to Catholicism. Another was Elisabeth Bentley, who had initially been attracted to the Party because "communism was the religion of the future." Many novitiates had had the same sense of a conversion experience, and, upon leave-taking, underwent a comparable spiritual crisis. As Whittaker Chambers tells us, "every break with communism is a religious conversion."

The Pact would destroy the Popular Front, with its emphasis upon the defense of democratic values and struggle against Nazism. About a third of the leadership of the League of American Writers, for instance, simply resigned. Garment center radicals in New York also left Front groups in droves, including the American Labor Party, and there were violent episodes among Jewish trade unionists. When the Communist-influenced *Freiheit* admitted that Jewish CP'ers no longer favored the boycott of German goods, there was further consternation and attrition in Party ranks. Divided down the middle in August 1939, the American League for Peace and Democracy formulated a compromise— "we neither condemn nor approve the actions of the Soviet Union"—which satisfied no one. Four months later it formally dissolved. So did the American Friends of the Soviet Union. The Left Book Club was deeply rent. And schisms tore apart the student left.

Student Front groups, at least those most completely penetrated by CP'ers, endorsed the change of line, which catalyzed dissent. Joseph Lash, the ASU's nominally socialist secretary, had cooperated with Communists in steering the organization from pacifism to collective security. Now criticizing the Pact and condemning the Finnish invasion, he was censured for his troubles at the December 1939 ASU convention—after Communist undergraduates seized control, bringing down the Popular Front in the process. The delegates then disowned collective security, affirmed that the European conflict was imperialist, and demanded that the United States remain aloof.

Trotskyites, it comes as no surprise, condemned both the trials and the Pact, and Max Schachtman denounced "the usurping masters of the Kremlin" in language of exceptional force and bitterness. But

Trotskyites did not then embrace American actions. Rather, they hammered away at the "financial oligarchy" which directed State Department policies, and arraigned United States overseas activities as "a thick cover for the mailed fist of dollar diplomacy."

Long opposed to the *New Leader* socialists, Norman Thomas now joined them in condemning the U.S.S.R. The Pact destroyed his vestigial faith in the Soviet Union and he wrote angrily: "Stalin's agreement with Hitler becomes a piece of infamy beside which Munich was an adventure in ethics and the hypocritical nonintervention agreement in Spain a model of international good faith."

The SP, with its central figure shaped by the pacifist left, never entirely resolved the problem of war and peace. Thomas opposed Fascism for a decade but nonetheless argued that America's entry into the war would only strengthen Hitler and delay meaningful social change. Yet Party members had been militantly anti-Fascist in the interwar years. They were on record, for example, as highly critical of Roosevelt's policy toward Spain. But SP'ers were also irreparably scarred by the domestic repression of World War I, and predicted something comparable should global conflict again break out. Thomas believed that war might well destroy civil liberties at home and bring Fascism in its wake. Much to the distress of the *New Leader* bloc, he testified before congressional committees against Lend-Lease and extension of the draft. Further distress was occasioned by his isolationist address at a May 1941 America First rally. *The New Leader*, in contrast, supported military assistance to the Allies, including Lend-Lease, and urged the United States to fight alongside England.

Even after Germany invaded Poland in September 1939, socialists would argue that Hitler's existence did not make the Allied cause a war for democracy. Their 1940 declaration concluded: "The working class must now present an unqualified demand: Keep America Out of War!" Thomas persisted in this position. Both FDR and Willkie, the 1940 Republican standard bearer, were, he believed, equally willing to "gamble the lives and fortunes of 132,000,000 people to preserve Western rather than Eastern imperialism." He endorsed the majority socialist view that steps "short of war" to aid the Allies would soon involve the United States in the conflict. Like the Communists, pacifists, Trotskyites, and *New Republic* liberals, he opposed Lend-Lease, "armament economics," and military conscription. These measures, he warned, were dangerously dishonest and would get us "into war crabwise."

Thomas was not unmoved by successive German victories. He watched the blitzkrieg with horror. The fall of France, he later recalled, "shook me as very few things ever shook me." Not even Pearl Harbor in December 1941, he confessed, "brought more anguish of mind" than the German advance on Paris and Dunkirk. He knew that "no choices that I could make" would be "wholly right." Nonetheless, American involvement on balance seemed more "evil" than "the uncertain good we might accomplish in a war."

Not all socialists endorsed this view, especially in the light of German aggression, and the Party suffered a drastic loss of membership. Those who left rejected the orthodox contention that the war was an imperialist rivalry. UAW chief Walter Reuther joined trade-union leader Sidney Hillman in defending Roosevelt's program of economic-military aid for those nations fighting Hitler. Reuther found the Democratic Party colors attractive, much like other former SP'ers, including about half the *Call*'s editorial board. When Thomas opposed Lend-Lease, a group of SP'ers, including Jack Altman and Gus Tyler, issued a dissenting minority opinion. And in February 1941, three national committee members resigned—as new factionalism, the so-called "silent split," divided the membership.

On the eve of war, then, foreign policy issues divided the Socialist Party into a number of competing blocs: absolute pacifists who would not support any war; waverers like Thomas, torn by old commitments to nonviolence and the urgent need to defeat Fascism; and a pro-Allied element. Communists, meanwhile, opposed Roosevelt's overseas policies from the time of the Pact until June 1941, when Germany invaded the Soviet Union—when they became win-the-war militants. They also suffered from a shrinkage in membership, but the war, we will see, brought new recruits and vitality, and an unprecedented and euphoric respectability.

8 War and Cold War: Shifting Radical Fortunes

THE SOCIALIST PARTY position was never unequivocally antiwar in these years. Even after Pearl Harbor it reiterated its "consistent opposition to all capitalist wars, including those fought by capitalist democracies against capitalist totalitarian states." Nor would delegates to the SP's first wartime convention give their "blessing to this war." And those attending the 1944 convention demanded "an immediate peace offensive based on the offer of an armistice." Thomas rejected "so negative a slogan as unconditional surrender," which was Roosevelt's, and the Party's unpopularity was reflected in the polls, where only 78,000 voters cast ballots for it in this presidential election year.

In effect, the SP returned to its World War I position, and thereby joined the isolated left, displacing the CP, which, after Russia had been invaded, turned to militant support of American belligerency. Thomas sought, in the interest of Party unity, to avoid foreign-policy debate and emphasize injustices at home. This formula permitted pacifists, antiwar and prowar members, reformists and radicals to remain within the Party structure—but SP influence, morale, and electoral strength reached their nadir.

The Pact, the trials, the war itself had vindicated the dark prophecies of Trotskyites and Lovestoneites, indeed of virtually all sectaries.

But these radical fragments did not join with Socialists and De Leonites. The polemics had been too lacerating, the battles too fierce, the legacy of factiousness too bitter for collaboration among non-Communist groups.

For instance, such stridently anti-imperialist sects as the clique around Abraham Ziegler, editor of *Modern Socialism,* endorsed the struggle against Hitler. A leader of the tiny Socialist Union Party, itself a splinter of the scarcely larger De Leonite SLP, Ziegler battled the SWP in a war of words that was sulfuric and very real to its participants. He insisted upon the priority of crushing Germany. Only then would it be "necessary to go the whole hog and destroy its evil genius and foster parent—decadent capitalism."

The Trotskyite SWP displayed a rigorous doctrinal consistency. It retained a trigger-like readiness to condemn Roosevelt—for Lend-Lease or his aim of a "great imperialist destiny" for the United States. Its position was like Thomas', but his spiritual ordeal never touched Trotskyites. They were convinced that Roosevelt-Churchill diplomacy aimed at provoking Japanese attack and as early as September 1940 declared that "Roosevelt and his boss-politician cronies" had committed the American people to war. *Labor Action,* a Trotskyite journal, warned in May 1940 that "two big rival camps are at each other's throat"; and a month later, commenting on the warfare in the Lowlands, the SWP's *Fourth International* asserted that "capitalism is in its death agony."

All was not peace among the Trotskyites, especially after the German invasion of Russia in June 1941. A minority faction seceded. Headed by Schachtman and James Burnham, co-editors of the *New International,* it established the Workers Party (WP) and preserved an uncompromising doctrinal purity.

Communist tactical somersaults over this two-year period continued. CP'ers, Browder stated after the Pact, "do not see valid grounds for suspecting" that Roosevelt's neutrality proclamation was a pretext for entry "in this imperialist war." The Party's National Committee expressed friendship for the Chief Executive at this time. "We wish to place on record," it stated in a letter to him and to Congress, "our firm accord with the stand of our country against

American involvement in the war.'' These words, however, were a brave face on the realities. For Roosevelt moved toward repeal of the embargo with the outbreak of European hostilities and obviously sought revision of the neutrality measures so as to give discretionary power to the executive. Shortly thereafter, an abrasive note began to appear in Party broadsides. "Unneutrality in thought," Browder observed, "has opened the door for a whole series of unneutral deeds which lead with inexorable logic to wholesale participation in the war." He gloomily predicted America's "eventual entry into the war as a belligerent in the process of switching the war against the Soviet Union," and proclaimed, "The War Party of the American bourgeoisie is on the march, and Roosevelt stands at its head."

On June 22, 1941, when Germany invaded the U.S.S.R., CP'ers made their legendary 360-degree turn—from condemnation of intervention, from isolationism and neutrality, while Hitler and Stalin were in partnership, to fierce support of military assistance to beleaguered Russia when the partnership had been dissolved. The "imperialist" war underwent an overnight transformation into a "People's War for National Liberation." The perpetual peace vigil quietly expired. *Communist* of July 1941, which included Foster's now obsolete argument describing the "present war" as a "violent division of the world among the great imperialist powers," also ran a hastily inserted editorial calling for support of Russia "in its struggle against Hitlerism." In June 1941, the *Young Communist Review* asserted that the forthcoming AYC convention would climax the antiwar struggle; then came the German attack and the "war mongering" imprecations were instantly transformed into support of Lend-Lease. *Clarity,* another YCL organ, had "justified doubts about the character of the war" in June 1941, but these were replaced "by the full confidence" that Hitlerism had to be smashed. Indeed YCL'ers openly admitted that Soviet involvement altered the character of the conflict from "imperialistic" to a "just democatic war of world humanity." Fellow-traveling congressman Vito Marcantonio, in 1939–40, opposed every measure which might involve the United States in overseas conflict. In October 1941, however, he declared that "a war which was predominantly imperialist has become essentially a war of national defense for the people of the United States." His volte-face duplicated that of the surviving Popular Front groups, such as the League of American Writers, which, in August 1941, candidly stated, "When there was peace in the world, we fought to maintain it. But now the alliance of Great Britain and the Soviet Union provides the people of all countries with an unprecedented opportunity to rid the world of Hitlerism."

Thus Communists, displaying the great resilience and opportunism which had always marked their policies, once again joined the liberal and non-Communist camp. They applauded the *Nation* and *New Republic* liberals who would mobilize the nation's resources for global war and who urged aid to the U.S.S.R.—since the enemies of Germany were friends of the United States. Sotto voce, they abandoned the earlier campaign against neutrality and imperialism. Now there was only the "democratic crusade," "the common struggle against fascism," and Browder's "broad, all-inclusive, anti-Fascist democratic camp."

As a consequence, the Party became more palatable to more Americans than it had ever been—in part because it lacked any independent political power which might have seemed threatening, in part because it returned to the coalition tactics of the Popular Front and, going further, increasingly adhered to a concept of class harmony. And it did so with gusto. No need for advice from the ever-friendly Corliss Lamont, who urged friends of Russia to have "mobile minds"; Communists had them *in excelsis*. And now one could support both the Soviet *and* the American cause. Hence this shift came easy, more so than the one in August 1939. The fact that membership grew, with the Party eventually doubling in size (to about 80,000) in the war years, simply confirmed the "correctness" of the current line. CP'ers reflectively basked in the national shift toward acceptance of the U.S.S.R., in the official Soviet-American cooperation, and in popular acclaim for Red Army victories.

The Party gradually moved into a position of unprecedented harmony with the government, a development made easier by the surprise Japanese attack on Pearl Harbor in December 1941. This attack, *The Nation* declared, "has made America one. Today we love each other and our country. We feel a happy sense of union." The Party agreed. The war was a relief: the primary business of defeating the Axis could now be pursued without any hesitation or ideological divisiveness. Its slogans became indistinguishable from those of the Administration and liberal Democrats. The rapprochement was further encouraged when Roosevelt, in May 1942, commuted Browder's jail sentence for passport fraud. For his part, Browder pledged "unconditional support" of the nation's war-service measures, which would have made every able-bodied man and woman liable for military or industrial duty, and which many liberals and all pacifists opposed.

For the Schachtman faction of Trotskyites, not even Hitler's invasion altered the fundamental character of the war. It remained an imperialist conflict "among the big bandit powers." The "criminal nature" of Stalinism caused the Schachtmanites to question the necessity of defending Russia. They claimed that the international proletariat and millions of wretched peasants "have been sacrificed upon the altar of Stalinism and the reformism of the Second International." They alone, so this minority bloc insisted, continued to build on the rock of socialism; and they were comforted by the thought that "other remnants of Marxism" abandoned "the Leninist analysis of the coming war. . . . We were the only proletarian party which remained faithful to the Marxist estimate of the imperialist contradictions leading to the war." Hence they rejected the commonplace—offered by "the Communist Party and the unions and organizations which it controls, its press, the Cannon group, the Oehler group, *The Nation* and the *New Republic*"—that "the character of the war has changed" with Hitler's attack in June 1941. The invasion altered nothing.

The SWP majority was led by James Cannon, who, with the schism, began a new journal, the *Fourth International* (1940–56). Cannon's followers exhorted Trotskyites to "defend the Soviet Union at all costs," Stalin's tyranny notwithstanding. They assaulted—and there is no other word for it—the Schachtmanites as if the fate of the Republic rested upon the outcome of their warfare.

In affirming the "People's War," Communists took a reductive ideological line: the war was a struggle between good and evil. Hence every development which might assist the forces of light, however pernicious ultimately—like the call for hemispheric solidarity, which would encourage American hegemony in Latin America—must be supported; every anti-Fascist film or novel was to be unreservedly praised. In sum, the political behavior which produced a suspension of critical judgment in the controversy over the trials, the Pact, the Finnish invasion, now shaped the Party's devotion to the Allied cause.

These, then, were the glory days. The Party had broken out of its sectarian isolation. Let pacifists and Trotskyites, and independents like Dwight Macdonald, resist United States intervention abroad! Communists, as they believed, would be in harmony with their fellow Americans. In a "flush of patriotism," CP'ers joined the Elks and American Legion members in collecting scrap metal, selling war bonds, giving blood. In Youngstown, the *Daily Worker* proudly reported, "as a result of the initiative of the Communists, thousands of school children, Boy Scouts and the people at large were involved in the collection of many tons of tin." Other Party members entered the armed forces, and CP journals chanted their genuinely heroic exploits. Ideological matters were quite forgotten. Browder, for example, hailed state capitalism in wartime, and also the Party's "integration . . . into our own American democratic life and national unity." All of this from a Party whose 1940 election campaign included the slogan: "No armaments or American soldiers for imperialist wars and adventures."

The Party's labor policy displayed the same uncritical enthusiasm for the war effort. It urged an unrestrained mobilization in the "battle of production," ceased fomenting labor unrest, and rejected any strikes in defense industries as "a hindrance to the war effort." It gave unqualified support to the no-strike pledge without even asking the Administration for a quid pro quo.

The war prompted CP'ers to join CIO officials in disavowing "trade unionism as usual" and, going even further than Gompers toward class collaboration, to scorn collective bargaining if it disrupted production. The views of Lee Pressman, CIO counsel and Party member, were typical: the steel workers' union "cannot permit its members to treat problems in the plant today in a similar manner as they were dealt with in the past. The labor union and its members must reorient their approach to all problems so that the prosecution of the war becomes the sole and major objective." Traveling a good distance beyond Gompers or CIO leaders like Murray, the CP even endorsed the Austin-Wadsworth bill, which unionists called a "slave labor" measure since it would destroy the seniority system and subject union members to criminal penalties for engaging in strike actions or refusal to work where they were directed.

CP labor policy was clearly on a collision course with UMW president John L. Lewis as well as with militant union locals. One of the heroes of American labor, Lewis vigorously upheld its right to strike. His 1943 strike call induced a vigorous reaction—from government, mine operators, CIO leadership, and Communists. Lewis' activities, Browder declared, were "a blow for Hitler" and "treason to the people." At another time he asserted, "There is not the slightest doubt that Lewis is working and has worked during the past two years at least as an integral part of the pro-Nazi fifth column, aiming at a negotiated peace with Hitler, and at the Nazi subjugation of the United States itself. . . . This is treason."

Nor was Lewis the only CP target. Any union leader who supported the miners' strike or endorsed a labor walkout risked being assailed for playing the German game. But, then, anyone who, in these war years, disagreed with CP labor policy would be arraigned on the "agent of Hitler" charge. This policy in effect undercut worker militancy and political independence, both hallowed goals of American radicalism. Conflict between union locals, which were instinctively militant, and the top union leadership, which sought to dampen workplace agitation, characterized much of labor's history in the twentieth century. In this period, for instance, delegates to SWOC conventions after 1940 urged local "autonomy," but union leaders such as Philip Murray blocked their demands. Similarly, UAW officials could not entirely suppress wildcat strikes. Nor could the CPUSA in those union locals which it dominated—like Ford's River Rouge local with its disruptive black foundry workers.

By the time of Pearl Harbor, the great organizing drives were over. The Party's contributions had been made, the trade-union apparatus refined and fixed, locked in place by an iron law of oligarchy. Youthful union militants in the 1930s had been increasingly integrated into society through relatively well-paying union jobs, family ties, community assimilation, and, not wishing to risk their status, now began to discourage militancy. Moreover, this now entrenched union bureaucracy, in partial duplication of Gompers' experience, sought to rationalize economic and social conflict, accommodate to the business-government demand for economic stability and to industry's twin goals of profits and efficiency. In this way the new CIO unions, under the shaping force of American foreign policy, were pushed into further collaboration. The war itself contributed, since it brought irresistible pressure for continuous production and social stability. It thereby strengthened conservatives among CIO officials who sought the same ends. Most union leaders perceived no other possible course except support of government policies. But in so doing they had to discourage internal debate, workplace agitation, and class awareness.

In June 1943, Stalin dissolved the Communist International, to facilitate "the organization of all freedom-loving nations against the common enemy—Hitlerism." By this time the Party's membership had peaked, and the CP was now *the* major socialist organization. But it is an empty, purely honorific claim—because, in reaching this goal, it had moved even further in the direction of collaboration. The Party, Browder declared, "will not raise any socialist proposals for the United States, in any form that can disturb this national unity." More specifically, it dissolved itself and re-formed as the Communist Political Association (CPA) in May 1944 to create a "broader democratic-progressive united front."

Meanwhile, Party spokesmen self-delusively argued that profound changes were occurring in the American business community, making it more progressive and responsive to social needs. "For the first time," Browder stated, "we are meeting and solving problems for which there are no precedents in history and no formulas from the classics to give us the answers." Such a departure from orthodoxy was heralded as flexibility. Corporate liberalism guaranteed progress, Browder and other CP officers believed, and also eliminated the possibility of imminent revolution in the United States. The CPA was the product of such thinking, another attempt at legitimation, renewed respectability, adaptation to the existing political system. Moreover, this "political-educational association" happily had Moscow's indirect blessings.

Browder, in December 1943, hailed the Teheran agreement promulgated by Churchill, Roosevelt, and De Gaulle as prefiguring a new and harmonious world order. It became the guide for Party policy. All

programs, he believed, could now "be solved by conference, conciliation and agreement, without either immediate or ultimate resort to the
arbitrament of war." In sum, as he declared, "Capitalism and Socialism have begun to find the way to peaceful coexistence and collaboration in the same world." Rising membership figures confirmed the
tactical rightness of the CPA and its readiness to "postpone until some
indefinite postwar period the basic problem of capitalism." The wartime blunting of anti-Communist drives further heightened Communist
euphoria about national unity; and, having taken hold, this sense of
well-being worked its will, feeding on the CP's instinctive social-
democratic tendencies.

It should not be thought wartime goodwill produced any substantial
conversion to Communism. Browder indirectly admitted as much in
1944, when he stated that "the American people are . . . ill-prepared
for any deep-going change in the direction of socialism"; all the more
reason, of course, for temporary collaboration. Unlike the CP's in
Europe, after all, where Communism was partially integrated into the
national subcultures, with deep roots in social-political life, the
CPUSA had nothing to draw upon. Communists sensed as much,
though never openly admitting it. Otherwise, how can one account for
their pathetic efforts to earn respectability? The war years brought
it—but at an enormous price. The Party lost its special credentials as
the militant radical organization. It contributed to a classless loyalty to
capitalism, which may have been understandable in wartime or even in
the Popular Front years, but which was not supposed to be the way of
the Marxist world.

In wartime, CP'ers basked in the glow of warm Soviet-American
cooperation. There was the exhilarating assurance of national respectability, the comfort that came from reading an entire issue of *Life*
magazine devoted to Soviet-American friendship and to finding the
Russians "one hell of a people" who look like, dress like, act like
Americans; or from the popularity of things Russian, whether folk
songs or Shostakovich symphonies; or from statements by long-time
conservatives such as Monsignor Fulton J. Sheen, Congressman John
Rankin, aviator hero Eddie Rickenbacker, and Douglas MacArthur,
who praised the Red Army and Stalin himself.

Thus bemused, the Party alone among radical groups did not share the same spontaneous cry of horror when atomic bombs were dropped on Japan. Pacifists, Yipsels, Trotskyites looked upon the doomsday weapon with loathing. So did Norman Thomas, who thought "we shall have to pay for all this in a horrifying hatred." Not the Party, however, its critical faculties dulled by years of wartime collaboration and the fragile hope that coexistence might continue.

Things began to fall apart for the CP with the famous April 1945 article of Jacques Duclos, France's Party chief. Most likely dictated by Stalin, it condemned the CPUSA, accused American Communists of "sowing dangerous opportunistic illusions," singled out Browder for having drawn "erroneous conclusions in no wise flowing from a Marxist analysis of society." In effect an accusation of "revisionism," a capital crime for Communists, the Duclos article signaled Browder's downfall.

It had been all so unexpected. Of Party officials, only Foster—at loggerheads with Browder since the 1930s—had had reservations about the Party's courtship of capitalism; only he had been apprehensive and thought Browder mistaken. "American imperialism virtually disappears," he privately complained, and "there remains hardly a trace of the class struggle, and socialism plays practically no role whatever." Others had expressed similar doubts, but they were mostly on the outside and largely unfriendly. Witness, for instance, one critical observer: "First we had the United Front, limited to working-class parties. Then we had the Popular Front, which included the liberal bourgeois parties as well. And now we have the National Front, which includes exactly everybody—everybody that's decent, that is." Within the Party, however, there was only Foster among the prominent and powerful and, collapsing under pressure, he made a public profession of loyalty to Browderism in the *Daily Worker*.

Browder, then, had been idolized among Communists as no Party leader before or since. And the abruptness of his fall from grace was traumatic for many. But most recovered with that swiftness which characterized their reactions to the substantive policy shifts of earlier days. Leading CP'ers turned savagely on their fallen chieftain, the more so when he refused the obligatory recantation. In the words of Bella V. Dodd, the Communist head of the New York City Teachers' Union, all CP'ers had to confess "in private and in public meetings that they had been remiss in their duty, that they had betrayed the workers by support of a program of class collaboration." Every Party official, except Browder, undertook the mandatory self-purging, and he was expelled. But "Browderism" was harder to exorcise. A denigrating slogan, it was conveniently trotted out for future occasions.

Thus Browderism continued to thrive, notwithstanding the official line against "class collaboration." Confronted by growing hostility to the U.S.S.R. after 1946, the penitents feared that a Soviet-American military confrontation was imminent. Consequently, they took to building a cross-class alliance of "democratic forces" against "monopoly capital." Such an alliance, Foster projected, would go "beyond anything in Roosevelt's time." It would develop into a broad third party including labor, in "organized cooperation with the poorer farmers, the Negro people, with the progressive professionals and middle classes, with the bulk of the veterans." Thus the Popular Front lived again—which was natural enough perhaps. And so did the old fratricide.

Thus veteran social-democratic leaders such as Dubinsky, who had fought Communists since the 1930s, intensified their old anti-Communist struggle. In these postwar years it produced irremediable division in the ALP leadership—with a "right" led by Dubinsky and Alex Rose, among others, and a "left," eventually victorious, headed by Vito Marcantonio and an assortment of trade-union leaders.

Gradually, the Party's rhetoric hardened. Foster's attack on "monopoly capital" indicated as much. CP leaders concluded that American overseas policies were "imperialistic" and that the country was going "fascist." Herbert Aptheker asserted that the nation's foreign policy "has been geared toward establishing hegemony over the world by the American ruling class"; Marcantonio concluded that the European Recovery Plan "is a big trust bill. World control by Wall Street trusts is written right into this bill"; and Party spokesmen believed the Truman Doctrine of 1947 was "unabashed imperialism." W. E. B. Du Bois, then unequivocally in the Communist camp, said bitterly, "Drunk with power, we are leading the world to hell in a new colonialism with the same old human slavery which once ruined us, and to a Third World War which will ruin the world."

In effect, unflagging efforts at collaboration, especially toward the goal of a cross-class third party, competed with countless Communist articles in the Du Bois vein, especially after Browder was purged. These tracts insisted that the United States wished to protect overseas investments, reduce Russia to weakness and isolate her by "a policy of hostile encirclement," shape Germany and Japan into political and economic satellites, strengthen American dominion over the Western Hemisphere, and use the United Nations as a device to reduce the power of "the peace-loving peoples."

Feeling increasingly trapped by massive anti-Communism at home and abroad, the Party embraced a postwar program that continued to be dominated by the lamentably simplistic formula: the United States was "the most aggressive empire in the world" (according to Foster), whereas Russia was the major force for peace and against imperialism. Such an uncomplicated equation, ingenuous to the point of fatuity, produced the expected linkage and conclusions. The "big American and British imperialists" did not "want to live and work harmoniously with the U.S.S.R." Why not? Because "they see the Soviet Union as the bulwark of world democracy, the friend of all oppressed people." When the UN Security Council considered the matter of Russian troop movements near Iran in 1946, Foster claimed with some justification that the affair was part of an attempt to ring the U.S.S.R. with hostile military bases: "They want to reduce that country to their sway, to put it in its place, so to speak, as they are now proceeding to do with the less capitalist countries of the world."

The Party was further propelled into sectarian isolationism when Communist-dominated unions were expelled from the CIO. By 1945, these unions accounted for about a quarter of all CIO members. CIO leader Philip Murray made no effort to drive them out. To the contrary, he discouraged attempts to do so—until the ascendancy of Walter Reuther (with the CP endorsing his opponent for the UAW presidency) and until the National Maritime Union chieftain, Joseph Curran, declared war on CP'ers who long dominated his union. The showdown became inevitable with the deepening Cold War and with the recognition that association with CP'ers could be a political liability. The purge must be seen against this background, and also as rooted in the failure of the CP to educate and indoctrinate its potential mass base, to relate organizing efforts to indigenous radical goals.

Murray moved slowly, but anti-Communist union leaders maintained their pressure on him and slowly won out. In May 1949, the CIO Executive Board resolved that "all members of the Board who are unwilling to enforce the Constitution are called upon to resign." Six months later the United Electrical Workers, a Party stronghold, was expelled for its defiance. Then the CIO constitution was amended so that the Executive Board could remove, by a two-thirds vote, any union that worked in behalf of a "totalitarian movement." The stage was now set for the massive expulsions to follow. And those not expelled were purified. Thus the Party's labor base, by the mid-1950s, was reduced to a pathetic passel of frightened Communist trade unionists.

Communists suffered a similar fate in other organizations, helped enormously by the Cold War and by domestic repression. Like all radicals, but more than most, CP'ers were pilloried by congressional committees, subject to investigation by state and federal agencies, harassed by loyalty-security oaths and questionnaires, deprived of jobs as screenwriters, stage producers, actors and actresses, schoolteachers, as well as expelled from unions, union leadership positions, even from factories. There were the Smith Act trials—only the most dramatic prosecutions of the day—with dozens going to jail and thousands cowed into silence or deserting the Party banner. Then came the Korean War and a further turn of the screw. The nation's anti-Communist mood hardened. Indeed, it was set in concrete for a generation.

The whole ugly record of illiberalism—of legal and extralegal actions, of public acquiescence and support—has been studied extensively and there is little point in retelling it. The Party virtually returned to the underground status of its first years, with the old insistence on undeviating loyalty and quasi-military discipline. It continued to urge that the working class, now faced with a "developing crisis and destruction," take "the road that eventually leads to socialism," as Foster stated in 1952. That workers had no sense of such crisis or of destruction never filtered into the never-never land of Party headquarters. No matter. Party leaders returned to the stale ideological stand, and Foster exhorted: "The axe must be applied to the root of the evil'': finance capital, that "breeder of economic chaos, fascism and war. . . ."

The Party, then, was faced with destruction owing to successive blows: Truman's intensive prosecutions, congressional and state legislative prosecutions, expulsion from the CIO, the disastrous presidential campaign of Henry Wallace, the "fall" of China, and the Korean War. More than ever, it dealt in the rhetoric of apocalypse—for itself and for the planet.

In the 1930s, Henry Wallace had been Secretary of Agriculture, perhaps the most effective in our history, and second to Roosevelt as the emblem of the New Deal. A midwestern progressive and Vice-President during Roosevelt's third term, he was in 1946 Secretary of Commerce in Truman's administration. It was of no small moment, therefore, when Wallace, a prominent and powerful figure, expressed dissatisfaction with American foreign policy. He sharply criticized it in a major foreign-policy address of September 1946. This speech cautioned against being "unnecessarily tough" toward the U.S.S.R. "The tougher we get with Russia," Wallace warned, "the tougher they will get with us," and he urged tacit acceptance of a Soviet sphere of influence in Eastern Europe, much as the Monroe Doctrine gave us domination in this hemisphere.

This speech was the opening gun in what would be a two-year debate on America's foreign policy. No serious questions would again be asked after it ended, no genuine alternatives offered the electorate for two decades. The pervasive anti-Communism of these years guaranteed as much: the belief—shared by Truman, his advisers, and virtually all Americans—that the sole threat to global order was Russian Communism. It was a vision, a demonology if you will, shared by Democratic and Republican Presidents alike. Surveying a prostrated Western Europe, Truman and those who counseled him failed to appreciate the near-mortal wounds inflicted on Russia or the rising nationalism in Asia and Africa. The non-Communist part of the planet, they concluded, must be protected by American arms, perhaps remade in the American image. A renascent globalism, a Pax Americana, resulted, and the Cold War with it. Not that the United States was wholly responsible for the ideological divisions, but it carried the major burden for a peaceful world. It alone among the nations emerging from global conflict remained strong and powerful; it had uncontestable military prowess, resting upon the atomic bomb; and the Soviet Union, while acting stupidly and aggressively at times, had been bled white by five years of savage warfare.

Wallace perceived much of this, as his speech indicated. Owing to this address, and the threatened resignation of Secretary of State James F. Byrnes—in essence it is either me or him—he was forced to leave the Administration eight days later. He then became part of the loyal opposition and carried his fight to the people. Contrary to the conventional wisdom of that day, he repeatedly urged coexistence, trade expansion, foreign aid channeled through the UN—in a word, détente. He would hit out at atomic-bomb tests, plans to arm Latin Americans, bomber production, and proposals "to secure air bases over half the globe from which the other half of the globe can be bombed."

The Party's first tentative groping toward Wallace and toward a third party began around the time of this September 1946 address. That it was, as James Reston observed, neither "pro- nor anti-Russia," that Wallace "talked of the need for Russian understanding of American aims," guaranteed a negative reception in Communist circles. "He advanced views," a *Daily Worker* editorial declared on the next morning, "which covered up American imperialism's aggressive role."

But the idea of a mass party began to be discussed around this time, though the Communists continued to work within the Democratic organization and thought of a third party only in tandem with it. That is, as general secretary Eugene Dennis visualized, they thought "a victory will be possible" in 1948 if "there can be a coalition candidate, backed by the independent and third party forces, running as a Democrat." Harry Bridges, fellow-traveling chief of the powerful West Coast longshoremen's union, stated it succinctly: his union would support "the progressive forces in the Democratic Party." On the East Coast, in New York, the ALP remained a conduit for labor votes for liberal Democratic candidates.

In December 1946, the CP's theoretical journal came out flatly "for a third party because we are of the opinion that the Democratic Party cannot be transformed into a people's party." But Communists remained equivocal, and continued to debate whether conditions were ready for a third party and whether to join up with Wallace, a critic of Soviet repression, a devout Christian, and a capitalist. As late as a year after Wallace's first major address, Party educational director Jack Stachel declared: it can "be accepted as a fact that the Communists alone, even with their left supporters in the labor and people's movement, will not and cannot organize a third party." Dennis agreed: "We communists are not adventurers. We are not going to isolate ourselves. We never did and do not now favor the launching of premature and unrepresentative third parties and tickets." By 1947, however, he admitted that concern over Wallace's religious rhetoric, open-door view of trade expansion, and criticism of Russia had blinded Communists to the fact that when he was Secretary of Commerce he had challenged "the main line of the Byrnes-Vandenberg policy and . . . the 'get tough with Russia' policy." By then the emerging Progressive Party would appear to CP'ers as a convenient political forum for the broad popular front against war and monopoly capitalism envisaged by Party leaders.

In October 1947, Moscow, taking a harder line, founded the Cominform and condemned the Marshall Plan. The CPUSA felt compelled to follow suit. Unfortunately for CP'ers, Communist trade unionists had already assented to a CIO convention resolution which urged that foreign aid be provided on the basis of need, the premise dominating Secretary of State George Marshall's proposal—which would give massive economic assistance to war-devastated nations. CP denunciation further eroded Communist influence in the CIO and accelerated the desertion of many of the ALP's original leaders—who joined the Liberal Party, founded by Alex Rose in 1944.

CP'ers knew that national labor leaders William Green of the AFL and Philip Murray of the CIO, despite the latter's initial flirtation with Wallace, were opposed to a third party. But Communists such as *Daily Worker* editor John Gates were also aware that "such unions as the United Auto Workers and the Amalgamated Clothing Workers must favor" a third party for it to succeed. They believed, as did Wallace, that such a party could receive substantial union support. Both were very wrong. Harry Truman would claim the trade unions in

1948. Indeed, labor and northern liberals, two critical constituencies for the Progressives, went Democratic. The social-economic elite's regnant values continued to govern subordinate classes; hence the working class and the liberal middle class retained what Talcott Parsons has called a "national supra party consensus."

Even before declaring, therefore, Wallace was attractive to the Communist Party, though not ideally so, as we have seen. He had begun to consider a third party in January 1947, but his larger hope was to influence Truman and modify the "get tough" policy. In March 1947, Truman delivered his famous Truman Doctrine address, perhaps the most important speech of any President on foreign affairs since World War II ended. It acknowledged that England had passed the burden as chief bulwark against Communism to the United States. It accepted that burden, warned of the domino theory—if Greece and Turkey fell, their neighbors would fall, then Western Europe, and then America would be in mortal peril—and offered a call to counterrevolution that set historic precedents for those interventions which stained our foreign policy over twenty years. It also made a third party all but inevitable.

Communists continued to move slowly toward endorsing a third party. They unhesitatingly approved of Wallace's speeches. They were pleased by his accusation that the United States was undercutting the UN, that "best, perhaps only, hope for peace." Nor could they be cold to Wallace's December 29, 1947, address, in which he declared himself and affirmed that "the new party must stand for a positive peace program."

The Party had little choice by this time, what with anti-Communism sweeping everything before it—Congress, the press, the Democratic Party, and most liberals as well. Fixing on Wallace as its hope for survival, the CP announced for him in January 1948. It still retained large hopes, since Party membership remained considerable and articulate, but dark clouds of repression and war loomed ever more menacing to the CP's existence. A dynamic movement headed by a prestigious political figure, then drawing enthusiastic crowds, was understandably attractive. Wallace, for his part, had always been hostile to Communists, feared the political stigma attached to being associated with them, and recognized that their continuing endorsement was "a political liability.'' He wanted, above all, only their unobtrusive support. But he refused to repudiate them, on grounds of principle: Communists should have the same right of political participation as other citizens, which was a bold assertion in those days.

Wallace, of course, fought a losing battle against being stigmatized. Everyone to the left of Attila the Hun was considered Communist or Communist-influenced in the late 1940s. And everything that the Progressive Party proposed seemed to be grist for the anti-Communist mill. Identifying its candidate with Communism became a deliberate administration tactic. The President usually remained in the background, though he added his voice on May 29, 1948: ''Communists are using and guiding the third party.'' Liberals, in their assault, gave unqualified support to Truman's basic foreign-policy assumptions—as they would those of successive presidencies.

Participating in the national debate touched off by the Truman Doctrine, Wallace concluded that it was not simply a Russian and not simply a ''Greek crisis that we face, it is an American crisis. It is a crisis in the American spirit.'' There were prophetic warnings about the danger inherent in ''being tough and building up armaments.'' He arraigned the symbiotic military-civilian relationship, ''the domination of the military'' in foreign affairs, and, a decade before Eisenhower's famous warning about the military-industrial complex, deplored ''the trend toward militarization of America which is so profitable to a few entrenched interests.'' On a positive note, he continued to urge coexistence, between ''communism and capitalism, regimentation and democracy,'' in an appeal for détente that was years ahead of its time. Equally in advance of contemporary opinion, Wallace proposed a general reduction of armaments, withdrawal of American troops from Korea, and a ''hands off'' policy toward China. ''We cannot stop great social movements,'' he declared, ''not even by raising the cry of 'communism' and pouring money, guns and bombing planes into the arsenals of Chiang Kai-shek. . . . Our position in China at the present time is morally bankrupt and indefensible even from the standpoint of practical power politics. In Indonesia and Southeast Asia our support of the colonial system in opposition to native peoples struggling to free themselves of it seems strange in view of our own beginnings.''

Truman's surprising victory at the polls simply hardened his foreign-policy responses. But despite the magnitude of Wallace's defeat, he remained the leader of the "peace" forces. Again and again he assailed the Truman Doctrine, rejected NATO, found the Cold War had saddled "Western Europe with an intolerable burden of armament expenditure." However, the steady barrage was increasingly ineffectual, the massive anti-Communism of these years bringing a massive conformity to the nation. In 1952, a markedly changed, more blatantly Communist-dominated Progressive Party would field another presidential ticket. Wallace had now retired from politics, the election results were a disaster by any count, and the Party expired without notice.

The CP had tried hard to maintain an identity separate from the Progressives. Wallaceites, it insisted, "believed that the badly crippled world capitalist system can be saved and transformed into 'progressive capitalism,' [but] we Marxist-Leninists do not." However, the Party after the war was as social democratic as any of Wallace's liberal followers. Though protected by an ideological shield, it readily succumbed to what Marx once called "parliamentary cretinism." And, we have noted, it condemned those radicals, such as SLP'ers, who proposed dual unionism and refused to join in the "progressive" coalition.

At about the time of Wallace's undoing came the Party's, at least in terms of the labor movement—when several hundred thousand workers in eleven "Communist-dominated unions were cast out into organizational exile. Those unions which remained with the CIO were purged of CP leadership and influence. Such expulsions, Wallace's defeat, repression at home, Cold War abroad, combined to make the 1950s troubled and disorienting for CP'ers. Their only defense became an appeal to liberals—to uphold traditional civil liberties. But the liberals were rarely listening. Dependent upon a coalition of liberals and union leaders in the 1930s and 1940s, the Party had failed to establish an independent political base. And now, deserted by both sectors, it was left naked to its enemies. Ironically, these included many former allies, since liberals and labor had enthusiastically joined in the national witch hunt.

9 The Fifties: Dangling in the Conservative Winds

SURVIVAL CONCERNED the Party's dwindling membership, as James Weinstein has shown, and became an end in itself. And with good reason. For the average American believed it inconceivable that China's Communists could win without conspiratorial efforts on the part of Communists in America's government; and it was equally unthinkable that Russian science could produce the atomic bomb without assistance from atomic spies. Other events further stimulated the already inflamed popular imagination. They contributed to the public's conviction that Americans were being spied upon, plotted against, betrayed; that repressive measures such as the 1950 McCarran Act, with its emergency detention camp provision, were essential; that Billy Graham's homily of February 1952—about "barbarians beating at our gates from without and moral termites from within" —represented the actual state of national affairs. Nor were Communists helped when the Chinese crossed the Yalu River into Korea and drubbed American forces. Such events, coming in quick succession—and following the 1948 Czech coup, the Berlin blockade of 1948, and the "loss" of China in 1949—profoundly affected all liberals and radicals, inhibited strong political expression, and dealt a nearly mortal blow to the Communist Party.

Foster spoke of the need for a "hard core" of members, prepared to withstand any assault; and yet the 1950 national convention warned that left-sectarian practices would impair Party activities. It further cautioned, in Foster's words, that "American big business has undoubtedly resolved upon . . . war against the U.S.S.R." Yet incredibly, in the midst of rising governmental repression and Cold War, Party leaders repeatedly argued that a peace movement was possible, that "World War III and fascism were not inevitable," that—as Communist youth affirmed—"the possibilities for peace are growing." At the same time they admitted that peace was a Browderite illusion unless capitalism were destroyed; but in issue after issue of *Political Affairs* and *New Foundations* (the CP's theoretical and student journals, respectively), CP'ers pressed for a peace campaign. And when the war which Foster predicted did not materialize, Foster found the facile explanation: capitalism was unready to fight.

Party spokesmen responded to the dark designs of capitalism by insistently pleading for a Soviet-American détente, which they called "peaceful coexistence," and which replaced "Popular Front" as the governing proposition. They continued to waver between a gloomy predestinarian theory of the inevitability of war under capitalism and, among other sanguine signs, the "life-giving hope" of the Khrushchev-Eisenhower meeting at Camp David. Thus Betty Gannett, of the CP's National Committee, declared that "our time can and must become a time of the triumph of great ideals, a time of peace and progress," while warning in the same breath of the "war preparations of American imperialism." The hallowed canon linking capitalism to conflict was balanced by her triumphant conclusion that Secretary of State Dulles' war "policy has failed," and by Foster's that the "vast system of socialist states" has neutralized the "monopolists."

Always the sensitive barometer of Soviet requirements, the CP matched Russia's massive "peace offensive" by launching an American version. It took the form of the Cultural and Scientific Conference for World Peace, the American Peace Crusade, and the Stockholm Peace Petition campaign. The last, which garnered over a million signatures in the United States, demanded the outlawing of atomic weapons, strict international enforcement of this ban, and a pledge against a first strike. The Party's "peace crusade," then, was in response to the threat of nuclear holocaust. Much as in the 1930s and thereafter, peace, not Communism, was the immediate goal. Translated into domestic proposals, CP'ers, again displaying doctrinal flaccidity, emphasized bread-and-butter issues. The 1954 draft of a new Party program described "the American way to jobs, Peace, Democracy." It retained the old tropism for Moscow and, contradictorily, sought to establish the CPUSA as "American," as "the inheritor and continuer of the best in American democratic, radical and labor thought and traditions." *Daily Worker* editor John Gates stressed the "constitutional path to socialism" and pledged Communist support for any administration seeking peaceful coexistence.

Despite these efforts at coalition, CP'ers were becoming increasingly isolated. Wallace now supported the UN "police action" in Korea. Pacifists reacted cautiously to Party peace initiatives, believing them, so FOR thought, directed "to building up the Communist Party rather than to pacifism or peace." Fellow travelers succumbed to a deep instinctual urge for hibernation at a time when China was "lost," Korea had become a battleground, and Russia exploded an atomic bomb. No viable successors to the prestigious Popular Front groups seemed possible, and though organizations like the Joint Council for Soviet-American Friendship continued, they were under the government gun by the late 1940s. In 1950–51, large-scale desertions sharply reduced Party cadres—to half their claimed membership of 80,000 two years earlier, to the steeled remnant Foster had urged; but Dennis, in 1956, lamented this development, for he found the CP was afflicted with "a deeply ingrained left-sectarian approach." This twin outcome was inevitable. Little was heard of the revolutionary talk that usually accompanied sectarianism. Survival, to repeat, had become the obsessive concern.

Ideology itself remained, or at least the crude distillations of Leninism. Thus CP'ers responded dependably to the Korean War. It was part of a larger design: the "colonial enslavement of all East Asia" and the establishment upon Korean soil of "powerful bases from which to make war upon the new China and the Soviet Union." For Communists, then, the polarities were as sharply drawn as for Americans generally: the heroic "Korean people's liberation forces" versus the Truman administration, which, "under the guise of opposing a 'third world war,' " is pursuing "a criminal policy which . . . if unchecked, can only lead . . . to a third world war." Communist youth journals like *New Foundations* voiced the same theme: Truman's foreign-policy initiative in Korea safeguarded J. P. Morgan's "billion and a half investment."

Party spokesmen went about their business of anti-administration tirades as if the world were unchanged. But they continued to be bewildered, if not staggered, by the fast-moving events. In 1956, Soviet Premier Nikita Khrushchev's revelations about Stalin's paranoia and about Russia's slave camps confirmed two decades of Trotskyite and anti-Stalinist criticism. Then came the Russian suppression of the 1956 Hungarian Revolution. For most Party members—who had defended the Moscow trials, rejected reports of Siberian labor camps as lies, followed every twist of Party line—such blows were traumatic. They had known that confidence which comes from being part of a small, embattled community of the pure; they had been dedicated singularly to the cause of truth and humanity. Now there was only disillusion and dismay.

Overseas events, of course, further eroded Communist hegemony over the American left. Radicals let loose a flood of heretical letters, articles, pamphlets, questioning and deploring the Party's policies, even its history. They prompted a great debate, what Arthur Koestler described, referring to any closed system of thought, as "a scholastic, Talmudic, hair-splitting brand of cleverness which affords no protection against committing the crudest imbecilities." Those who remained faithful after the mid-1950s turned inward, went underground, and thus reduced the CP to one of a number of powerless radical sects. America's left, consequently, was back where it had been in the mid-1920s; as Lasch has observed, it had again "acquired the characteristics it has retained until the present day: sectarianism, marginality, and alienation from American life." Indeed, the retreat was such that, for the first time since 1900, it lacked an influential organizational base anywhere.

The aging Foster and his aging followers were doctrinally reliable if nothing else. Undisturbed by Khrushchev's disclosures, they praised the wisdom of the Soviet leaders whose wise initiatives were eliminating "the Stalin anti-democratic cult." But things were not the same after these disclosures. Though Party members were besieged on all sides by "class enemies," they fought their own deadly war: the "deviationists"—the group around Gates—were accused of encouraging the Party's "liberalization." Gates was called "right-winger, Social Democrat, reformist, Browderite, people's capitalist, Trotskyist, Titoite, Stracheyite, revisionist, anti-Leninist, anti-Party element, liquidationist, white chauvinist, national communist, American exceptionalist, Lovestoneite, Bernsteinist," etc. and forced to resign. His followers would eventually stand trial and be purged for their sins.

In still another virulent internal struggle, CP'ers were torn by a campaign against racism, which involved the purification of Party rhetoric. Such terms as "whitewash," "black sheep," etc., were found to have racist connotations—and those using such language had to confess their "errors" or be expelled for them. These strains, exacerbated by Khrushchev's revelations, further demoralized Party members. By now little remained save their franchise.

It followed that political radicalism survived in the postwar decades only as a collection of tiny, antiquated parties—Communist, socialist, several Trotskyite splinters, and an assortment of other marginal groups. In addition, there was a gaggle of unattached radicals, usually programless, sometimes experimental and homegrown, like Paul Goodman and C. Wright Mills. Goodman, for one, attacked the "multiversity" for complicity in larger social evils, concluded that an affluent society had produced disaffiliated youth, claimed that students were not simply marginally alienated but in fact an "exploited class." His *Growing Up Absurd* became the Bible of a generation of students who, as Jack Newfield recalls, never touched the works of Dewey, Marx, Lenin, or Peter Kropotkin. Mills took a different tack. A middle-aged Texas maverick who taught sociology at Columbia University, he condemned his discipline for its proclaimed "value-free" and facts-oriented perspective, and concluded that, notwithstanding this façade, it was dominated by a powerful conservative thrust, that it had trivialized matters, and that it had failed to wrestle directly and ethically with human relations. In *The Power Elite*, Mills explored the structure of American society, while his celebrated "Letter to the New Left" as well as other works condemned labor bureaucrats for betraying the working class, depicted white-collar labor as a work force scarcely different from the industrial proletariat, and suggested that students and intellectuals—rather than the working class—were the potential source of revolutionary protest and change.

Such social critics were early inspiration for youthful radicals. Their theories would gain devotees and stimulate a growing body of student leftists when the sixties got under way; and theoretical continuities between the two decades should be noted. But for the moment these critics were almost as irrelevant to the American scene as the radical sects and parties. Indeed, radical theory existed only at the interstices of society, and lacked a mass movement to give it meaning in the form of political activism.

Though some former Communists did move into Trotskyite or SWP ranks, in New York and the Northwest, respectively, most of the departed did not join ideological peers, unlike the deserters of the 1920s and 1930s. Thus in the 1950s students, who normally could be recruited to campus radicalism, were caught up in personal affairs, not surprisingly made *The Catcher in the Rye* a best seller, and had varied reactions to the emphases upon money, conformism, and technology in American life. Among their responses, which would eventually become national trends, were a return to the soil, a revival of old craft arts, alienation from middle-class affluence. Of the last, the Beats were perhaps the most conspicuous example. Most of them middle-aged poets and artists out of San Francisco's Bay Area, they contributed to the apolitical, dropout culture spawned primarily in Berkeley's hothouse atmosphere. Their followers offered no "blueprint for the future," Lawrence Lipton commented. Rather, they would escape from the world, seek spontaneity in human relations, disdain the uses of reason, and flee what Henry Miller called the "air-conditioned nightmare" that was American society. They had no use for the conventional social standards pertaining to drugs and sex, and they would bequeath their legacy of alienation to another bohemian subculture that was a decade away.

The New Leader, the Thomasite socialists, the Schachtmanite and Cannonite Trotskyites, the De Leonites, *et al.* had unceasingly denounced Stalinism before 1940. Their postwar views changed only in being more extreme and uncompromising. Bolshevik Russia still hung over their lives like Spanish moss, and they remained consistently hostile to her repressive ways. Every development of the late 1940s and early 1950s was seen through this anti-Soviet prism. Thus the entire non-Communist left—from *Common Sense* liberals to both wings of Trotskyism—denounced the Yalta agreement by which the Allied powers yielded to Russia on the question of reparations, the Polish border, and control of the Polish government. SWP'ers actually had it both ways. They cried a plague on both your houses, while condemning the United States for surrendering Eastern Europe to the U.S.S.R. They denounced the "heinous conspiracy" of all the powers, and yet asserted that American strength and blood had been used "for the benefit of Russian and American imperialism."

Dwight Macdonald's *Politics* (1944–49) was the most interesting effort in these years to formulate a democratic socialism, a new radical social theory. It warned against unqualified rejection of the German people, attacked the "liblabs" of *The New Republic* and *The Nation,* undertook an exuberant and overdrawn hatchet job on Henry Wallace. Yet it was intelligent enough to recognize gloomily that the Truman Doctrine and the Marshall Plan supported reactionary post-war governments as well as resisted Soviet aggression. Like the Trotskyites from whom he derived, Macdonald concluded that both super powers were "imperialistic" and "oppressive," kicking their respective peoples "around from cradle to grave."

Such views were shared by the entire non-Communist left. Events drove them to greater heights of denunciation. Russia's aggressive moves in Eastern Europe, such as the 1948 Czech coup, intensified both Cold War and nationalist perspectives. Thomas, for instance, though always angrily anti-Communist, had also been "very sceptical" of Dulles' containment policy. But the coup changed his mind and he would come to uphold such policy in the next decade. Many non-Communist radicals traveled the same route and would soon admit to a community of interests with the political establishment. And virtually all would join Thomas in embracing the slogan of "Red Fascism." This simplistic limning of the U.S.S.R. had been advanced in equally superficial form by interwar dissidents such as Eastman and J. B. S. Hardman, and they handed down a legacy of Cold War ideology to postwar liberals and non-Communists. Norman Thomas joined men such as George Meany, George Counts, Eugene Lyons, and William

Borah—labor leader, educator, journalist, and senator, respectively—and most Americans, like them, transferred hostility from Hitler's Germany to Stalin's Russia with easy assurance.

All of them could agree with the majority report of the 1946 SWP national convention that Soviet aggression and denials of human freedom matched those of the defeated enemy. "The Kremlin oligarchy," the report concluded, was "counter-revolutionary through and through, fearing and hating the workers' revolution no less than the imperialists themselves." It was a "foreign conqueror and a savage oppressor," and had converted "Eastern Europe into its closed preserve."

Surprisingly, Communist and Cannonite views corresponded on other critical foreign-policy matters. Cannonite analysis of overseas developments seemed more balanced than those of the Schachtmanites, the Thomas socialists, or Macdonald and his followers. There is nothing like Macdonald's grudging praise of the Truman Doctrine in Cannonite tracts; none of his or Thomas' fearful cries of appeasement by Roosevelt at Teheran and Yalta. The Truman Doctrine, for this Trotskyite splinter, was simply one more commitment "to imperialist intervention on a world scale." Cannonites had good words for Wallace, expressing admiration for his "condemnation of the Truman-Marshall proposals for Greece and Turkey" in May 1947. They even defended North Korea's "social programs and measures of agrarian reform," and interpreted its attack on South Korea as one more sign that "the surging Asian masses [were] ready to throw off the shackles of oppression."

Naturally, readers of Cannon's *Fourth International* and readers of the *Daily Worker* would never admit to a rough coincidence of their views. Nonetheless, both radical sectors were controlled by the same crude analytical propositions. CP'ers emphatically shared the Cannonite contention that "the 'cold war' is not only a tactic in the grand strategy of American imperialism for the destruction of the Soviet Union and for world domination; it has become a way of life." Nor would Communists disapprove when the *Fourth International* asserted that "a termination of the 'cold war' will embarrass and possibly upset the armaments and military aid program and thus hasten the coming of the crisis."

Cannonites were locked in mortal combat with the Stalinites, the Schachtmanites, and the Thomasite socialists. They chided Thomas for "his vulgar anti-Stalinism" in the 1948 campaign and concluded that he "stood cheek-by-jowl" with "the crudest of the war-mongers and State Department Brass Hats."

Generally they were endowed with virtues of realism and political sagacity otherwise lacking on the left. Their balance is further confirmed by the SWP's freewheeling criticism of such anti-Communist heroes as Sidney Hook and Max Eastman. For the record, both Trotskyite factions remained ideologically unyielding in these years. They evenhandedly condemned "the new Russian imperialism" and "American world domination," whereas socialists exclusively assailed the former. Schachtman's Independent Socialist League (ISL), for instance, sought Secretary of State Dulles' goal of "liberation" for colonial peoples "oppressed by the capitalist nations" as well as for those under Stalin's rule. The Korean War is not "our war," Schachtmanites further declared; it is the war of the two great imperialist powers.

Socialists never made such an equation in villainies. Possessed of a soured hostility toward the past, they forgot their once-slashing assaults on "mass culture," their insistence upon the sanctity of revolutionary movements, their old vehement crusade against imperialism. For decades now they had been converging on the central theme of American liberalism and conservatism—the utter evil of Communism.

And this so compromised non-Communist radicals that Cold War liberalism and even McCarthyism—both dedicated to the commonly held goal of frustrating Communism—appeared palatable.

Socialists had been on a downhill course for years owing to a number of developments: Wilsonian liberalism, post-World War I repression, the viability of the two-party system, the resilience of capitalism, the Cold War. And by now they had surrendered to an appealing opportunism. Succumbing to consensual politics, they ineluctably absorbed liberal Democratic assumptions and thereby contributed to the suffocating complacency of the Eisenhower years. American actions abroad failed to divert them from an implacable hostility toward the U.S.S.R.; their domestic programs hardly differed from those of any group of liberal reformers; hence their final vision of

socialism lacked clarity and imaginative appeal. SP'ers simply con-
tented themselves with scoring the critics of national policy or those
who, like the Cuban or Vietnamese rebels, had taken up arms against
repressive ruling elites. They even contemplated the risks of nuclear
war—in order to resist and defeat Communist aggression.

Socialists, it needs emphasis, were hardly alone in the mid-1950s.
Eastman and Dos Passos, for instance, had already journeyed down
the road into anti-Communism, and had gone further into a pathological Russophobia than most socialists would ever contemplate. But the
socialists accompanied them much of the way. For instance, replying
to Muste's appeal for America's "unilateral initiative" in disarmament, the onetime pacifist Thomas asserted: "For America to avoid
war simply by surrender to communism would in no way avoid the ultimate violence" of Stalinism.

It follows that the SP viewpoint was indistinguishable from that of
the government. The Party accepted Thomas' strictures about the
"economy" of the "garrison state," about the refusal to admit China
to the UN, which was essential "if any program of peace and disarmament is to be other than a pious aspiration," and about the inadequacy of efforts made to avert nuclear war and the "wanton suicide of
our civilization." But it demonstrated no intention of transforming
American society, and it frequently rubber-stamped liberal Democratic
candidates at election time.

The defection of a major radical party was an unmitigated disaster.
It created a vacuum impossible to fill. United States foreign policy at
this time encountered no sustained or effective criticism. Those who
still were in the opposition carried no weight in the citadels of power.
These were years of crises and malaise for America's radicals. There
was scarcely a demurrer from the conventional picture—of a Manichaean struggle between the forces of goodness, led by the United
States, and the forces of evil, in the form of an aggressive international Communist conspiracy. The Communist Party was broken on
the twin racks of repression and disillusion. What had been its source
of prestige and strength for thirty years—correspondence of program
and outlook with the U.S.S.R.—had become a crippling legacy. The
SP was deeply riven and maimed by a role reversal. Most of the
remaining radical blocs—Schachtmanites, Cannonites, De Leon's SLP,

etc.—never had centrality in radical affairs, and, in any case (with the possible exception of the Cannonites), they were so frozen in an anti-Communist posture as to have lost critical integrity and the capacity to consider a neutralist alternative.

For the orthodox, the tired remnant of Trotskyism, together with the CPUSA and most socialists, the demons remained to be exorcised. These old leftists tenaciously held to the grand traditions. They continued to purchase the old tracts, were locked in debate on surplus value and dialectics, sustained their sectarian exclusiveness and their readiness to expel "deviationists." They competed for recruits, fought each other with ferocity, and, more than ever, were shadow organizations.

Defections from radicalism made the 1950s less interesting than the 1920s and 1930s. Marxist thought had once been exciting and produced disciplined and incandescent polemical thinking. Nothing of this hard and exhilarating intellectual play remained in the 1950s. Those faithful to traditions of dissent were continuously in the shadow of congressional investigatory committees and of prison, overwhelmed by a sense of the futility of efforts to alter the nation's course. Understandably the non-Communist editors of *Liberation* worried about "the gradual falling into silence of prophetic and rebellious voices." Radical "inspiration appears to be used up," they observed, and "old labels . . . simply do not apply any more." The *Monthly Review,* an older left-wing publication, agreed. The U.S.S.R., its editors concluded, failed "to make a creative Marxian critique of capitalism's post-war expansion."

Criticism of Russia by a friendly journal like the *Monthly Review,* published by "independent socialists," further confirms a quiet trend developing over the decade—namely, the rise of a new force of unattached radicals who were capable of discriminating, even disapproving commentary on the U.S.S.R. without the usually related and predictable anti-Communism. Thus *Liberation,* founded in 1956 by Muste, Bayard Rustin, and David Dellinger, was *the* voice of radical pacifism, but it reached beyond it to an endorsement of black nonviolent protest and broadsides against corporate America for seeking imperialist conflict.

Many of these unattached radicals were not blindly obedient to

Marxist orthodoxy, and some were acutely discomforted by the questionable relevance of Marxist propositions to postwar conditions. The extreme claims for the "end of ideology" given currency by Daniel Bell and Seymour Martin Lipset, among others, seem indefensible, but disillusion with traditional doctrine did exist—owing to prosperity under capitalism; the system's successful adoption of a pragmatic blend of laissez-faire, government intervention, and government spending; the Cold War climate; and Russia's internal and external policies. And for many, this amalgam conspired to make Marxist thought seem inappropriate as a mode of social analysis. In this manner old radicals were stripped of a theoretical base that once had given their lives a powerful sustaining belief.

Consequently, radical and socialist ideology markedly declined in midcentury America, and many of its former votaries made the short journey into liberalism or beyond. Liberalism and radicalism now muted doctrinal differences, confronted as each conceived it by the requirements of an *union sacrée* against Communism. This had bizarre results at times, such as liberal Irving Kristol's defense of the "anti-Communist" Joseph McCarthy or Trotskyite James T. Farrell's endorsement of the 1950 Internal Security Act. It produced a vindication of capitalist society by ex-radicals that was both unnecessary and undignified.

Those who clung to SWP and SLP membership, like those who remained Communist—whether Moscow or "Mao" variety—continued to be captive to a nostalgia for apocalypse. The CP never repudiated the axial belief that Russia was a model for any radical reconstruction of society. It responded mechanistically to global crises. It would not admit that the New Deal's welfare-state institutions had been retained and enlarged, that these had a stabilizing effect upon the nation, and that Communists faced a time of genuine historical indeterminacy. Whether SWP, SLP, CP, or spin-offs—radicals refused to recognize that the world had passed them by and that their millennial dreams were little more than summer butterflies.

The CP had suffered a marked decline in numbers and energy. It was now limited to a few thousand, mostly elderly romantics who fed upon memories of the Golden Age which followed the November 1917 Bolshevik Revolution. Indeed, the entire hereditary left totaled no more than 10,000, fragmented into the complete spectrum of sectarian convictions, and most were aging leaders, veterans of countless internal wars and soon to pass off the stage.

The Socialist Party, for example, had only a thousand members in the late 1950s and was, as Jack Newfield aptly observed, merely "a holding company for an ideal." That is, it largely ceased to exist. Michael Harrington attributed its problems to the "discontinuities" created by McCarthyism, but its own internal weaknesses, its social-democratic character, the nature of the working class, and the very structure of capitalism were at least as responsible. Harrington's LID was little more than the social-democratic left wing of the ADA or, depending on one's angle of vision, the right wing of the SP. As such, its members had become Cold War recruits; they scorned the rising New Leftists and inadvertently contributed to the strength of right-wing ideologues like McCarthy. The Yipsels, continuing this survey, would expand in the middle and late 1950s, be captured by the "left wing," suspended for ultra-leftism in 1964, and virtually cease to exist, thereby becoming another casualty of that intra-party warfare which continued to enfeeble the American left. The SLP, meanwhile, lived on sectarian frustration, much as did the Trotskyite SWP, and both remained troubled by dissent and schism. Seemingly more relevant in the 1950s than when uttered in May 1965 was Irving Horowitz's grim prophecy: "American radicalism has no future." The popularity of the Beats, the growing youthful audience for Goodman and Mills, the stirrings among black students in the South, the rise of such journals as the *Monthly Review* and *Liberation,* these were harbingers of a new and unattached radicalism. The 1950s were a transitional decade, serving as prelude to a burst of militancy and non-Communist radicalism quite unlike anything which appeared in the preceding half century.

10 The Beginnings of the New Left, 1960-1965

ONLY IN the early 1960s did the "silent generation" of the 1950s, those who grew up in the Eisenhower years, begin to find its voice. It was drawn to a new radicalism out of the shaping events of childhood and adolescence. Its members had been born toward the end of possibly the most savage and destructive war in our history. Their earliest consciousness of outside life was associated with Auschwitz and with genocide. They began their "maturity with Hiroshima." These "children of the bomb" lived through violence, atrocities, atomic bombs, the possibility of global cataclysm, and a growing sense of powerlessness. Their adolescence was played out against a background of nuclear terror, involvement in Korea, America's military presence around the planet, the Cuban Revolution, followed by those which swept Algeria and Vietnam; against a setting of swollen governmental bureaucracies and special interests, the rigidities of a homogenized two-party system; against public unresponsiveness to social needs and priorities, and the violation of civil liberties on an unprecedented scale. They became sensitive to the paradox of a national creed of social equality and the grim facts of bigotry; the myth of affluence and the realities of poverty; the pronouncements of peaceful goals and the preparations for nuclear conflict. Government misstatement and decep-

182

tion became ever more visible to them; the circle of awareness widened, penetrating ever more into an adolescence of relative ease. Bomb testing, Caryl Chessman's execution, the discovery of poverty, the threat of urban violence—still only on the perimeter of America's consciousness—began to touch impressionable youth. There came, as Robert Lifton describes it, "the sense of being betrayed by a nation, a government, by specific political leaders, or by the older generation in general." And their instinctive conclusion was Yeats's—that innocence had been drowned in the blood-dimmed tide.

Thus innumerable national and international crises formed their lives. And all of it made vividly real by, among the bewildering actualities, air-raid drills in small communities and the requirement to huddle under schoolroom desks. Commenting on these realities of childhood, David Horowitz recalled: "We have been made to live as no other generation has, on the edge of the world's doom." They received an early awakening with the 1960 San Francisco demonstration against the House Un-American Activities Committee—and students remote from Berkeley were left troubled by the police response to undergraduate demonstrators. For most, too young to be aware of McCarthyism, it was the first conscious instance of repression and official lies in their own country. For this small sector of students, itself a minor segment of America's youth, a crisis of legitimacy had begun to unfold.

It would take time. These future radicals, after all, were shaped by the facts of economic opportunity as well as by domestic turbulence. They were not brutalized peasants or products of the ghetto; they were not social and economic failures; they were, as the 1962 Port Huron statement (the founding document of SDS) affirmed, the children of an affluent generation, "bred in at least modest comfort." They were mostly white, well-educated, suburban youth of similar backgrounds. Their parents had frequently been left-of-center, usually liberal Democrats, and often politically aware in their own student days. Their offspring, however, would not be radicalized in the home, but by society at large and specifically on the campus. In college, they were customarily enrolled in the humanities and the social sciences—which transmitted the strong Western traditions of skepticism and dissent—and they usually did impressive academic work. They grew unhappy with their classes because they were too large and impersonal; and they became scornful of fraternity and sorority life and even of athletic competition.

By the late 1950s, these students were numerous enough to form a genuine subculture. And their political liberalism was rooted in cultural changes which had begun to take shape, with such harbingers as folk music and the Beats, those alienated and apolitical poets of the Eisenhower years. This embryonic "counterculture," as it would be called, was a tocsin—for those who groped for ways to question society's fundamental assumptions. At first pointedly anti-middle-class, this counterculture would become pervasive and nationwide within a decade. It would turn into a highly commercial enterprise, filter down to working-class and non-college youth, and be absorbed into the middle class. That such a counterculture should spring up first on college campuses is understandable. Students, as Daniel Cohn-Bendit has pointed out, were under less pressure to conform. The campus permitted an unusual degree of social latitude. It offered hothouse conditions for germinating culture radicalism.

One segment of the counterculture never turned overtly political. Its tastes ran to D. H. Lawrence, who wanted the revolution "for fun," not for the proletariat. Becoming known as "hippies," this minority never made the great leap forward into the political activism of the Movement, sharing only its sense of alienation, the belief that impersonal powers controlled their lives. They engaged in love-ins and rock festivals rather than sit-ins and antiwar protests. But whether the counterculture was political or not, one thing is certain: there was a rising hostility to the dominant ethos of consumerism, materialism, and personal success—a repudiation of money, work, career, marriage.

The counterculture first appeared on selected campuses. Berkeley became a shrine for student pilgrims from across the country. But even here, it should be cautioned, the radicalized students were only a minority of undergraduates—and even when bitterly anti-militarist, antiwar sentiment neared its peak, some 63 percent of students polled thought that "the ROTC belongs on campus." In the late 1960s, to jump ahead momentarily, three fifths of the nation's students were "getting tired of all the campus unrest." They were at best reform-oriented and non-alienated, with only 8 percent seeking to replace the existing social system. Still, as New Left leader Al Haber prophesied, "if any really radical liberal force is going to develop in America, it is going to come from the colleges and the young." Moreover, it became an unspoken assumption that such a force would be concentrated in the liberal arts programs.

New Left students were the product of a class society and enjoyed its best advantages. They could never really cross over to white working-class youth, whom they charged—as they did all of America's labor force—with having "a false consciousness of their role and status." Their sentiments were reciprocated, for their values and long hair were offensive to labor. Behind the workers' pique was a powerful class hostility which AFL–CIO head George Meany and others effectively exploited.

The New Left's attitude toward labor bureaucrats was much like its reaction to government or to the Communist Party. It was hostile to virtually all discipline and all authoritarian forms—whether that of parent, teacher, lawgiver, or priest; it was deeply distrustful of the state, opposed to the bigness and remoteness of both government and trade union. Appalled by the quality of American life and its institutions, New Leftists would shift to localism, community organizing, decentralized controls, and, a favored term, "participatory democracy."

What occurred, then, was a moral rebellion, a protest by the middle class against the middle class, a kind of anguished children's crusade against "the careful young men" (as *The Nation* described the class of '58) who never expressed any political discontents. As such, it was unlike the leftist student movements of earlier days, which were umbilically linked to adult political groups. The New Left was a genuine youth movement, mostly of white undergraduates. Their youthfulness was perhaps their outstanding feature. Except for the middle-aged Christian pacifists and some aging gurus like philosopher Herbert Marcuse, most New Leftists were born after 1940. No wonder the admonition of Berkeley's Free Speech Movement (FSM), "Don't trust anyone over thirty," seemed appropriate.

Unlike the Old Left in many respects, the New Left also differed from countless other groups in our history who felt pushed out, left behind by change, unable to transmit their legacy; they rejected the legacy offered to them. They were different, too, in that they rose spontaneously and lacked the hopefulness of interwar radicals, with their concrete model of an alternative economic order. Having no faith in the great October Revolution, they combined instead an insouciant disregard for revered radical systems with antagonism toward the existing order and with vague utopian longings. They were in a way even more romantic than the older radicals and bore virtually all the stigmata of romanticism, though some of its features matured only in the late 1960s. They were more inclined toward the intuitive and emotional, unlike their Depression liberal-radical parents, who had trusted in reason. They displayed an intense subjectivity, a preoccupation with private problems, a propensity for physical violence, a revulsion against theory, an attraction to mysticism, a cultish worship of youth as the repository of wisdom and beauty.

They shared with their radical predecessors a sense of purpose, solidarity, and urgency which drove them steadily leftward. The sixty-four-page Port Huron statement of 1962—which emerged from a national convention of the three-year-old Students for a Democratic Society (SDS)—caught the spirit of this new radical world, with its spacious idealism and highly developed sense of moral responsibility. Significantly, LID objected to the political content of the Port Huron statement—to such ideas as "denuclearization" of the Third World and "universal controlled disarmament" in order to end the Cold War—and refused to permit SLID, its student unit, to distribute it.

For this New Left, the values of the Port Huron statement—anti-elitism, anti-bureaucracy, participation, community—were crystallized by the civil rights movement then germinating in the South. Indeed, the blacks would virtually replace the working class as central to radical social change—as student radicals identified emotionally with southern civil rights workers and transferred student discontent and humanistic values onto the civil rights movement. Of the eventual black reaction, more will be said later. For the moment it should be noted that the civil rights movement preceded the New Left. First came the monumental desegregation decision of 1954, *Brown* v. *Board of Education*. Then, in 1955, the Montgomery bus boycott led by Martin Luther King, which induced Irving Howe to hope "that the mute should find their voices." The boycott involved the entire black community in a sustained confrontation with the white power structure, something unprecedented in our history. Five years later came the real catalyst for blacks and for college students: four neatly dressed black undergraduates deliberately challenged state racial segregation by sitting down at the "whites only" lunch counters of Greensboro, North Carolina, stores; they asked for coffee and refused to leave until the stores closed. Thus new tactics were developed. These needed an organization not "subject to the authority of anyone but themselves"; consequently, southern blacks founded the Student Nonviolent Coordinating Committee (SNCC) in October 1960. Its goal was the elimination of segregation—and not simply at lunch counters, "but in every aspect of life." Its focus was on the immediate situation—not one involving a socialist future.

In 1961 came a first climax, the "freedom rides" organized by the Congress of Racial Equality (CORE)—in which northern "riders," many of them whites, flooded southern cities and refused to accept segregated accommodations at bus terminals, lunch counters, and rest rooms. SNCC's greatest achievement would be the voter registration drives across the South, in which it was joined by CORE and staffed by 500 organizers, many of them northern white undergraduates. Always living in the shadow of the noose, these organizers would work alongside rural blacks from 1961 to 1965. Their efforts were shaped by non-resistant black leaders, such as Martin Luther King, and by those radical pacifists who founded *Liberation* in 1956 and who immediately endorsed nonviolent protest.

The Greensboro tactics quickly caught on. By the end of 1960, an estimated 50,000 had participated in some civil rights protest across the South, and over 3,600 had spent some time in jail for violation of local ordinances. Many were Northerners, galvanized into action by the notes of high idealism which John Kennedy had early struck. Southern treatment of the black and the poor seemed like a blot on the promise of American life and, for the first time in their comfortable existence, suburban white youth saw how the other half lived; for the first time dogs attacked them and hoses were turned on them; for the first time they were witness to the poverty and illiteracy of rural black labor and exposed to the brutality of American life—to arrests, beatings, occasionally to murder. These experiences were traumatizing.

They would return to college with a new awareness of the national ills and with a new sense of camaraderie and purpose.

Thus a new breed of civil rights activists gathered in SNCC, CORE, and the Southern Christian Leadership Conference (SCLC). Primarily middle-class in origins, they were now "trying to heighten consciousness," as SNCC leader James Foreman declared, to reduce black powerlessness. They sought at first legal and formal equality with whites in such matters as public education and the right to vote, but their goal would shift somewhat to a political struggle for socioeconomic parity; it would also evolve into a racially exclusive movement, as blacks increasingly took over. They fought for those rights already possessed by the white middle class. Hardly revolutionary goals, but essential to integrating the rural black work force into the capitalist system. To find their demands governed by a social-democratic, not revolutionary, perspective, does not suggest that they were any less worthwhile; they were in response to immediate need and they were a cry for justice. That student liberals and leftists should equate the aims and objectives of the civil rights movement with their own, that SDS in the early 1960s sought to deepen its ties with militant southern blacks, that the Port Huron statement expressed hope that a new movement for social change could be enfolded within a broadened civil rights campaign, was natural and inevitable.

Thus a new radical mood began to percolate in the early 1960s. It would become immensely complicated, striking out in many directions and including many groupings, with a few, the offspring of the Old Left—YPSL, the Young Socialist Alliance (YSA), Progressive Labor, the Du Bois Clubs—invoking the theorists of the past. But the Movement, as the new radicalism came to be called, was far more inclusive. Lacking a long-range perspective, it was able to create and maintain a powerful student crusade. It came to believe that such a crusade could be a potent agency for change. Massive protest demonstrations confirmed this belief. Students could indeed make history.

No survey of this loose coalition which comprised the New Left would be complete without the pacifists. Only a small segment persevered in the grand tradition of resistance to the claims of the state on theological grounds. Virtually all, as their style evolved in the 1950s—and Dellinger and the *Alternative* are exemplars—helped to transform pacifism and make it the basis of protest against the nation's social structure. Accordingly, they would have a major impact on the nonviolent left. They worked for peace by means of vigils and fasts, civil disobedience, draft resistance, non-registration for conscription, protests against Polaris submarines and the ROTC on campus, sit-downs at entrances to rocket sites or Selective Service headquarters—that is, by using passive disobedience and nonviolent means rather than by political activities.

Peace workers, by the mid-1950s, could read the *Catholic Worker* or the tracts of the Quaker-dominated American Friends Service Committee, both of which urged "coexistence" with the U.S.S.R. and condemned the Truman Doctrine and "its assumption that military force is the only language understood by the Communist high command." The aging and irrepressible Muste—he was seventy-five years old in 1959—attempted to build a viable non-Communist radicalism, much as he had tried to do twenty years earlier (in his American Workers Party). He also persisted in opposing militarism and poverty as well as the regimes which harnessed both Russians and Americans "in the service of global atomic war." Standing firm, he and FOR now concluded that there was little "decisive difference between Norman Thomas' position on war and peace and Truman-Eisenhower."

Throughout the 1950s, the great menace to mankind was the threat of nuclear war. Driven by mutual suspicions and animosities, the superpowers were building up formidable arsenals and continuously testing nuclear weaponry. The 1954 hydrogen-bomb test in the Pacific gave new life to pacifists. Led by Muste, they organized a new liberal coalition—SANE—for a sane nuclear policy. It included Communist sympathizers, World Federalists, and veteran peace workers like Thomas, and rallied radicals and liberals, such as Mrs. Roosevelt and publisher Norman Cousins, around the single issue of "cessation of nuclear weapons testing." Politically moderate, SANE operated in counterpoint to the more radical Committee for Nonviolent Direct Action (CNVDA), which proposed unilateral disarmament and, in the autumn of 1958, caught the public imagination when it sponsored the dramatic protest voyage of the ketch *Golden Rule* into the Pacific nuclear testing area.

The tactics of the late 1950s—the picketing, vigils, peace

marches—were directed by a pacifist core of Christian radicals. And they went beyond peace work and advocated a social revolution, thereby standing to the left of liberal and Democratic opinion. They stood apart from Marx as well, since they would make the revolution by nonviolent means. They reacted angrily to the mounting arms race, and the pages of their journal, *Liberation,* were crowded with articles attacking American foreign policy.

Radical pacifists gradually broadened their attack. *Liberation* launched a direct frontal assault on every administration redoubt. It condemned America's "neocolonialism" in Puerto Rico, hailed the Cuban Revolution as "the most important event in this hemisphere since the Mexican revolution," challenged the brink-of-war and massive-retaliation assumptions of Eisenhower's Secretary of State, John Foster Dulles, and flayed "imperialists" for trying "to stop the awakening of the Asian and African nations." Pacifism stood for a congeries of values and reactions enfolded into the very discrete New Left. Pacifists ranged from nonviolent Quaker groups, such as the American Friends Service Committee, to the militantly radical May 2nd Movement (M-2-M), a faction that was influenced by Maoist doctrine and that emerged out of the protest against the war in Vietnam. Between the two extremes of M-2-M and AFSC stood the traditional agencies—FOR and the Women's Strike for Peace among them—and a variety of New Left groups which included pacifist-oriented members. Thus was pacifism in the 1960s divided along religious, tactical, and social lines, and such divisions usually made only ad hoc arrangements feasible.

The peace issue was a broad umbrella in still another way. It sheltered issues-oriented members of the fraternity—those who, say, opposed atmospheric testing and bomb shelters—and those, like the Quakers, who took high ethical grounds. This very spread of interests and outlook made for a similarity between peace workers and Depression radicals in some significant details. They both displayed energies and passions beyond their numbers, and they also featured internal struggle. SANE, for instance, was crippled by disputes, and its student affiliate withdrew and disbanded in February 1962. There were deep divisions between those who sought nuclear controls and those who were unilateralists; those who sympathized with the Vietcong and those who were absolute pacifists; those amenable to working within the legal-political framework and those who would transform the growing antiwar movement into a revolutionary crusade. How different were the latter from socialists among the peace workers who would move in traditional political channels!

Most peace workers were still liberal in outlook in the early 1960s and anxious to work within these existing channels. Hence they stood in ambiguous relation to the New Left. They shared its concern for peace and several of its basic foreign-policy assumptions. Unlike the New Left, however, they were not held by a vision of the revolutionary potential of the laboring poor, and they sought change within the existing political structure. After 1960, these liberal peace workers began to lose their modest influence—or at least were forced to share the pacifist spotlight with radical pacifists. The latter, Christian radicals much like those of the 1840s, stood on the high ground of conscience. They invoked the "higher law" or something ethically comparable and rejected governmental measures which were in conflict with it. Unlike the antislavery Garrisonians of over a century earlier, these radical non-resistants sought the remedy for unjust laws, such as the Conscription Act, within the political framework. But increasingly working outside it as well, they would come to endorse the actions of draft resisters and of those army men who refused to obey orders which would send them to Vietnam. They did not invoke the memory of nineteenth-century Christian pacifism, such as the Garrisonian non-resistants; they had the contemporary model of Nuremberg, with its approval of resistance to the illegal commands of a higher authority. And they displayed the readiness of their forebears to confront civil authority, to violate—violently if need be—federal measures which conflicted with the "higher law" of conscience. Therefore, while possibly unaware of it, they were drawing upon the historic proposition that a Christian must avoid participation in an unjust society and its unjust wars—not merely by refusing to become a soldier, but by rejecting any service in government.

The very uncoordinated and non-programmatic nature of the New Left facilitated cooperation with pacifists. New Leftists cared more for informal and improvised forms of social action, as Kenneth Keniston has observed, than for explicit programs that would restructure society. And being a mood, a mode of life, an élan rather than a prospectus, the Movement was thus thrown open to a variety of tactical as well as philosophical perspectives, some of which were readily shared by peace workers—whether these be social-democratic efforts to elect peace candidates on the Democratic Party ticket or confrontation politics against nuclear testing. Since even such confrontations were nonviolent before 1965, a working alliance was all the easier. So pacifists joined student radicals in collecting signatures for petitions and in fasting against nuclear tests in the autumn of 1961. The New Left rekindled pacifist energies, eventually communicated a sense of crisis, and turned peace workers into militant critics of society.

Reflecting an ex officio collaboration between Christian pacifists and the New Left, *Liberation* opened its columns to those who held deep ethical convictions about war, specifically the war in Vietnam—with appeals by Bertrand Russell, the doyen of pacifism, and by Staughton Lynd, a major New Left spokesman. Both writers, indeed all who called themselves "radical," affirmed, as *Liberation* stated, that "our role in Indochina has always been immoral." "Stop shooting and get out!" it exhorted. Muste expressed similar sentiments. He found overwhelming evidence that "the United States' part in that war is foolish, illegal, immoral, unspeakably atrocious." To the New Left, its radicalism grounded in genuine moral conviction, such sentiments had a powerful appeal.

Radical activism was equally appealing. It was necessarily so in a society that historically reflected a tension between the athletic and the contemplative—and that invariably chose the former. Thus even those most committed to the life of the mind frequently found action superior to theory. Hence activism, and activism of a violent sort, would become increasingly fashionable. In more recent times, it lost its remedial purpose and became a means without any coherent end.

In any case, a mounting number of peace workers would soon reject democratic processes and gradualism. Pacifist David McReynolds soberly noted their departure—with Dellinger endorsing the Cuban Revolution and Lynd "disengaging from his pacifism as it applies to Vietnam." And, McReynolds concluded, the real dilemma confronting the peace movement was its wavering between peaceful change and violence, with one bloc adhering to traditional pacific modes of action and the other, growing powerful, seeking peace through violent means. So it would fall out. Suffice to note that pacifist non-resistance mingled with the pure streams of antiwar radicalism from the outset.

The inclusiveness of the New Left is one of its most striking characteristics. It would comprise anarchists, antiwar students, draft resisters, GI dissidents, radically inclined intellectuals, liberals, libertarians, socialists, young professionals, apostate Catholics, syndicalists, followers of R. D. Laing, who sought personalism, the first generation of liberated women, high school dropouts, brilliant graduate students, and a growing number of black nationalists. It would embrace SDS, SNCC, ad hoc groups such as the Free Speech Movement (FSM) and the successor Vietnam Day Committee (VDC), the Mississippi Freedom Democratic Party (MFDP), as well as social idealists from Vista and the Peace Corps. It would attract nihilists off the Columbia University campus, single-issue antiwar religious or radical organizations like the National Mobilization, Vietnam Summer (1967), the Moratorium (1969), Clergymen Concerned, Women's Strike for Peace. This left-liberal coalition welcomed college faculty, high school and college students, doctoral candidates. Some were unsophisticated, unable to distinguish between a Maoist and a liberal; others were refreshingly trenchant voices like Mills and Paul Goodman, writing in *Studies on the Left*. Still others, including Adlai Stevenson's followers and Young Democrats, sought only campus reform; while more rejected Stevenson, owing to his defense of the Bay of Pigs, and rejected that misadventure as well, and they found New Deal liberalism and Stalinism, capitalism and socialism, equally flawed.

The Movement transcended any single individual or organization. Its massive reunions in the streets of New York, Washington, and San Francisco were conducted by ad hoc coalitions—in which SDS, so often synonymous with the New Left in the popular mind, was only one among many sponsoring or participating organizations. The April 1965 demonstration, for instance, brought together former Peace Corps volunteers, SANE members out of white suburbs, urban black teen-agers, Berkeley activists, members of MFDP, short-haired freshmen out of Catholic colleges, liberals drawn from the ADA, Communists who belonged to the Du Bois Clubs. A "new generation of American radicals," Jack Newfield has written, they were not nourished "by the alien cob-webbed dogmas of Marx, Lenin, and Trotsky. . . . They were there not to protest anything so simple as war or capitalism."

The New Left, then, was a most capacious vessel of change. It was much like the Popular Front, the product of a symbiotic relation between liberals and radicals, between those who sought reform and those who were indifferent to politics, those who were dogmatic radicals and those who were bohemians. Thus one sector of the Movement would turn its back on society, its sexual morality, technology, rationalism, militarism, social regimentation. These rebels against the culture were themselves not an undifferentiated whole. Some, for instance, copied the "life style" of the now widespread counterculture, superficially identifying with its appearances—its scatological speech, eccentric dress and behavior, use of drugs, wearing of flowers and bells—and they were the "love, peace, groovy" flower children of the mid-1960s.

Others, more profoundly troubled by the prevailing work ethic and social norms, questioned the conventional pieties and authority of any kind. They exalted the spontaneous and unexplored, the individual and personal relationships, existential experience for its own sake. They proposed a pastoral ethos and a romantic celebration of nature and of the senses. They wanted to feel and be, not to know. They were convinced that sex, rock, drugs, and meditation were avenues to a new culture, and these values, not changes in doctrines and institutions, were fundamental and would reshape the world.

Though largely indifferent to politics, at times they did make common cause with the political rebels and with the civil rights movement. After all, they shared some of the same grievances and sources of inspiration; they had a common enemy in the vaguely defined "establishment"; they also searched for communal involvement, displayed contempt for the authorities of the past, sought a decisive break with the nation's bureaucratic systems.

It is a mistake, then, to separate entirely political and cultural rebels in these early years. Indeed, the Movement's partisans deliberately linked antiwar and counterculture politics. There is, furthermore, a linkage that is political in a less obvious way. Those converted to the counterculture, including the hippy-acidhead sector, gradually created an underculture, involving dress, drugs, community, and rejection of democratic processes. Largely unaware of it, this non-doctrinal segment inadvertently undermined the politics of legitimacy. No Movement component, at least not until the late 1960s, would elect to mount the barricades. Rather, they all joined in a campaign that, as Keniston has observed, was not "a movement in the traditional sense," but a cluster of customarily uncoordinated groups which attacked poverty, racism, discrimination against women—a nearly inexhaustible list of domestic ills—and, turning overseas, condemned the traditional "liberal" orientation in foreign affairs.

The discrete, often ephemeral nature of the constituent parts would be debilitating for the whole. Different political styles and social emphases made it unlikely that a single guideline could be maintained. Moreover, each group, rather than combining and then mediating among the needs of the diverse elements, locked into one stratum—blacks, youth, labor—as the catalyst for change. Some groups rejected the hereditary left and its objectives; others secretly lionized it. And there was still another sector which, being pacifist, was not ideological, though rejecting America's "imperialism" and her role as global policeman.

The Movement surely had no clear political program, no viable organization, and, early on, no substantial constituency. All of which made it relatively easy for many of its votaries, over the objections of the doctrinally pure, to join the McCarthy and Robert Kennedy primary campaigns and thereby work their way back into the system. It is useful to note that the "new politics"—of the McCarthy and then the McGovern presidential drive—was entirely conventional. It involved precinct organizing and endless canvassing, among other activities, to fight for reform-radical goals within the existing party structure. And, ironically, seeking such goals meant cooperating with politicians who were themselves implicated in the Vietnam War or unable to break from it, unable to repudiate its growing horrors even after Richard Nixon made those horrors his own.

The relative ease with which many in the Movement crossed over into Democratic Party work further confirms the flexibility of most of its components. At the outset more open to ideas than most, the New Leftists stressed, as Keniston tells us, immediate tactics, limited goals, short-range activities. They refused to deify theoretical schema or to develop a revolutionary strategy. To the contrary, they scorned those trapped in the theoretical dustbins of Europe, neglecting the saints and renegades who so preoccupied the radical imagination for nearly a century. Their governing tone was proclaimed at the December 1965 SDS conference: "We have slogans which take the place of thought: 'There's a change gonna come' is our substitute for social theory. . . . What sociology, what psychology, what history do we need to know the answers?" The question itself discloses an implicit skepticism and cognitive sterility. New Leftists attacked not so much "the world of ideas," as Irving Louis Horowitz shrewdly concludes, as "the idea that reason is the only mode of knowing." Or, as a contemporary found, contemptuous of theory, they "rarely read anything unless it came from the underground press." In this manner they abandoned the Old Left's certainties and reductivism, its doctrinal rigidity and historical inevitability. They were in "revolt against *Capital,*" to adapt Gramsci's phrase, and drawn to Marx's sociology and philosophy rather than to his passion for exactness or his body of economic theorems. Hence they ignored surplus value but were attracted to his doctrine of alienation and made it, in altered form, their major philosophical construct.

Their guru was Herbert Marcuse, the elderly Marxist scholar whose *One Dimensional Man* (1964) made him a culture hero. Americans, Marcuse found, were basically alienated—man from other men, from nature, from work, from his true self. They were, in addition, absorbed in bread and circuses, such as split-level homes and *Playboy* magazine, which "militates against qualitative change." Combined, these factors created a "false consciousness" and made revolt next to impossible. Marcuse's celebration of youth and its "new sensibility," however, encouraged the belief that a collaboration between students and workers could galvanize a revolutionary consciousness.

Marcuse met the New Left's conditions for acceptance by his romantic and unorthodox Marxism. New Leftists were simply hostile to those "smelly little ideologies" that George Orwell once described. Rather, most held themselves personally responsible in a way previous generations had not done (as Colin MacInnes observes), and regarded their social critique as grounded in very personal moral convictions, the theoretical sources of which were obscure. They were anti-capitalist of course, but not necessarily Communist, and they were as critical of Russia as of the United States and emphatically opposed to the Cold War. Consequently, they resisted Party blandishments, refusing an unqualified commitment to any nation or intellectual system, something that both Communists and non-Communists in the 1930s failed to do.

The children of the Old Leftists have been called "red diaper babies" with good reason. Many came out of radical backgrounds and remained committed to the faith of their fathers. Like their parents, they remained trapped in the same tired rhetoric and posture, and were nourished on imported ideologies and delusions of imminent insurrection. The Du Bois Clubs and Progressive Labor were the major groups which housed them and their doctrines.

Du Bois Clubbers were surprised by the sudden ascent of the New Left, as were all established radical groups. They failed to "adequately get into SDS," as they later admitted, but sought rather to "build Du Bois as a substitute for other movements." Caught off guard, they raced to catch up and would join the New Left in criticism of national policy in Vietnam and in condemning the draft. They would not smoke pot, go unshaven, endorse sexual experimentation or mysticism. Nor did they accept the personalism of drugs and the personalist politics which expressed itself in natural language and dress, in guerrilla theater and underground presses. Nor would they disavow the trade-union bureaucracy and the Democratic Party; to the contrary, they took the orthodox Communist position and would work with both. They accepted the CP directive of December 1965—"join in struggle with the New Left whenever it is possible"—and joined the Movement and infiltrated the civil rights campaign as well.

Progressive Labor, like the Du Bois Clubs, possessed qualities reminiscent of Depression-decade Communism. Both were entangled in musty Marxist dogma—e.g., the working class as the instrument of revolutionary change—and both would press for labor's immediate demands. Both sought centralization and Party control by an elite; both were pure churches and, in contrast to major New Left groups, unwilling to admit deviants from the true faith; both turned to external models, with Progressive Labor looking to China and Du Bois Clubbers to Russia, though the members of each did not ignore domestic affairs and sang "We Shall Overcome" in Harlem and in Alabama during the civil rights protests. But there were marked differences. PL was more tightly knit, organizationally less flexible, more militant than the Clubs. Its members were called "ultra-leftists" by CP'ers and Club members, a sobriquet meaning a falling out of line. It indicates a familiar tropism, drenched in hostility toward anyone, anywhere, who rejected the CP because it was too moderate and too willing to enter into coalition with reformist elements. "Ultra-leftists" were, varying the rhetoric, "adventurists," "left sectarians," or "agents of the Albanian Party." Trading verbal charges, PL claimed CP'ers and Clubbers alike were "revisionists" and "class collaborationists."

Progressive Labor would ceaselessly fight its enemies on the left, indict their nonviolent tactics and "counter-revolutionary policies," arraign their support of Russia's policy of peaceful coexistence. PL's provenance, like its rhetoric, reminds one of so much of the radical past. It, too, was the product of schism, being an expelled Communist splinter. Thus its founders were mostly CP'ers who, beginning in December 1961, upheld China's position in the Sino-Soviet rift, rejected the Party's social-democratic drift, and were purged for their troubles. At the June 1964 founding convention of the Du Bois Clubs, after three years of earlier disputes, and together with Trotskyite students and unaffiliated radicals, they bolted and formally organized as PL. PL'ers accused the Russians, the CP, and the Clubs of the heresy of "revisionism." They rang the praises of labor militancy and of China; they enshrined Mao Tse-tung as the new divinity, glorified strikers as victims of class war, and made confrontation politics on Harlem streets and college campuses the order of the day. While talking about socialism, they did not conduct a political struggle for it. Rather, like past militants, they fought for immediate gains for the socially marginal and oppressed.

PL'ers were not necessarily identified with the New Left. They were clean-shaven, neatly dressed, opposed to the Movement's emotional anarchy, and critical of the counterculture. Much like the Trotskyites, whom they found reprehensible, they felt that the American working class must be drawn into the antiwar movement, that otherwise it could not succeed.

Completing this survey of the Old Left are two smaller and less influential Marxist youth groups—YPSL and the Young Socialist Alliance (YSA), the Trotskyite (SWP) affiliate founded in 1960. Each of these radical bodies was, in its own way, Old Left to the bone. Fortified by Trotsky's theorems, YSA believed that both Russia and China have betrayed the revolutionary proletariat and it unceasingly assailed "Stalinism." The Yipsels, in the mirror image of their socialist parents, denounced all other Marxist groups. Both organizations totaled no more than a few hundred students, but, then, all four Marxist groups had a combined membership of only about 2,000. They carried on the old tribal vendettas as if the nation's destiny hung on the outcome. YSA, for example, attacked Du Bois Clubbers for betraying the working class; and the latter in turn accused the Trotskyites of ideological rigidity. Occasionally they put aside conflicting doctrinal emphases to collaborate on ad hoc committees protesting, say, United States intervention in Cuba or in the Dominican Republic, or later in Southeast Asia. YSA campaigned as early as 1964 for complete American withdrawal from Vietnam; and the May 2nd Movement (M-2-M), a peace group organized by PL, focused on the war as an example of American imperialism.

Lacking the massive certainties of the hereditary left, the new radicals were pluralistic and amorphous. They willingly accepted recruits with divergent social and political views—anarchist, Trotskyite, socialist, pacifist, Communist. Because of their refusal to exclude Communists, or even express anxiety about them, they were viewed with growing alarm by old-time social-democratic trade unionists and groups like SANE, LID, and ADA, by over-thirty liberals as well as by socialists. After all, for those scarred by Depression-decade struggle with the Communist *apparatchiki,* such indifference and lack of selectivity seemed naïve and hopeless. Hence the response of Robert Gilmore, executive director of Turn Toward Peace (TTP), when SDS failed to exclude Du Bois Club members from its April 1965 antiwar demonstration. He quietly sought to convince several peace leaders to withdraw from the march and, whether or not he influenced them, some prominent socialists as well as liberals and pacifists (including Thomas, Rustin, and Muste) signed a statement which obliquely slapped at SDS. "We welcome the cooperation of all those groups and individuals who, like ourselves, believe in the need for an independent peace movement," they declared, but not those "committed to any form of totalitarianism nor drawing inspiration or direction from the foreign policy of any government." Their language seemed unexceptionable; however, for those touched by McCarthyism it was clear warning that even the most courageous of over-thirty pacifists were not inured to red-baiting.

Berkeley's FSM was equally suspect to old radicals. Like SDS, it swept in Maoist PL'ers, Du Bois Clubbers, YSA'ers, SNCC members, and Trotskyites from M-2-M. And it, too, was most vehemently attacked, not by conservatives as one might expect, but by liberals and those whose social idealism derived from the 1930s. Their onslaught demonstrates, in words of exceptional emotional force, the incipient and actual conflict between the New Left and ex-leftists. Lewis Feuer's animadversions in *The New Leader*, directed, it must be remembered, toward some of his best students at Berkeley, are extraordinary and require no comment: The FSM "acts as a magnet for the morally corrupt; intellectual lumpen proletarians, lumpen beatniks, and lumpen agitators who wend their ways to the university campus to advocate a melange of narcotics, sexual perversion, collegiate Castroism and campus Maoism."

SDS did not spring full-blown from the brow of Zeus. There were the ties to an earlier radicalism: the members who also belonged to the Communist Labor Youth League (LYL), the youthful passions and innocence that were so reminiscent of the prewar *Masses*, the concern for immediate issues, and so forth. It was a direct descendant of SLID, itself the offspring of the ISS of 1905 and organized by LID in 1930. Closely allied to the SP, LID was revived by Cold War socialists after 1945 and SLID had been reorganized in 1959 and renamed SDS.

That LID should object to the Port Huron statement and censure its authors was predictable. It had been deeply stained by the deadening atmosphere of repression and the Cold War ideologues who officered it. SDS refusal to be unconditionally anti-Communist—its rejection of Laidler's resolution to this effect—was unpardonable in the eyes of LID spokesmen. SLID's 1965 statement (drawn up by Rustin, Harrington, Lewis Coser, and Irving Howe) reflected LID's position. Angered by the "anti-anti-Communism" of SDS'ers, it claimed that they sought to "give explicit or covert political support to the Vietcong," which made both their pacifism and personal morality suspect.

In contrast, these socialist intellectuals shunned any critique of imperialism, tried to torpedo the planned 1965 antiwar March in Washington, and disavowed such radical tactics as blocking the movement of troops to Vietnam. These tactics, affirmed Tom Kahn in *Dissent,* are "not related to a strategy for building a mass movement." Rejecting direct action, "which alienates potential allies," he advocated legislative activities, a parliamentarianism reminiscent of old-time socialists and pacifists.

The SDS split from its parent group was inevitable. That it took three years was the only surprise. The students themselves contributed to the schism by their insistent disregard of theory and strategy, their failure to embrace the ideological birthright. But who could they turn to? The Lovestone-Meany labor bureaucracy had been implicated in CIA operations in Africa and Latin America. The liberal Democrats had invented counter-insurgency and conspired to bring about the Bay of Pigs. If the unions had not excluded blacks, if the old-line socialists had not supported the war in Vietnam, if the forces around Kennedy had not bloodied their hands in Cuba and Southeast Asia, SDS'ers might have had options. But they did not. Their rupture, as it turned out, was a decisive break with the spirit of the 1950s, a move toward uninhibited and full-scale debate on American society and foreign policy. When the rupture finally came, at the fourth SDS convention, it left social democrats bitterly antagonistic to the youthful renegades and they would cast splenetic barbs at their heirs throughout the decade.

The New Left would eventually succumb to the compelling simplicities of historical myth and of revolutionary romanticism. But at first it refused to see things in Manichaean terms. Life seemed just not that simple. Conceivably it might have been in the 1930s, when the crisis appeared limited to the Depression. But no longer. In any case, no prewar liberal and radical could be trusted. As to postwar America, New Leftists recalled that the original commitment in Southeast Asia had been made by a main-line liberal, Harry Truman, and escalated by another, John Kennedy; and the men who engineered that conflict

(McGeorge Bundy, Robert McNamara, Dean Rusk, Dean Acheson, etc.) were all liberals, Democrat or Republican as the case might be.

The New Left did endorse some classic liberal goals as well as an issues-oriented perspective. But it had contempt for what was thought to be the cant of liberalism, was estranged from civil rights and trade-union moderates when they endorsed Lyndon Johnson's candidacy in 1964 and asked, to the vast discomfort of Democratic liberals, "How can we continue to sack the ports of Asia and still dream of Jesus?" New Leftists were ready to condemn American actions in Vietnam without voicing comparable imprecations against repression by Hanoi, a prerequisite for holding unimpeachable liberal and anti-Communist credentials in these years. Both powers were equally culpable, Movement leaders thought, a conclusion violating historic guidelines for both Communists and anti-Communists. The Port Huron statement, for example, was typically evenhanded in assessing the failure to promulgate a nuclear test-ban treaty: "Our paranoia about the Soviet Union has made us incapable of achieving agreements absolutely necessary for disarmament and the preservation of peace. We are hardly able to see the possibility that the Soviet Union, though not 'peace loving,' may be seriously interested in disarmament."

Subsequent New Left tracts made much of the sins of "corporate liberalism," and it became a major theoretical construct of SDS'ers. It was responsible for such reprehensible facts as segregation in the South, for social welfare programs which were at best palliatives, for the effort to subvert Cuba's revolution, for the slow escalation of war in Vietnam. SDS arraigned Adlai Stevenson, a liberal darling, for his bald lies at the time of the Bay of Pigs. *Studies on the Left*, perhaps the earliest theoretical journal of the Movement, first appeared in 1959 and three years later was assailing the Kennedy liberals and the CIA in the same breath: one failed to "recognize the nature of anticolonial revolutions," and the other sought to subvert them. Liberals and New Leftists, of course, appealed largely to the same constituency, and they went some way down the same road together; witness the civil rights and antiwar movements. Perhaps that is why liberals were the "chief enemy." Because, as Michael Walzer has wisely speculated, SDS was searching for an independent identity.

Though the differences were very substantial, the public understandably failed to discriminate between New and Old Leftists; and the popular view was confirmed by the political rhetoric which scarcely differed quantitatively. They shared the capitalism-cum-war conviction; the cult of the personality; and the factionalism which replaced the Movement's non-ideological beginnings and which eventually consumed it. How different from those early years! The system appeared tenacious. Lenins did not spring up. It required study, application, discipline, consistent work to make them. It was so much simpler for these self-indulgent radicals to take a vow of poverty and work in the ghetto than to wrestle with theory that seemed inapplicable or to engage in the lifetime work of building a revolutionary movement.

It bears repeating that the Movement found trade unions politically assimilated, socially domesticated, intellectually sterile. There was some justification for these opinions. American capitalism had revived and prospered in the postwar decades, and labor swerved away from militancy and its friends in the socialist vanguard, moving toward accommodation to management. Militancy revived in the early 1960s, in opposition to automation, inflation, and undemocratic trade-union practices—that is, militancy directed toward immediate issues. Those who protested, furthermore, did not comprise that impoverished and revolutionary labor force presumably spawned by capitalism. Their experiences did not suggest fundamental changes were possible. Nor did they find such changes desirable. They accepted the inevitable constraints of the existing social-economic structure. They thought, as the Hammonds observed of early English industrial society, "that their society was to be judged solely by its commercial success."

In this way, America's economic system continued to provide its own standards of legitimization and a content-free ideology. These ruling-class standards, an entire complex of ideas and attitudes that indirectly supported and validated the power of the dominant elites, were readily absorbed by the working class. It is worth repeating, then, that workers did not perceive themselves as such. Thus the revolutionary intelligentsia was drawn from the middle class, and these beneficiaries of bourgeois culture were its chief antagonists. Finally, a twofold observation: (1) the labor militancy of the 1960s was spontaneous and the Movement's efforts at best complemented it rather than controlled or shaped it; and (2) the Movement, with its casual sexuality, drugs, and abrasive campus activities, elicited intense hostility from the working class.

That the New Left would in turn abandon the historic pro-labor perspective of the hereditary left is understandable. It shifted from the view of labor as the vehicle of social change to that of youth as the revolutionary class, including the politically powerless minorities. It leveled a threefold charge against labor: it was indifferent to social movements; it was a mainstay of the Cold War and interventionist foreign policy; and it was part of the power structure.

The New Left shifted to the poor and to the university campus, which was, in the words of the Port Huron statement, "an overlooked seat of influence." There was some hidden ambivalence to this view. On the one hand, the university was central to "social change" and an untapped locus of power; on the other, it reflected the society itself and was governed by repressive elites. The latter view, alien to 1930s radicalism, which thought the university a refuge for humanism and social experimentation, made for a murky equation of capitalism and campus; and New Leftists would attempt to bring the university to its knees.

11 Challenge, Confrontation, and Division, 1965-1969

PROFOUND BLACK disaffection and turbulence, especially in the nation's ghettos, was made manifest in a wave of riots that began in August 1965 with arson and looting in Watts, a high-crime and high-unemployment section of Los Angeles. Riots exploded in a score of northern cities in the summers to come. They caused widespread fear, violence, and destruction, and left burnt-out homes, sullen hatred, deserted streets, and social decay. New Leftists, driven by a missionary impulse to improve the conditions of blacks, became involved in campaigns against ghetto poverty and for social justice. They often worked through SNCC, which, as Jack Newfield observed, had grown into the first incipiently revolutionary movement since the IWW. SNCC, by the mid-1960s, was engaged in a moralistic critique of American society. If the New Left's attack on the racist character of the Vietnam conflict spilled over into criticism of the nation's treatment of blacks and Chicanos at home, SNCC's leaders also discerned a connection between events in Vietnam and in Mississippi. In so doing, they did not speak for the black community as a whole, since most blacks did not perceive events at home and abroad as inextricably enmeshed. But, as its chairman, John Lewis, affirmed, SNCC "assumes its right to dissent with United States foreign policy on any issue" and did so on Southeast Asia. His statement prefigured the position of Martin Luther King's non-resistant SCLC and the MFDP. "No Mississippi Negroes," declared the latter, "should be fighting in Vietnam for the White Man's freedom until all the Negro People are free in Mississippi."

New Leftists would soon find themselves unwelcome in the civil rights movement. For blacks, in and out of SNCC, were becoming increasingly militant after the mid-1960s. Thus they began to look to Che Guevara, the Argentine-born guerrilla leader—dark and romantic, with his combat boots and black beret, leading the masses to revolution—or to Malcolm X, the black nationalist who strongly influenced SNCC workers, particularly after his assassination in 1965. In May 1966, SNCC had abandoned many of its former ideals and elected black nationalist Stokely Carmichael as chairman. Out of the ashes of its nonviolent, integrationist past a new SNCC emerged: nationalist, revolutionary, oriented toward the struggles of the Third World.

For a brief time, however, New Leftists, especially SDS'ers, managed to collaborate with SNCC and other blacks in the urban ghettos and won some small victories— welfare funding in Baltimore and garbage collection in Newark, hardly the stuff of revolution. SDS cadres, mostly white, worked out of shabby storefronts in Chicago, Cleveland, Newark, and elsewhere. They sought to establish educational and community projects in the slums. They hoped to organize local power bases—at least until they themselves shifted to campus activism. Their work was marked by tolerance, disavowal of the cult of leadership, the refusal to silence any speaker, insistence that each person had an equal voice in decision making ("participatory democracy"). They lasted about a half dozen years in this grass-roots activism, their minor advances and class perceptions not being sufficient to sustain a lifetime commitment to the slum poor.

Students are not generally disposed to revolutionary militancy. Even those most touched by the malaise and violence of their times are not born-again radicals ready to mount the barricades and shed blood. Only a traumatic event which directly affected their lives, like the 1930s Depression or the military draft of the mid-1960s, could force a significant minority of students into radicalism. Such events came in quick succession in Johnson's administration: the mounting commitment of men and resources funneled into Vietnam at the expense of urgent domestic priorities, the escalating air raids and ground fighting. Then, too, students were confronted with the absurdity of such hallowed formulas as "Communist imperialism" or "Sino-Soviet conspiracy"; the presidential denials that the war would be expanded, followed by new escalations and by conscription of a growing number of youth. The draft, of course, touched them in an immediate way, but all of these measures produced mounting disenchantment, the "credibility gap," and campaigns of resistance—which would block troop trains in Oakland, halt draft board operations, destroy federal property, obstruct recruiting. These actions would lose their remedial purpose, becoming very nearly ends in themselves. Moreover, they would not only deepen antiwar sentiment but also trigger the activism of groups with long-standing grievances which antedated the war itself. Thus did protest against the war spill over into a generalized social ferment.

Overseas events would produce a series of crises at home, and these spanned the whole range of civic obligations—from simple obedience to law to pacifist non-resistance and disobedience. Until 1965 these trends were not obvious. SDS grew slowly, with only about fifty members in 1962, at the time of Port Huron. Until the 1965 March on Washington, it was only one of many ad hoc groups, mostly springing up in response to immediate issues. Until then it fought on southern battlefields and out of these struggles evolved a sense of fraternity. It was destined to become the focal point for the growing antiwar sentiment and resistance to the draft. It would sponsor the campus protests and then the "teach-ins," which began in Ann Arbor, in March 1965, and soon spread across the nation. Johnson's decision to begin systematic bombing of North Vietnam was the catalyst. Until it occurred, the antiwar movement attracted little public notice; with it came the April 1965 Washington demonstration, which was the largest assemblage in our history. Vietnam, then, fueled the protest. There was a growing horror of it, and a departure from the basically reformist outlook of the early 1960s. But even after the Democratic Party nominated Hubert Humphrey in 1968, it was democratic practices rather than democratic goals which many New Leftists were abandoning.

In any case, Johnson's 1965 bombing decisions were the trip hammer. The war now opened a Pandora's box of disturbing issues: the mass destruction of a non-white, non-Protestant culture by a white Protestant one; the blind and excessive reliance on a destructive technology; the economic and political power of the military-industrial complex. It dramatized a score of social evils and unloosed a score of often unrelated demands. It "is only one arm of a two-fisted crisis," declared *The Insurgent,* the Du Bois Clubs' quarterly; it "is matched by the fire in the nation's ghettoes." But the ghetto fires were seasonal dramas, while the war was unceasing. Indeed, the protest movement would have atrophied if not for Vietnam. It alone brought the vaguely liberal students out of their dormitories en masse; and it alone made undergraduates aware of university ties to the military.

Such ties were made more obvious by the presence of campus recruiters for the armed services and for corporations engaged in war production, such as Dow Chemical—which led to riotous confrontations at an increasing number of schools. These developments in turn yielded to the conviction that higher education was part of the larger capitalist structure and led to a reckless indictment of capitalism.

The war—always the war! It became surrogate for all other issues— the symbol of what was wrong with America, of that corporate liberalism and imperialism which would continue after the war ended. Thus those who participated in the 1965 Washington March were not only protesting Vietnam. Some, by this gesture, would tell the world of their opposition to a government which engaged in such actions; some would thus revise the Nuremberg code that every individual is responsible for his actions and his nation's.

Thus the war, spilling over into a generalized indictment of American foreign and domestic affairs, funneled an imprecise anger against society itself. Vietnam became a symbol for cultural alienation, and a diffuse symbol at that—which made it a simple matter for the New Left to absorb and mobilize its varied force of sympathizers. That New Leftists had no ideology also helped. Then, too, the very intensity of antiwar sentiment further contributed to the blurring of critical distinctions among those who sponsored or joined in protest activities.

The Movement's tack to antiwar resistance as a full-time action became evident in mid-1966, after the Selective Service decided upon special standardized examinations for male college students—in order to determine eligibility for the draft. Several schools were the site for sit-ins against the university practice of furnishing draft boards with information about the class standings of male students. New Leftists joined the 1966 election campaigns for local peace candidates. The SDS national convention of that year reflected delegate hostility to such antiwar electoral politics and urged a "return to the campus" as the organizing focal point for what later came to be called "student power." That is, SDS'ers emphasized internal university control and the struggle for power on the college level. They were not, in other words, prepared for even a mild anti-draft program at this time; but the escalating conflict would force a different set of priorities.

Draft resistance before the winter of 1966–67 had been almost entirely an individual matter, and frequently the labor of peace workers alone. Pacifists, of course, were often enfolded within the New Left, participating in efforts to elect "peace candidates" on the Democratic Party ticket, in confrontation politics involving nuclear tests and fallout shelters, and even in the Movement's belief that American intervention abroad was rooted in the structural needs of capitalism. Earlier, in the spring of 1965, a number of veteran pacifists signed a statement in *Liberation* urging those opposed to the war on grounds of conscience to refuse induction. Events of this sort, however, attracted little attention. Draft-card burnings in the summer of 1965 produced the predictable congressional measure declaring them illegal. Finally, in December 1966, anti-draft tactics began to be developed in earnest and the SDS national council called for opposition to conscription, which "in any form is coercive and anti-democratic, and . . . is used by the United States Government to oppress people in the United States and around the world."

The march on the Pentagon in 1967 was the climax to a wide variety of dramatic tactics by New Leftists, all of which riveted national attention upon them. The march became a media event: the sit-downs of pacifists, the attempt by the New York Revolutionary Contingent to force entry, the Cornell University flag on the Pentagon wall, the direct and dramatic face-to-face encounter between middle-class participants and federal troops and marshals. There were two obvious, sometimes overlapping, sometimes distinct sectors involved: the militants walking under the revolutionary banners of the Vietcong, and the short-lived flower children with their carefree mockery of the system. Their styles were different, but the enemy was the same.

The Pentagon confrontation came in the midst of a series of brief and savage encounters between student radicals and campus or state authorities. In mid-October 1967, a Stop-the-Draft week featured symbolic acts of draft refusal and ceremonies at which draft cards were collected, to be handed over to local Justice Department officials or to federal authorities in Washington. At the Oakland Induction Center and elsewhere, campus radicals organized demonstrations which led to beatings and arrests.

These nightmarish scenes reflect the Movement's sweep, its concern for issues unrelated or at best tangentially related to the war. They had a powerful effect upon many relatively unconcerned students on the big state university campuses. They led to a quantum jump in radicalization among those already converted, owing to a growing sense of frustration and betrayal. And, of course, they produced an escalation in police repression. They shifted from implementing participatory democracy to the self-defeating dialectics of revolution, from work within the political process to insurrectionary politics.

These shifts were locked into the escalating war, and fueled a politics which became more dogmatic and more desperate, stoned on rhetoric and increasingly disconnected from reality. The near-unanimous agreement about the need for confrontation politics was encouraged by the doctrinal poverty of the Movement, which left it vulnerable to any tactical emphasis upon individual militancy.

By the mid-1960s, then, the nonviolent populist fraternity was abandoning its liberal critique of war and of society. Beliefs that incremental adjustments, reforms within the established political-economic framework, were sufficient had been eclipsed. The April 1968 march, the largest of its kind, and the rallies and sit-ins that followed, made this period the most explosive in the history of American higher education. Participatory democracy began to lapse, black and Chicano resistance mounted, street fighting broke out in some cities. An "existential commitment to action," a growing disposition to indulge in or exalt acts of violence, was further stimulated by what Gordon Allport has called "the sense of oneness, of belonging" which such acts produce and which "appeases . . . feelings of insecurity, of helplessness, of isolation."

After the 1967 Pentagon march, SNCC, formerly pacifist-oriented, began to cut loose from nonviolence. It talked of "guerrilla war" and of "liberation struggles"—rhetoric which came easier with the death of King and Muste, those twin anchors of restraint and reasonableness. Militant factions appeared in other organizations: e.g., New York's Crazies and Berkeley's Molotov Cocktail Party—described in *New Left Notes* as "a group of anarcho-Communists inspired by Hell's Angels, a cycle club; Herbert Marcuse; the Mother Fuckers of New York; and the peculiar state of war in which they now find themselves." Departing from the naïve idealism of Port Huron, SDS imported revolutionary perspectives from Cuba or China or Vietnam. Thus it canonized legends in their lifetime like Che Guevara, dashing and courageous, the very model of the model guerrilla fighter. It also held aloft Frantz Fanon's *Wretched of the Earth,* which found violence therapeutic and redemptive, as well as Régis Debray's *Revolution,* a technical primer on insurrectionary warfare.

SDS was now the best known and most influential campus-based group, having outdistanced its rivals. M-2-M and Student Peace Union (SPU) had folded. The Du Bois Clubs were breathing their last. YPSL and YSA were barely visible. But SDS had begun to decay. Mississippi summers, ghetto projects, and peaceful picketing of military bases had been replaced by *ressentiment* and desperado tactics.

These tactics were born of bitter lessons. The gap between national pretensions and national practices had widened; the election campaigning had produced no more than the usual choice between Tweedledee and Tweedledum; the egalitarian promises of the national tradition had not been implemented. New Leftists could not halt the escalating conflict. No more than the IWW in Lawrence could they maintain a radical organization beyond the crisis period—as the dominant social values continued to make such organization virtually impossible. The national pledge of integration remained just that, after a decade; the inevitable promise of every candidate that he would bring peace produced only a rising savagery; Presidents violated constitutional politics by waging war without the mandatory congressional declaration; a peace-loving people continued to build the greatest military machine on the planet, permitting it to take precedence over all social priorities.

No wonder, then, the "end of politics," the "holy disobedience" of Christian pacifists, the "call to resist illegitimate authority" which evolved an individual morality of action. No wonder a romantic anarchism appeared, nourished by a strain of nihilism, subjectivism, and anti-intellectualism which was always dormant in American radical thought; and which, Hannah Arendt reminds us, Bolsheviks and Marxists alike never recognized as the way to revolution.

The tactical variables which were advanced reflected emerging internal troubles. Deep divisions began to appear in what was once a more or less unified Movement with generally accepted leadership. The latent conflict ignited in 1966 when PL, the most disciplined Old Left group, dissolved its Trotskyite satellite, M-2-M, and began in semi-secret fashion to infiltrate SDS chapters and to establish a front group, the Worker-Student Alliance (WSA). PL's decision, more than anything else, introduced Old Left slogans and factionalism into SDS. It imported Maoist cadres, haircuts, an anti-drug mentality. It also brought its own incoherent Maoism and its own unreality of proletarian revolution. Saturated with Marxist clichés, PL'ers tried to force this dogma upon the non-ideological SDS and found it relatively easy to fill the existing theoretical vacuum.

Partly for defensive reasons and partly driven by events, SDS went looking for revolutionary positions and prophets. Such trends produced increasingly intense doctrinal hairsplitting and Marxicology, and began to tear apart New Left groups, much as it had done to Depression radicalism. And much as in the 1930s, the same hopeful mood appeared—only it was now measured by a Vietcong ambush and a Detroit riot—and these were harbingers of the inevitable revolution.

Thus SDS'ers took a distinctly sectarian turn, repudiated their earlier mission of being a mass student body, and abandoned their natural constituency. They had been shut out of community organizing and civil rights by growing black nationalism and machismo as well as by their failure to build alternative political structures that would compete with existing political parties. Their varied components had varied loyalties. They identified with labor if professed Old Left Marxists, with Third World revolutionaries if violence-addicted extremists, with minorities if Black Panthers. The Du Bois Clubs were pulled in contrary directions—toward SDS and toward black militants. The disciplined PL'ers wanted to remain close to the proletariat and thought in terms of a revolutionary labor force—the fantasy of youthful radicals through much of the century. The Black Panthers, broadening the theoretical underpinnings of their party, became a "Marxist-Leninist" group, which provided a doctrinal framework for nationalism. Thus SDS acquired the familiar symptoms of organizational exhaustion—sectarianism, isolation, dogmatism, elitism. Each splinter identified with one or another "true" revolutionary sector—industrial workers, culture radicals, Third World revolutionaries, ghetto blacks. And with this trend went whatever hope remained for an effective organized left.

When the SNCC-influenced Mississippi Freedom Democratic Party, then seeking to unseat the state's segregationist delegation, was rebuffed at the 1964 Democratic Convention, cynicism about politics mounted among student militants, especially among blacks. The painfully slow progress of southern registration drives also contributed to disenchantment. Then came that most predictable of events: the white summer soldiers returned to the comparative safety of northern campuses. Natural enough, since white student militancy was always seasonal: education in the fall, demonstrations in the spring, activism in the summer, particularly when the summers were jobless. But such a rhythm had expected consequences. Black nonviolent tacticians were compromised. The rapid rise of the Black Panthers and SNCC's break with its white radical allies as well as with liberal respectability ensued. CORE endorsed a "Black Power" orientation, and SNCC's Carmichael affirmed that blacks would go their own way, build their own institutions, serve their own needs and interests. Thus did the ghetto black–New Left coalition break apart, an event that would prove disastrous for the Movement. It ended the hope that a new revolutionary tandem was about to take the stage of history.

SDS disintegration was well advanced by the time of the June 1968 East Lansing convention, where Black Panther leader Bobby Seale presented his party's ultimatum—any coalition with the Panthers had to exclude PL—and where delegates voiced strong anarchist sentiments. Shortly thereafter, the National Office Collective, as SDS leadership was then known, began to formulate a program which could compete successfully with PL, then making substantial gains among SDS'ers. In this effort to compete, and to block PL's take-over of SDS, Mike Klonsky, SDS national secretary, wrote "Toward a Revolutionary Youth Movement" (RYM). "The main task," it declared, "is to begin moving beyond the limitations of struggle placed on the student movement."

Inspired by France's general strike of students and workers in 1968, RYM now also emphasized such a collaboration, finding the past emphasis upon students in isolation had been too narrow. Black youth, black labor in particular, was central to this shift in SDS thinking. RYM would embrace the Black Panthers as "the vanguard force," and recognized "the dialectical relationship between the liberation of the black colony and socialist revolution for the whole society."

By 1969, PL had emerged as a major force in SDS, comprising two fifths of the delegates to the national convention of that year, and it mounted a clear challenge for organizational control. But PL'ers hurt their cause by condemning youth culture and "student power." Strongly opposed to nationalist movements of every kind, they also attacked Cuba, Castro, Guevara, North Vietnam, women's liberation, and black nationalism—specifically black students and the Black Panthers—as reactionary. The Panthers, charged PL, were bourgeois nationalists and opposed to proletarian "internationalism."

Delegate feuding broke out into open conflict on the convention floor. Slogan-chanting PL members cried out, "Mao, Mao," and the newly formed RYM grimly responded, "Ho, Ho, Ho Chi Minh." And watching in the wings were the Panthers, especially those from Chicago, who were close to the National Office faction of Klonsky and Bernardine Dohrn, SDS organizational secretary. This configuration of Panthers and revolutionary youth—the insurrection's shock troops—together with followers of the Third World, distinguished RYM from PL, with many SDS members supporting RYM as the instrument which might eliminate PL.

The inevitable division occurred. The anti-PL forces walked out, reassembled nearby, and proceeded thereafter as if they had expelled PL. Mark Rudd was elected national secretary. When both meetings adjourned, the public learned there were now two SDS groups and no

SDS at all. Certainly neither organization resembled the original, whose end came with bewildering suddenness. And with it, as Lynd sorrowfully observed, something was gone—that "shared commitment to certain ways of behaving toward each other and toward all human beings."

The Weatherman bureau then moved into the Chicago national office, forged a political collective, and perceived itself as a suicide squad providing cover for black urban terrorists, the "true" revolutionary vanguard. They assigned the leadership role to black labor, and proposed "two, three, many John Browns." But the Panthers refused to follow this script. Under murderous attack by city police departments, they sought united defense efforts rather than guerrilla violence. Weathermen and RYM then went it alone and in so doing slipped the traces of a revolutionary politics, with the repudiation of both white labor and white student militants indicating as much.

Thus another rite of radical passage began. The rhetoric of civil disobedience was now forgotten, drowned by the rhetoric of revolution—with isolation, political marginality, and intensified feelings of alienation resulting. SDS had its pyrrhic victory and PL achieved nominal control. Klonsky's RYM II bloc, which was conventionally left of center, adopted a number of PL proposals. It sought recruits in working-class districts, ridiculed "student power," criticized Black Power as bourgeois nationalism, reduced New Left theory to a vulgar Marxism, and claimed to be the only SDS. There were other spin-offs, a further splintering that marked a final stage in the organizational disarray and dissolution of the New Left.

The Weathermen's attempts to escalate the confrontation would complete the demolition. The nation, they were convinced, had become a Fascist state, a racist one with a ceaselessly imperial appetite. Soured by the failed dream of a popular revolutionary movement, embittered by the Panthers' refusal to correspond to their image, they shifted to a politics of *frisson*. Armed struggle alone, they believed, would raise labor's "revolutionary consciousness." Their elite radicalism, their belief in themselves as the insurrectionary vanguard, shaped the ultimate conclusion: a frenzied overreach of protest which took the form of terrorism, a deliberate assault on persons and property, beginning with the October 1969 "Days of Rage." Now a Red Army, a vanguard of shock troops standing alone, the Weathermen settled for street bravura, which they dignified as "armed struggle." Theirs was the fantasy of victory in hand-to-hand combat. They thus severed all connection with daily life, sacrificing everything for a revolutionary totality. In this way, the politics of radical faction was transformed into fantasies of violence, of impossible revolution, and of cleansing redemption; and thus, as Peter Clecak observes, "the tragic rhythm of American radicalism" had been re-enacted within a decade.

12 The Radical Scene in the Seventies

BY 1970, in reaction to the pathology of violence, there was a growing trend away from extremism, a mounting disillusionment within the radical remnant. To be sure, the elite militants and the fierce factionalism within the tiny sects continued. Some romantic anarchists would accidentally blow themselves up with homemade bombs. Other SDS stragglers organized the National Labor Committee and the International Socialists, both of which were soon divided into two hostile camps. Completing the picture, there were the major Trotskyite groups, the SLP and YSA, and a host of dissident sects like Spartacus and Youth Against War and Fascism.

The Cambodian invasion, the My Lai massacre, and the Kent State shootings in the spring of 1970 produced a final radical gasp. But it was now the moderate, politically middle students who were stunned and who joined those already radicalized in the largest student demonstrations ever held in the United States. Even then, however, it could not be claimed that most students were truly alienated and, indeed, polls indicated that only 4 percent "considered themselves to be members of the radical left." Such figures, moreover, confirmed the general movement away from ultraism and even from sweeping social change. If many political moderates now perceived their nation as the

New Left did, they nonetheless rebuffed political extremism and turned to electoral activity—in the belief that they might change things through the use of the customary political machinery. Thus they responded in traditional social-democratic terms—much as their predecessors in the New Left had done when, some years back, radicals sought to promote economic and social gains for the urban poor within the usual channels, though their efforts had often been blocked by the pressure of local political-economic interests; or when they joined the McCarthy campaign and worked for George McGovern in 1972.

Thus radicals turned back to the democratic polity and norms. They committed the familiar resources of energy and idealism, but they were not pushed over the brink—into holistic dreams of sweeping change. Rather, their critique of national policies and priorities proved undogmatic. By the fall of 1970, campus protest had clearly waned and "the focus . . . switched . . . from antiwar demonstrations to demands for minority recognition."

Most students in the 1970s, like most youth, had not been scarred by the New Left and its wars. They were politically passive, socially conservative, morally conventional, largely preoccupied with private pursuits. Still others, being isolated and demoralized, lost the old headlong passion and vital sense of involvement and simply dropped out. But the New Left nonetheless left its mark. Buoyed by evangelical, even apocalyptic, expectations, it had been a gathering of forces, a coming together of styles of discontent, a genuine social movement which expressed fundamental grievances—even when it tried for immediate ends within customary channels and defined political issues in personal terms.

That the Movement died was inevitable. The reasons for its end are less apparent and highly complex, a mix that is generic to radical failures after 1900. And we may claim continuities even while recognizing that specific historical factors are partly responsible—the antiwar movement, after all, was a function of a specific and unique event in our history.

The war brought prominence and power to the Movement. It was the primary passion, providing the glue which bound abrasive elements. Moreover, Vietnam provided the common denominator, even a set of common grievances against society, and, with its end, each element—e.g., women and blacks—lapsed into the usual pluralistic pattern of pressure-group action on behalf of its own limited constituency. Paradoxically, then, the war which cemented discrete segments was the Movement's undoing. The changed historical situation contributed to radical loss and disintegration. For when Nixon, under enormous pressure, ended the draft and began withdrawing American forces from Vietnam, he defused public concern and irreparably damaged the Movement.

The Movement's inability to develop a new radical theory beyond liberalism left it deeply flawed. For it meant that the United States produced no Gramsci, Lukács, Lenin, Luxemburg, no theoreticians who might go beyond the contributions of Marx over a century ago, no school of social analysis comparable to the Frankfurt group of Marxists today. It meant, too, that gesture and rhetoric would replace good, tough theoretical system building. It virtually guaranteed that radicals would end up reinforcing the business civilization they proposed to change. It also assured that when the overseas conflict ground to a halt, the New Left would lose its *raison d'être*.

The war heightened domestic social tensions but could not be the basis for a viable revolutionary movement. For that a sustained theoretical overview was needed. None developed—which partly explains the New Left's abrupt departure from the scene. It also helps us understand why a decade of militancy and social turbulence has left virtually no institutional remnants, no ongoing parties, no nationally recognized radical cadres or leadership, no established formulas, as Walzer concludes, by which one can keep on being radical.

Political protest of the early 1960s, which had been directed by the blacks or the New Left, shifted after 1966, when important black groups and sectors excluded whites from participation and adopted disciplined organizational forms incompatible with the spontaneous protest that had brought them numbers and visibility. Then, too, the antiwar movement was gradually taken over by the Old Left, which had different goals and more rigid practices than earlier activists.

In sum, the New Left never possessed what George Vickers has called "historical self-consciousness" which would provide theoretical coherence. It failed to supply the normative framework which would encourage workers to understand their society and provide a durable mass base. Spawned by the most highly educated and most privileged sectors of society, New Leftists distinguished themselves both from capitalists and from the proletariat. They confused their own protest and interests with those of the blacks and the unskilled; and they confused their desire "to rationalize social relationships *within* a system of structured social inequality," as Vickers shrewdly observes, with the truly radical desire to abolish social inequality—which would mean abolition of the very structures which shaped their desire.

There are other factors to consider in explaining this latest failure of the left. First, the very encounter with American politics was a bruising if not fatal one. For the political system again demonstrated its immense flexibility. Assimilative in function, adapted to gradualism, it easily reincorporated groups which had moved out of it. For such disaffected, a non-ideological *Realpolitik* governed, which meant devising tactics that would preserve their ideals and yet respect fixed political and cultural guidelines. Specifically, it meant boring from within trade unions and the Democratic Party. Thus radicals, as in the interwar years, could not be insensitive to immediate human needs. They permitted narrowly reformist activity to take priority over any doctrinal perspective, thereby serving the purposes of liberal capitalism. Explicitly socialist groups, not serving their socialist integrity, became left-liberal and populist, pragmatic and non-ideological— which is itself an ideology and not simply an automatic response to structural constraints. The New American Movement (NAM) is an obvious example. It seeks to mobilize the female work force, but it has shallow roots in the labor movement. As such, it resembles the new populists who, with their media groups and resource centers, are of mounting influence in community and consumer affairs. Both the NAM and the multi-organizational populists are engaged in struggles on the local and state level that involve a wide range of immediate issues—from housing repairs to bank loans for slum dwellers to lower taxes and insurance rates.

The NAM, unlike the new populists, explicitly seeks to build a mass movement for radical social transformation, but it has largely lost sight of the initial socialist objectives. Those organizations which have not, which have refused to engage in accommodation, have gone the predictable way of elitism and sectarian isolation. Witness, for instance, the Communist Party—about 8,000 members in the 1970s—with Gus Hall, the Party chief, fantasying that his 1976 presidential campaign was a "great break through" and "left an enormous impact on the electorate." The CP coupled such distortion of the political realities—itself the inevitable product of closed cells—with a primitive Marxism, with the recurrent claim that capitalism is in crisis, and with an opportunistic call for the thirty-hour week as the solution. Lacking the sweep of the Popular Front of the 1930s, the CP's recent versions—like the National Anti-Imperialist Movement in Solidarity with African Liberation or the Trade Unionists for Action and Democracy—began as large conferences and concluded as clique-like Party-staffed organizations.

Then there is the minuscule U.S. Communist Party (Marxist-Leninist), formerly the October League. One of a number of tiny underground cabals that have littered the history of America's left, it is distinguished only by a religious devotion to the Chinese Communist Party, unlike the CP, which proclaimed in 1975 that "Maoism is opportunism on the level of betrayal." None of these radical sects have surfaced into the popular consciousness, except when they have engaged in acts of political terrorism: e.g., the bombings of the Armed Forces of Puerto Rican National Liberation (FALN) or those of the New World Liberation Front on the West Coast. The NAM is not, true enough, an underground group, but, secret or not, its impact on the nation is about the same.

Still another fact merits a final mention: working-class indifference or hostility to the New Left, indeed to radicalism generally. In explaining the reasons for the Movement's disappearance, it bears repeating that radicals were deprived of what was always thought the essential revolutionary base. America's union bureaucrats enjoyed the sun at Miami Beach, and making capitalism work more efficiently governed their strategic vision. Much like Gompers then and George Meany today, they believed in a fundamental identity of interests between business and labor, and endorsed goals of liberal capitalism: anti-Communism, social welfare, democratic practices; and both worried over workplace insurgency. Nor did it cease in the 1960s. Rather, labor's resistance to management practices intensified. Usually it took the form of controlling the pace of work, combating unsafe labor conditions, establishing production-output quotas, organizing slowdowns, evading speedups, sabotaging machinery, and comparable forms of resistance, rather than direct confrontation with corporate power. But such tactics, such fitful working-class dissidence, should not suggest revolutionary restlessness. Labor was not even nominally socialist. It lacked the insurrectionary voice which, given the opportunity, would—like E. P. Thompson's yeomanry or Richard Cobb's artisans of pre-revolutionary Paris—prompt rebellion. True enough, its most depressed elements, such as farm workers and coal miners, did have a real sense of class identity, but class antagonisms were only infrequently expressed and they were articulated, as Gramsci noted, "within the existing fundamental structure." Hence even those elements within the labor movement which had a sense of their identity were contained. Their goals were mediated and formulated—to some extent reformulated, adapted to their situation—by the dominant class ideology and its complex network of values and institutions.

Labor's tactics, to be sure, indicated a declining respect for the work ethic, which reflected a comparable decline in society at large. But this did not produce class solidarity or a challenge to the dominant social ethic. It failed to threaten a value system which measured class divisions primarily in terms of income and material possessions. By the 1960s, there were obvious changes in the occupational structure of American capitalism—with the sharp growth of white-collar and service workers as well as the rise of a "new middle class" of salaried wage earners—unlike an "old middle class" of self-employed small entrepreneurs. But the changes in class structure reflected the growth, not the breakdown, of capitalist economic organization. These changes possibly rendered some dominant cultural forms obsolete, but the interaction between structure and consciousness was uninterrupted. Consequently, middle-class ideology, while undergoing adjustments, remained relatively stable. It still transmuted labor's values, consciousness, and institutions. The result: the self-legitimizing capacity of industrial capitalism went on apace and radicals over the last decade became more isolated from the work force than at any other time in our history.

Thus the Movement came to an end, though in some ways its consequences have never wholly disappeared. Marxism, for instance, experienced a modest revival after being dormant for at least a generation. It reappeared in the social sciences, as Warren Susman has noted, but it took on a new form. No longer a test of political orthodoxy, Marxism is studied for its relevance to American society or as a legitimate academic exercise. And in one of the twists of history, those who study it are frequently the very New Leftists who had once eschewed theory.

This is not to suggest that all former New Leftists turned to a serious study of Marxist thought. Most settled for liberalism—which meant the old drift toward the left, the party of humanity and generosity, the durable enemy of ignorance and injustice. They remained obstinately, if quietly, reformist. Many simply settled for the retention of private doubts about the government, internalizing their cynicism and dissent. They continued to be repelled by its manipulative and repressive character, and to find it less credible and "obeyable" than ever. No less than 79 percent believed that American foreign policy was governed by economic interests, and 94 percent charged that business was too concerned with profits and too indifferent to public responsibility. In this sense the Movement also left its mark. It contributed a legacy of cultural opposition. It created a substantial body of young men and women who could no longer clearly identify our "enemies" abroad, who had their doubts about capitalism, and who, when Watergate became part of the amalgam, helped produce a crisis in legitimacy shared by many non-radicals as well.

The veterans of the early radical campaigns are not terribly interested in renewing the political contests, in undertaking the hard work necessary to build institutional bases. They now seek careers and assured incomes, but they have also retained the earlier premises about money, competition, sexual openness. As novitiates in the law, medicine, social work, education, they are caught between personal ambitions and the social implications of these ambitions. They take on jobs, join institutions, begin families, assume positions of authority, but still have reservations about these matters and remain stubbornly loyal to the new departures in family structure, child rearing, the meaning of work, sexual relations, which the 1960s generated.

So this earlier decade transmitted a wide-ranging spirit of inquiry, nourished a tradition of cultural insurgency that did not suddenly expire. There were the religious cults devoted to personal salvation or charismatic expression. There were the continuing articulation of black identity, the Indians' growing sense of their history, the effort to build women's consciousness, the new journals focusing on drugs, music, sexual behavior—in lieu of political interests. And gradually these cultural features became for many transmuted substitutes for the old political enthusiasms.

But the drugs, music, and sexual openness of the 1970s were no longer part of the highly visible counterculture of the Movement. Rather than being "counter"—part of Raymond Williams' "oppositional culture"—they were absorbed into the residual culture. The government provided token support for women and blacks in the national political and economic life, gave verbal fealty to ecology, closed its eyes to homosexuality and marijuana—and hence made for a more smoothly functioning and better integrated society.

The new populism is a case in point. Evolving out of the social turbulence of the 1960s, it had an anti-corporate bias but was far more concerned with "bread and butter" issues than with explicit ideology. It would not, unlike Marxism, seek a social transformation or depend upon the working class as the agent of change. Rather, it would defend the democratic system against corporate depredations, expose bureaucratic muddles, and appeal to the "citizenry" at large, much as populists have always done. It displayed little more than an unfocused suspicion of great power—whether in public or private hands—and would balance private interests against countervailing public power, thereby demonstrating a hostility to privilege that has been deeply engrained in the nation's past. It had no other options. It is, at this time, engaged in only a piecemeal attack on the business-government alliance, one that is largely localist in orientation.

Some of these observations apply to the minority groups which emerged in the late 1960s and found their voice in the early 1970s. The black movement, for instance, took a separatist cultural form and pre-capitalist emphasis—with its Afro hairstyles and "black is beautiful" slogans—but simply sought its share of the capitalist pie. The claims of the blacks, like those of the new populists and the feminists, like those of virtually all marginal and excluded groups, have been easily accommodated by the system.

The women's movement had its beginnings in the late 1960s, given impetus in part by the women's caucuses in SDS, but it rapidly developed into an autonomous crusade to end the systematic oppression of all women. Recognizing that all women were oppressed, the feminist movement mushroomed out of its radical matrix and developed separate issues and organizations. That it split off from traditional radicalism, Weinstein notes, was due to a number of factors: the socially conservative character of most segments of the left, which would do no more than imitate Old Left views of revolution and insist upon the primacy of the working class. But the social base of the feminist movement remained among college-educated and professional women, without deep roots among blacks or working-class women. Like the New Left from which it issued, women's lib had an anti-intellectual animus and has thus far failed to develop a political theory adequate to bona fide radicalism. Hence it became easy for feminists to target men as the primary enemy, to focus upon entry into the male world, rather than consider transforming the social relations and political economy of that world, rather than analyze women's oppression within the context of advanced capitalism. The women's movement has also suffered from as much divisiveness as the Old Left, the New Left, and the black movement. Its one stable national movement—the National Organization of Women (NOW)—is no more than a lobbying group within the existing political institutions, state and federal legislatures as well as the Democratic Party. It would work for liberal reforms— like equal pay, equal opportunity, elimination of job discrimination and of inequitable representation for women in politics and business. Another feminist sector is outside of politics altogether. Deriving from the consciousness-raising and support groups of the first years, it seeks alternative styles in family life and child rearing and, as Weinstein notes, is "largely anti-male, and radical Lesbianism in its ultimate form of expression." A small segment, lacking an organizational voice, has a socialist-feminist viewpoint. It is concerned with "private" relations but understands them to be determined by the prevailing cultural values and class structure.

In effect, minority groups sought legitimacy within the residual culture. By their tendency to separatism, they would unintentionally divide socio-cultural opposition to the existing attitudes and institutions.

They are all, like the New Left, lacking in a coherent theory, and they have a taste for patient and pedestrian strategies unknown to the radicalism of the late 1960s. Certainly, however socialism is defined, none of these new movements and trends may be subsumed under its rubric, though they are suggestive of the continuity of American radicalism, as well as the variables in its expression. All of these post-1960s groups and movements were also manifestations of a changing capitalism and its cultural values. Virtually all would merely mitigate one or another evil existing under capitalism. Such was frequently the way of a failed American radicalism.

What has been said at the outset of this study bears repeating: one must be careful about the assumption hidden in these observations, for it cannot be concluded that, had organized radicals acted differently in the 1960s and 1970s, or in the interwar years for that matter, their story or America's future would have been qualitatively altered. It is a mistake to assume that had factionalism not existed—that had Los Angeles Communists not formed the all-black Che-Lumumba Club, which deeply divided a Party membership, that had Berkeley's YSA (the SWP student affiliate) not formally recognized the right of dissident opinion, thereby evoking SWP cries of heresy—socialism would have succeeded. Whether or not radical organizations became sterile sects, descended into irrelevance, engaged in "Mecca watching," deteriorated into bureaucratic rigidity—whether or not they became basically reformist or still voiced the opinions of Lenin and looked forward to the Götterdämmerung—it is doubtful that a durable socialist consciousness could have developed.

Radicals have ever been caught in the dilemma created by concrete historical conditions and by the nature of capitalism—by the facts of a vaunted occupational mobility; by the celebrated, if partly mythic, fluidity of class structure; by the absence of a feudal tradition; by the flexibility of the political process, the capacity of the two-party system to accommodate and absorb radicals and radical issues; by the popularly held conviction of a democratic and egalitarian ethos, which, as Hillquit observed, was "another check to the progress of the socialist movement in America." These factors suggested, for Gramsci, an "Americanism" which was a distinct ideological alternative to socialism. Laslett, agreeing with him and elaborating, concludes that in the

United States "the ideals of bourgeois civilization—individualism, the sanctity of private property, antipathy toward state interference in the economy, as well as a whole host of other factors—have become diffused throughout society in all its institutional and private manifestations, informing with its spirit all taste, morality, customs, religions and political principles." Marcuse would add the media, growing leisure, relative affluence as more recent phenomena that produced the "spontaneous" consent of the masses in capitalism. Then, too, there were two world wars and the spoils of imperialism which benefited favored sectors of the labor force. Thus a large mix of economic, political, social, and ideological factors shaped a non-revolutionary society and militated against a sustained socialist tradition in the United States. There is every reason to believe that these factors, which have always presented a critical problem for America's socialists and for an effective radical movement, are still operative.

Acronyms in the Text

ADA	Americans for Democratic Action
AFL	American Federation of Labor
AFSC	American Friends Service Committee
ALP	American Labor Party
ASU	American Student Union
AUAM	American Union Against Militarism
AWU	Auto Workers Union
AYC	American Youth Congress
CCC	Civilian Conservation Corps
CIO	Congress of Industrial Organizations
CLP	Communist Labor Party
CNVDA	Committee for Nonviolent Direct Action
CORE	Congress of Racial Equality
CP	Communist Party
CPA	Communist Political Association
CPPA	Conference for Progressive Political Action
EPF	Emergency Peace Federation
EPIC	End Poverty in California
FALN	Armed Forces of Puerto Rican National Liberation
FOR	Fellowship of Reconciliation
FSM	Free Speech Movement
ILD	International Labor Defense
ILGWU	International Ladies' Garment Workers' Union
ISL	Independent Socialist League
ISS	Intercollegiate Socialist Society
IWW	Industrial Workers of the World
KAOW	Keep America Out of War
LID	League for Industrial Democracy
LIPA	League for Independent Political Action
LYL	Labor Youth League
MFDP	Mississippi Freedom Democratic Party
M-2-M	May 2nd Movement
NAACP	National Association for the Advancement of Colored People

229

NAM	New American Movement
NCF	National Civic Federation
NEC	National Executive Committee
NNC	National Negro Congress
NOW	National Organization of Women
NPL	Non-Partisan League
NRA	National Recovery Administration
NSL	National Student League
PL	Progressive Labor
PWA	Public Works Administration
ROTC	Reserve Officers' Training Corps
RYM	Revolutionary Youth Movement
SCLC	Southern Christian Leadership Conference
SDF	Social Democratic Federation
SDP	Social Democratic Party
SDS	Students for a Democratic Society
SLID	Student League for Industrial Democracy
SLP	Socialist Labor Party
SNCC	Student Nonviolent Coordinating Committee
SP(A)	Socialist Party (of America)
SPU	Student Peace Union
STLA	Socialist Trade and Labor Alliance
SWOC	Steel Workers Organizing Committee
SWP	Socialist Workers Party
TTP	Turn Toward Peace
TUEL	Trade Union Educational League
TUUL	Trade Union Unity League
UAW	United Auto Workers
UCP	United Communist Party
UMW	United Mine Workers
VDC	Vietnam Day Committee
WILPF	Women's International League for Peace and Freedom
WP	Workers Party
WPA	Works Progress Administration
WPP	Women's Peace Party
WRL	War Resisters League
WSA	Worker-Student Alliance
YCL	Young Communist League
YPSL	Young People's Socialist League
YSA	Young Socialist Alliance

Bibliography

THERE IS no major comprehensive study of the failure of American socialism, none at least that provides a major overview of radicalism from 1900 to the present. True enough, Werner Sombart's inquiry *Why Is There No Socialism in the United States?* was hardly the first on the subject and will surely not be the last. Numerous books and articles have examined the greater success of socialism abroad and the invariably unfavorable public response in the United States. But most academic studies, though useful, are usually too narrow in approach.

An indispensable overview of American socialism itself is provided by the two-volume *Socialism and American Life* (Princeton, 1952), edited by Stow Persons and Donald Drew Egbert. The centerpiece is Daniel Bell's "The Background and Development of Marxian Socialism in the United States," which was subsequently published separately as *Marxian Socialism in the United States* (Princeton, 1967). Factually impressive and highly influential, Bell's work includes some crude categories, albeit elegantly expressed, and a number of dubious generalizations. One of them, for instance, is his emphasis upon "political messianism"—the "not of this world" axiom—as if the Party's unreality were comprehensive, consistent, or sustained throughout its history. Moreover, as Arthur Schlesinger has observed (*The New Leader*, November 7, 1952, p. 21), overseas socialists had much the same difficulty and orientation and yet were more successful politically. Bell's stress on the ideological rigidity of the Party, moreover, compels him to ignore the reformist wing. Volume II of *Socialism and American Life* is devoted completely to bibliography and, while now dated, it is the standard bibliographical source, an absolutely essential reference work for the study of American radical thought. Ira Kipnis, *The American Socialist Movement, 1897–1913* (also published in 1952, by Columbia University Press), is an important study of the socialist movement, one of a number which conclude that both Party membership and propaganda were too middle-class. It provides the reader with a running account of the schismatic factionalism within the SP down to 1912. Kipnis has been rightly criticized for his arbitrary "left" and "right" labels and for not probing the internal dynamics of Party life. His argument that the SP would have been more successful had it been more "militant" is unconvincing, given the nature of the American working class and structural and cultural facts of life. His study is supplemented by Howard Quint's *The Forging of American Socialism* (Columbia, S.C., 1953), a monograph that is especially valuable for its recognition of grass-roots elements in early American socialism—the Nationalist movement of Edward Bellamy and the Christian Socialists, for instance—since these are customarily neglected. David Shannon's *The Socialist Party of America* (New York, 1955) is a carefully detailed account of the Party's history, but written from a conventional viewpoint. Hence, while concluding that the SP was "just like" the major political parties, it neglects the importance of working-class culture, structural forces, consensual middle-class ideology, social status aspirations—that is, those questions which political sociologists and social historians have recently been asking. Like Bell, Shannon attributes SP decline after 1912 to the expulsion of Haywood and the syndicalist left, to Wilsonian reforms, and to government repression. James Weinstein, however, in *The Decline of Socialism in America, 1912–1925* (New York, 1967), rejects this view; and unlike Bell and Kipnis as well, he concludes that the Party actually grew in strength in 1917 and 1918. Nor was it destroyed by its right-wing leadership, as Kipnis alleged; nor by Haywood's removal from the National Executive Committee of the SP or by wartime illiberalism. His painstaking scholarship has forced scholars to re-evaluate the 1912–19 period; and one of those who has, and who takes a middle ground—the Party slipped sharply after 1912 but still contained reserves of strength—is Michael Bassett, in "The Socialist Party of America, 1912–1919, Years of Decline" (Ph.D. dissertation, Duke University, 1963).

Frank Warren's *An Alternative Vision: The Socialist Party in the 1930s* (Bloomington, Ind., 1974) carries the socialist narrative into the 1930s and is a defense of the Party's tactical position. Disagreeing with Bell and Bernard Johnpoll as well—with those who have characterized Norman Thomas as "utopian," "impractical," "doctrinaire"—Warren argues that Thomas was a realist who steered a correct course in insisting upon the struggle for union democracy and industrial unionism. Warren examines Bell's claim that the SP would have been more successful if it had been less radical and doctrinaire, and concludes that this would have meant abandoning socialism altogether. Finally, he concludes, fear of government repression justified SP opposition to America's entry into World War II. Warren, unfortunately, is one-sided in his claim that the Party sustained an unequivocally radical and utopian vision in this prewar decade. Nonetheless, the book is an improvement over his earlier *Liberals and Communism* (Bloomington, Indiana, 1966), a study which demonstrates Warren's failure to understand 1930s radicalism. Alfred Kazin's *A Walker in the City* (New York, 1951) conveys a much better "feel" for these years. So, for that matter, do Rita Simon's *As We Saw the Thirties* (Urbana, Ill., 1967), especially the vignettes rendered by Hal Draper, Max Schachtman, Granville Hicks, and Earl Browder; and Murray Kempton's *Part of Our Time* (New York, 1955). For a detailed account of Party organization, tactics, rifts, and the like, one should consult William Seyler's "The Rise and Decline of the Socialist Party of the United States" (Ph.D. dissertation, Duke University, 1952), which makes good use of the Duke University collection on the SP and which is useful for its careful presentation of the Party's internal affairs.

Unlike his study of the Socialist Party, which avoids virtually all theoretical questions, Shannon's *Decline of American Communism* (New York, 1959) acknowledges the embourgeoisement of American labor. To be sure, he accounts for it in wholly economic terms and attributes labor's non-revolutionary impulses to trade unions, health insurance, and relative economic prosperity. He neglects to tell the reader very much about the Communist Party in the 1930s, which makes Joseph Starobin's *American Communism in Crisis, 1943–1957* (Cambridge, 1972) useful and complementary. Relying on sources largely unavailable to Shannon, Starobin is most helpful in tracing the postwar policies of the CP, from its roots in the interwar years and its early infatuation with the Bolshevik model. Spanning the same post-1945 period as Shannon, he explores in much more thorough fashion the theoretical dispute between Foster and Browder, Duclos and the CP. Nor does he neglect the Wallace movement and post-Wallace developments, such as the virtual underground status of the Party in the 1950s. Starobin's book is valuable, too, for capturing the Party's inner life and world view in these years. Perceiving the CP's collapse as a result of seeking to operate a nationalist strategy at home while paying obeisance to Russia abroad, he thus explores issues which are at once topical and timeless. A most useful companion volume, though largely valuable for its detailed coverage of earlier decades, is Lewis Coser and Irving Howe's *The American Communist Party* (New York, 1962). Their book surveys the entire history of the CP. Though not dependent on primary sources, it presents a syncretic view not offered by any other study of Communism and possesses panache, stylistic grace, and theoretical boldness. The most authoritative study of the emergent years of American Communism may be found in Theodore Draper's *Roots of American Communism* (New York, 1957), which meticulously unravels the tangled skein of factionalism and organizational chaos.

Less specialized than the above books, since it surveys the most significant radical groups and movements, is John Diggins, *The American Left in the Twentieth Century* (New York, 1973). Diggins writes easily and forcefully, with a gift for portraiture that is impressive. He maintains a level of analysis that is rich and thoughtful, well above most of the studies which he synthesizes, and his short work is deceptively simple and occasionally brilliant. The more regrettable, then, that Diggins feels obliged to defend New Deal liberalism and that he fails to examine the permanent Cold War economy and its impact upon labor and radicalism as well as the New Left's counterculture with any degree of completeness. His book, nevertheless, is a first-rate introduction to the American left for student and novitiate alike. More significant perhaps is James Weinstein's *Ambiguous Legacy: The Left in American Politics* (New York, 1975), since it most nearly approximates our need for a structural overview, including the nature of the work force and the two-party system, which explains radicalism and its failure. A forcefully argued account, part history and part polemic, and drenched in shrewd aperçus, Weinstein's study ranges from the pre-World War I period to the New Left. It surveys the failure of the pre-1917 socialists and of the CP from 1919 to 1956; and in the course of it emphasizes the historical determinism that animated the leadership of both parties and the disastrous consequences of such an emphasis and of taking on the Soviet model. Weinstein also devotes a substantial portion of his work to the New Left, which, he concludes, was much like its predecessors in some highly significant ways: it also failed to understand twentieth-century capitalism, and it shared their revisionist Marxist stress upon "immediatism"—in the workplace and in the community—and thereby failed to transcend the differences and characteristics of the Old Left. Another attempt to lay out theoretical guidelines is provided by John H. M. Laslett and Seymour M. Lipset, who have edited *Failure of a Dream* (Garden City, N.Y., 1974). This very significant collection, of the discrete views of a number of radical/social historians, grapples with the interpretative issues which earlier scholarship has largely avoided. Of the contributors, Laslett's and Susman's essays are most impressive; Bell reaffirms his earlier, and now sadly dated, thesis; and Johnpoll and Paul Buhle offer important insights on the subject. Other than Diggins and Weinstein, and the contributors to this collection, there are few generalists at work. Kenneth McNaught, the Canadian historian, is perhaps the most significant. He has explored the inclination of American radicals and intellectuals to work within the established political parties, and shrewdly dissected the relation of socialism and culture within a Tocquevillian context—in "American Progressivism and the Great Society," *Journal of American History,* 53 (December 1966), 504–20.

There are two books notable for the speculative insights they offer into American radicalism. Roberta Ash's *Social Movements in America* (Chicago, 1972) has been neglected by historians and possibly for good reason. An uneven book, it mixes arrestingly original perceptions with crude generalizations. Almost as provocative, and a more balanced exploration, is Peter Clecak's *Radical Paradoxes* (New York, 1973). It is a serious and thoughtful study which divides radical theorists into two factions: the anti-Stalinists and plain Marxists. He dismisses the former as anachronisms and clearly sympathizes with the anti-Stalinist democratic socialists like Michael Harrington. Selecting Mills and Marcuse among other plain Marxists, Clecak deals with that most salient of questions confronting them: can a socialist society be created in a nation that is non-revolutionary and that can mobilize at will overwhelming state power? Clecak also surveys the New Left, and concludes by offering a "radical conservatism," a formula which would reaffirm Marx's Hegelian view of reforms building upon one another, thus retaining historical continuity. As such, his book is flawed by elements of fantasy: it finds that a feasible socialist alternative is now in the offing.

Of the recent studies of the New Left, there are three that merit consideration. The first is Irwin Unger's *A History of the New Left* (New York, 1974), a survey of the Movement of the 1960s and of the social and intellectual forces which generated it. His discussion of the New Left is unclear at times and also unsympathetic, betraying a hostility toward the sources of its radicalism. Kirkpatrick Sale's *The SDS* (Random House, 1973) chronicles the rise and fall of the New Left's major organization. Drawing on SDS archives and interviews, among other sources, Sale tells a good story. Admittedly, he praises the SDS and exaggerates its contributions to the Cambodian protests, but has sufficient balance to note its romanticism, especially in its view of the ghetto poor, and draws a parallel between it and the Russian *narodniki*. Sale attributes SDS's failure to Progressive Labor, which was dogmatic and manipulative, but fails to perceive how its insularity and inability to reach working-class youth also contributed to its downfall. George Vickers' *The Formation of the New Left: The Early Years* (Lexington, Mass., 1975) is one of its kind: it describes the New Left's development, the personal background of its followers, their self-activity, which he understands in terms of praxis, and the substructure and superstructure which shaped their outlook and efforts.

Possibly the best books, and there are a score to choose from, that deal with the culture radicals are those by James Gilbert, Daniel Aaron, and Richard Pells. Gilbert's *Writers and Partisans* (New York, 1968) is the most narrowly focused of the trio. It treats of the left-wing journalists of the 1930s, especially those who were New York-based and contributed to *Partisan Review*. Among its virtues, *Writers and Partisans* analyzes the ways in which politics and literature coalesce and splinter, doing so in the course of outlining the Trotskyite-Stalinist division and how it shaped the culturally schizoid 1930s. Aaron's *Writers on the Left* (New York, 1961) gives us a thoughtful account of the literary wars of this same decade, commenting upon such culture radicals as Eastman, Calvert, and Joseph Freeman. Richard Pells's *Radical Visions and American Dreams: Culture and Social Thought in the Depression Years* (New York, 1973) casts a wider net. More ambitious and inclusive than either Gilbert or Aaron, it offers first-rate analyses of such diverse figures as Orson Welles, Dwight Macdonald, James Agee, Edmund Wilson; of such artists and writers and social commentators as John Sloan, Malcolm Cowley, Sherwood

Anderson; of such members of the intellectual establishment as John Dewey and George Counts, their reaction to the Depression and their failed efforts to construct a new culture and a new social philosophy. Pells's book is destined to become the standard work for all those interested in such figures and in these years.

Of the notables in twentieth-century radical history and thought, John Reed has received the fullest treatment. The most recent biography, Robert Rosenstone's *Romantic Revolutionary: A Biography of John Reed* (New York, 1975), is the most balanced and acute of them all; more intelligent and perceptive than Hicks's portrait of 1937 or the popular biography by Richard O'Connor and Dale Walker of thirty years later. It is short on interpretation, but cares for the subject while not perceiving him as a hero; and it wisely confirms Christopher Lasch's view of the culture radicals as implicitly anti-intellectual —devoted to activism, direct experience, exhilarating revolutionary militancy. Norman Thomas has also received a great deal of attention from both scholars and popular biographers. Murray Seidler's *Norman Thomas* (Syracuse, 1961) is a straightforward but rather average performance; Harry Fleischman's *Norman Thomas* (New York, 1964) has more personal reminiscences but is largely uncritical; Johnpoll's *Pacifist Progress* (Chicago, 1970) is the most informed and also the most abrasive. Thomas, he concludes, was basically a social gospel minister, a middle-class intellectual who "neither understood nor appreciated the aspirations of the workingclass"; and he unfairly attributes the SP's decline to Thomas, when it clearly antedated him. Johnpoll's focus on the middle-class, educated socialists versus old-line, labor-oriented socialists is most illuminating. Edward Muzik has written a respectable account in *Victor Berger: A Biography* (Evanston, Ill., 1960); and so has Sally Miller in *Victor Berger and the Promise of Constructive Socialism* (Westport, Conn., 1973). Daniel De Leon and the SWP are the subject of an excellent dissertation by Don McKee, "The Intellectual and Historical Influences Shaping the Political Theory of Daniel De Leon" (Ph.D. dissertation, Columbia University, 1955). A thoughtful account of Algie M. Simons, the right-wing SP leader, may be found in Kent and Gretchen Kreuter, *An American Dissenter: The Life of Algie Martin Simons, 1870–1950* (Lexington, Ky., 1969). Of the studies on Haywood and the IWW, the most significant are Joseph Conlin's *Big Bill Haywood and the Radical Union Movement* (Syracuse, 1969), which was the first full-scale study of Haywood's activities and provides a careful examination of his successes and failures; and Melvyn Dubofsky's *We Shall Be All* (Chicago, 1969), a big, fascinating, and instructive study of the IWW. Although not entirely convincing in explaining the alienation and radicalization of native-born Wobblies—he uses the Oscar Lewis model—Dubofsky has written a solid work which demystifies the IWW'ers, refuses to regard them as aberrant, and relates them to the conditions of contemporary life in America. There are also a number of books on Eugene V. Debs, naturally enough, of which Ray Ginger's is outstanding. His

The Bending Cross (New Brunswick, N.J., 1949) is vivid and exciting biography, a first-rate account of this charismatic labor leader and socialist.

The best study of American Trotskyism is a most recent book, and the only full-length scholarly account: Constance A. Myers' *The Prophet's Army: Trotsky in America, 1928–1941* (Westport, Conn., 1977). The pacifists have been examined in a number of solidly researched monographs. The best of them are C. Roland Marchand, *The Peace Movement and Social Reform, 1898–1918* (Princeton, 1972), which skillfully and exhaustively explores the early leaders and groups; and Charles Chatfield, *For Peace and Justice: Pacifism in America, 1914–1941* (Knoxville, Tenn., 1971), a thoroughly researched study of those activists and organizations involved in peace work in the first half of the twentieth century; it describes how pacifists increasingly sought political realism within the Christian framework and how they became radicalized in a Christian sense. And, finally, there is Lawrence Wittner's *Rebels Against War: The American Peace Movement, 1941–1960* (New York, 1969), the only full-length account, and a superb one, of peace workers in the Cold War years and of their growing secular orientation and search for radical panaceas.

There are a number of books that deal with Henry Wallace. Among the most notable are J. Samuel Walaker, *Henry Wallace and American Foreign Policy* (Westport, Conn., 1976), a scrupulously researched monograph that recognizes the significance of Wallace's foreign-policy opinions and seeks out their roots and their historical continuity; Edward and Frederick Schapsmeier's *Prophet in Politics: Henry A. Wallace and the War Years* (Ames, Iowa, 1970), which, while not uncritical, finds the period after 1946 to be Wallace's "noblest moment"; Norman Markowitz, *The Rise and Fall of the People's Century: Henry Agard Wallace and American Liberalism, 1941–1948* (New York, 1973), which is possibly the most interesting account of the lot, examining how Wallace reflected or refracted American liberalism; and, finally, Richard Walton's recent *Henry Wallace, Harry Truman and the Cold War* (New York, 1976), which, drawing on Wallace's diaries and various archival sources, seeks to rescue his subject from the abuses of liberal democrats and to demonstrate that Wallace "has been vindicated by history." Wallace is depicted as a premature advocate of détente and of Kissinger's sphere-of-interest politics, and Truman and the democratic liberals condemned as Cold War warriors.

Index

239